THE SMALL HO
TODAY AND TOMO

LIBRARIES NI
WITHDRAWN FROM STOCK

BELFAST
REFERENCE
LIBRARY

PLATE I. Group of houses in the Three Bridges neighbourhood of the new town of Crawley forming part of the development which was awarded a Ministry of Housing Medal in 1953. At the far end of the lawn are semi-detached houses roofed with redland silver grey tiles and faced with Midhurst sand-lime bricks, colour-washed broken white. On the left are maisonettes which are similarly treated but centre sections are colour-washed light tan. *Architect: A. G. Sheppard Fidler, F.R.I.B.A.*

THE SMALL HOUSE:
TODAY AND TOMORROW

by

ARNOLD WHITTICK

in collaboration with

JOHANNES SCHREINER
DIPL. ARCH., F.R.I.B.A.

LONDON
LEONARD HILL [BOOKS] LIMITED
9 EDEN STREET, N.W.1
1957

BELFAST
REFERENCE
LIBRARY

728.[1]
WHIT

c/u

Eaom
FA[?
18.7.
At

First published . . 1947
Second edition . . 1957

To Gillian Margaret
and her generation who will make
homes of the houses of tomorrow

PRINTED IN GREAT BRITAIN AT
THE UNIVERSITY PRESS
ABERDEEN

PREFACE TO THE FIRST EDITION

BEFORE the war I was much influenced in thoughts on housing by the ideas of such progressive architects as Walter Gropius, Le Corbusier and others in sympathy with their ideas. During the war I gave a large number of lectures and conducted numerous discussions among the Forces on reconstruction, planning and housing. I was particularly anxious to discover what the majority of men and women desired in housing, and I was able to collect much information concerning their ideas and preferences. I put before them many of the modern ideas that I had previously cherished. Many of these ideas were received with enthusiasm and were whole-heartedly supported; opinion on some was almost evenly divided, while others evoked steady, consistent and almost unanimous antagonism.

It sometimes happens that the student of social ideas may be greatly influenced by the attractive nature and plausible character of many of those ideas, and that he does not always refer the questions involved to his own experience and ask what he really feels about the matter. There are three ways of determining the needs of people in any branch of social life; one is by asking the people themselves; the second is by consulting the views of experts (these two thus providing the external evidence), and the third is by asking oneself by the method of introspection. All are necessary, and two without the third give incomplete and therefore unreliable results. One may be turned too easily from introspection by the attractive ideas of apparently progressive experts. That was partially my experience. When encountering the resistance among men and women in the Forces to many of these ideas, I did not ask myself for some time: What do you yourself really want; what do you feel about it? What does your own personal experience suggest as the best? At last I did and in many matters my allegiance was transferred from the experts to the ordinary man and woman.

It is desirable, I think, that housing should be the result of a happy union between the ideas of the expert and the wishes of the ordinary man. Either alone would not, I am convinced, give us the best houses. In this book I have tried to bring about that union. The men and women in the Forces (the Navy, Army and Air Force) represent the layman (there were a few experts among them who seemed to stimulate discussion among others), while those, to whom I have already referred, and Johannes Schreiner, the well-known European architect, represent the expert. I am more than the priest performing the ceremony, because I helped the expert and laymen to become acquainted and look kindly at each other. Many of the ideas put forward in this book, and illustrated in the designs made by Schreiner emerged from discussions I had had with the Forces, while other designs emerged more from Schreiner independently, but were related to the needs that I always tried to stress. But then Schreiner is a very human expert, and that was one reason I asked him to collaborate, in addition to his wide experience of housing abroad. A pupil of Peter Behrens, he was for many years principal assistant to Eric Mendelsohn before he practised on his own. My thanks are due, therefore, to Schreiner for his most sympathetic collaboration.

My grateful thanks are also due to the proprietors of *Building* and the *Building Digest* for permission to reproduce certain parts of the book that appeared in their journals; to Sydney J. Hunt of the Hunt Construction Co. for advice on the chapter on cost; to Mrs. R. Edwards for her work on the index, and to my wife for reading the proofs and making some helpful suggestions.

ARNOLD WHITTICK

Beckenham,
March 1947

PREFACE TO SECOND EDITION

Several new chapters have been added in this second edition, other chapters have been rewritten to bring them up-to-date and to incorporate developments that have occurred since the publication of the first edition nearly ten years ago. This has also necessitated changing many of the illustrations; while their number has been increased by about fifty.

Not long after the publication of the first edition my collaborator Johannes Schreiner died while making a survey for housing and industrial development at Kampala in Uganda in May 1948. The designs and several of the ideas in this book were his and I cannot say whether, if he had lived he would, as the result of further experience, have wished to change or modify them. My conviction is that there has been no need to change the essential principles by which the book was first actuated.

I am indebted to several architects, to the development corporations of new towns, and to firms responsible for various methods of construction for the loan of photographs. The captions in each case should make identification clear. I am also indebted to the British Electrical Development Association, the Lighting Service Bureau of the Electric Lamp Manufacturers' Association, the Gas Council, the Coal Utilization Council and the British Coal Utilization Research Association for much helpful advice and for the loan of photographs. I am further grateful to the manufacturers of appliances for information and photographs for illustrations. I have as far as possible given the trade names of these appliances to facilitate identification.

ARNOLD WHITTICK

Beckenham,
Janaury 1957

CONTENTS

vii

BELFAST
REFERENCE
LIBRARY

LIST OF ILLUSTRATIONS

Figures

BELFAST
REFERENCE
LIBRARY

PLATES

Chapter I

INTRODUCTORY—THE REQUIREMENTS THAT THE SMALL HOUSE SHOULD SATISFY

Fʀᴏᴍ a study of people's needs and wants and of family life it is possible to enumerate broadly certain essential requirements that the small house should satisfy if families are to have the necessary setting for a happy life. I suggest eight requirements which appear to me to cover essentials:

1. The house should provide good, reliable and durable shelter with adequate protection from the inclemencies of the weather.

2. The house should be designed and constructed with full consideration for the health of the occupants; it should consequently admit a fair measure of fresh air and sunlight; it should have heating provided so as to allow comfortable movement about the house in all weathers; it should be easy to keep clean; it should provide adequate facilities for personal cleanliness, and hygienic removal of refuse.

3. The house should provide facilities for the convenient storage, efficient preparation and agreeable consumption of food.

4. The house should admit light by day and be lighted by night so as to provide the utmost visual comfort.

5. The house should permit a fair degree of privacy, seclusion and quiet when required.

6. The house should be of a size and plan to give adequate space and facilities to its occupants for domestic and cultural pursuits, social intercourse, recreation, relaxation and rest.

7. The house should be sited on a plot of ground of a size adequate to provide a large outdoor room in summer, and space for flowers and a degree of verdancy as surrounding to the house.

8. The house should be pleasing to contemplate.

In the following chapters each of these requirements is more specifically defined and considered. Introductory to this the present housing situation is considered, and questions like the existing shortage and demand, means of satisfying this demand, and speed and economy in production are discussed, because it is important to relate family requirements to present realities. The conditions produced by the Second World War have become less difficult and housing in a few years will have a less urgent character; but if the people of this country are to be well housed it is of value to envisage some sort of standard for the family, some approximation of an ideal small house for the majority at which we should aim as a part of housing policy.[1] This

---

[1] The Report of the Standards of Fitness for Habitation Sub-Committee of the Central Housing Advisory Committee (Sir Miles E. Mitchell, chairman) 1947, recommended that The dwelling should (i) be in all respects dry; (ii) be in a good state of repair; (iii) have each room properly lighted and ventilated; (iv) have an adequate supply of wholesome water laid on for all purposes inside the dwelling; (v) be provided with efficient and adequate

1

BELFAST
REFERENCE
LIBRARY

house should not be just a technician's or sociologist's dream, but should be based upon the wishes of the people themselves. Thus, in one chapter the value of these expressed wishes and the extent to which they should influence the expert is considered.

means of supplying hot water for domestic purposes; (vi) have an internal or otherwise readily accessible water-closet; (vii) have a fixed bath preferably in a separate room; (viii) be provided with a sink or sinks and with suitable arrangements for the disposal of waste water; (ix) be provided with facilities for domestic washing, including a copper, preferably in a separate room; (x) have a proper drainage system; (xi) be provided with adequate points for artificial lighting in each room; (xii) be provided with adequate facilities for heating each habitable room; (xiii) have satisfactory facilities for preparing and cooking food; (xiv) have a well-ventilated larder or food store; (xv) have proper provision for the storage of fuel; (xvi) have a satisfactory surfaced path to outbuildings and convenient access from a street to the back door.

These sixteen points are covered in the first four requirements that I give (1 and 2 by 1; 3 to 10 and 12, 15 and 16 by 2; 13 and 14 by 3; and 11 by 4 and also by 3). These standards of the Mitchell Committee are for existing houses which should be brought up to these standards by means of conversion as soon as is practicable. They are regarded as essential to comfortable domestic life. The committee refrained from including in the standards any items which might be regarded as being in the nature of luxuries. The requirements I suggest in items 5 to 8 could hardly be regarded only as luxuries, but it can be appreciated that it might be difficult to provide these by converting existing houses as they involve questions of size and siting. They are standards for new houses.

CHAPTER II

THE NEED AND THE OUTPUT

How can the need for new houses be defined, and what is its extent? The minimum need may be defined, I think, as the number of new houses required to give every family of whatever size a separate dwelling in accordance with the standards of the Housing Act of 1935, and in accordance with what would be regarded by responsible medical opinion as providing healthy accommodation. This means providing houses for the large number who have married during and since the war and who do not want to live with their parents, or in other people's dwellings, but want to have a home of their own as soon as possible. It also means replacing the numerous obsolescent and overcrowded dwellings.

In 1945 various estimates were made of the housing need at that time, and a widely accepted figure was 4,000,000, which it was felt to be within the capacity of the building industry to provide in ten or twelve years. The Minister of Health had said in Parliament at the end of 1943 that the generally accepted estimate of 3,000,000 to 4,000,000 is a broad indication of the probable housing need during the first ten to twelve years of peace. The estimate was based on the number of dwellings in a poor condition or grossly deficient in modern amenities, for which 1,500,000 to 2,000,000 was allowed and the number required to give each family a separate dwelling and so eliminate overcrowding, for which 1,500,000 was allowed. In the first edition of this book a rough calculation of the need for new houses was made as follows:

Number required to eradicate slums and over-crowding and replace obsolete dwellings	1,000,000
Number destroyed or irreparable through enemy action and too much damaged to be worth repairing, and the number that it will be necessary to destroy in conformity with planning schemes in war-damaged areas	400,000
Additional houses required because of the increase in number of families in a period of six years (number of marriages from 1st October 1939 to 30th September 1945 was 2,259,097, less number of houses vacated through death, say 810,015 on the basis of average size of family 3·8, which was the average size of family at the 1931 census, while number of deaths for the same period was 3,078,058)	1,449,082
Average yearly accumulated future demand (350,000 marriages per year, which was the approximate average for 1935-6-7-8, less houses vacated by death on the basis of family of 3·8 and 500,000 annual deaths which is 131,579) deducted from 350,000; thus 218,421 per year. For a period of ten years	2,184,210
Total necessary to build in ten years to satisfy the need	5,033,292

The actual number of permanent houses built in Great Britain in about eleven years since the war (to 30th June 1956) was 2,383,862, which is very much short of the need estimated in 1945 and as calculated to be within the capacity of the building industry to provide. But, as in the period following the First World War,[1] we were

[1] See Appendix 1.

slow in making a start and only really achieved big scale production, comparable with the output in the record years immediately preceding the war, since 1952. The progress of the production of permanent houses in Great Britain is as follows:

1945	...	...	3,014
1946	...	...	55,400
1947	...	...	139,690
1948	...	...	227,616
1949	...	...	197,627
1950	...	...	198,171
1951	...	...	194,831
1952	...	...	239,922
1953	...	...	318,779
1954	...	...	347,605
1955	...	...	316,995
1956	...	...	300,225
			2,539,875

This is over a million less than was generally hoped and expected would be built in the period. It means that there is still in 1957 a very serious housing shortage and it is useful to make some attempt to estimate what the present shortage is, and what should be the annual rate of production at which we should aim.

There are two main sources of information which would give some indication of this shortage—one is the number of families still without a separate dwelling, the other is the number of dwellings that it would be necessary to replace in slum clearance and planning schemes and in the elimination of obsolescent dwellings. To estimate what should be the annual rate of production it is necessary also to consider the probable future trend of population and the desirable period of replacement of houses.

In the analysis of 1 per cent. sample tables of the 1951 Census, the number of structurally separate dwellings is given as 13,311,900. The number of private householders is given as 14,481,500, which probably means that in 1951 about 1,169,600 families were without a home of their own. Although in the five years from 1st April 1951 to 31st March 1956 1,441,835 houses have been built in Great Britain, not all would have gone to those who married in the period.

The position in the five years would have been roughly as follows:

Houses built	1,441,835
Houses vacated by death (deaths in the five years 1st April 1951 to 31st March 1956=2,841,414 divided by 3·21 being the average size of household as given in the 1 per cent census sample table	885,175
The number of marriages for the five years was	1,960,542
Thus the accumulated demand in the five years would have been nearly	1,075,367

Thus the shortage at March 31st 1956 might be estimated as:

Number without homes of their own in April 1951	1,169,600
Plus accumulated demand in four years	1,075,367
	2,244,967
Less number of houses built in five years	1,441,835
	803,132

To which must be added the number of houses it would be necessary to replace in accordance with a good standard.

Some indication of the number of obsolescent dwellings and slum property that it would be necessary to replace to secure a good standard of housing can be derived from the 1 per cent. sample tables of the 1951 Census. A large number of households were still without certain essentials in a good standard of housing, as follows:

Without exclusive use of	Could share with another household	Entirely without
Piped water	1,638,900	810,500
Cooking stove	791,100	334,100
Kitchen sink	944,700	905,200
W.C.	2,179,200	1,114,500
Fixed bath	1,086,900	5,435,700

To take what is perhaps the most important item, the W.C., it would mean that to provide a W.C. for all the households that have not the exclusive use of one, on the basis of 1,114,500 entirely without, plus a proportion of 2,179,200 determined by the extent of the sharing, the total is unlikely to be less than two millions. Some would have been accommodated in the 1,441,835 houses built since the Census, but this would not reduce the total very much. Without a fixed bath implies the absence of a bathroom, which cannot be regarded as a good standard of housing. In a number of these houses a fixed bath could be installed, or additions or conversions could be made to accommodate a bathroom. It is not such a guide as the absence of a W.C. which indicates an approximate minimum of new houses required as about $1\frac{1}{2}$ million. There would be a certain overlapping of this figure and the 803,132, but it would not be far out to suggest that the shortage at the middle of 1956 was about 2 millions.

In estimating a desirable annual rate of production it is necessary, as previously mentioned, to consider the probable growth of population. Present signs indicate that population in Great Britain will continue to rise very gradually for another ten years, then become stationary for a few years, and then possibly decline slightly, but it is very difficult to forecast anything beyond ten years. In estimating the future population in 1939 the Registrars-General working from an estimated population in 1937 of 46,008,000 made the forecasts of 46,565,000 in 1941, 47,501,000 in 1951, 47,192,000 in 1961 and 45,980,000 in 1971. It will be seen that from this forecast the population is estimated as roughly stationary between 1951 and 1961. Actually the population was 48,840,893 in 1951, and has increased in the five years to 31st March 1956 by about 860,000, the population at that date being approximately 49,700,000. Emigrants in the period would probably be balanced by immigrants. Assuming that an increase of about 175,000 a year will continue for a few years, it is not unreasonable to suppose that the population of Great Britain in 1960 will be approximately 50½ millions, and not less than 51 millions in 1965.

The average size of household according to the Census sample tables is 3·21, which means that this has gradually been getting less. This decrease may continue, but the figure may remain nearly stationary, or even increase a little; but the signs are that fluctuations will not be marked.

The question remains of the period of replacement of houses.

The belief has been growing during the present century that building, if it is to serve modern life to the utmost should be adapted to changing needs and should make possible constant renewal. Lewis Mumford remarks in *The Culture of Cities* that 'one of the most important attributes of a vital urban environment is one that has rarely been achieved in past civilisations: the capacity of renewal'. Modern building technique in which a frame can be rapidly erected and in which walls have become comparatively thin insulating screens, makes this renewal in comparatively short periods possible. The advantages are apparent in most types of structure and particularly in domestic building. A house fifty years old has disadvantages in convenience and equipment compared with one built with all the experience of modern planning and technique. This line of thought has suggested that houses should be built for a definitely limited period and then renewed. This process of renewing houses in a certain period, indicates that a housing policy should aim at a definite tempo of building which should determine a long-term housing programme. Two major points would have to be decided; the desirable life of a house, and the total stock of houses necessary for family life.

Various estimates have been made of what is the most desirable life for a house. Some have suggested that technical developments and improvements now occur so rapidly that a house remains modern for a much shorter period and that forty years is a reasonable life for a house by which time it should be renewed. Others take the view that this is far too short a period because it must be related to the economies of renewal. A more moderate view is that the life of a house should be approximately sixty years, and that is the period in which we should aim to renew our stock of houses. Yet when confronted with a shortage it would be difficult if not impossible to base housing production on a period of sixty years, and eighty years suggests itself as the more reasonable and within the capacity of the country to achieve.

The total stock of dwellings if every household or family is to have a separate dwelling, say in 1965, when the population would be about 51 millions, would be that number divided by about 3·2, which is 15,937,500, approximately 16 millions. To replace these every eighty years would mean building at the rate of 200,000 a year, which is easily within the capacity of the building industry. But before such a production would be adequate it is necessary to overcome an existing shortage, which has been indicated as being in the region of 2 millions as the minimum. In the Census the number of structurally separate dwellings is given as 13,312,000, which means that about 2,700,000 plus replacements of obsolete dwellings should be built by 1965.[1]

[1] The local authorities' returns in the report of Slum Clearance published in October 1955 gives the number of houses unfit for human habitation as 847,112, for England and Wales, out of a total of 12,935,117. A few local authorities failed to send in returns but the total on the same basis would probably not be more than 850,000. It is doubtful, however, if these returns can be considered as very reliable. It is not surprising to learn that out of

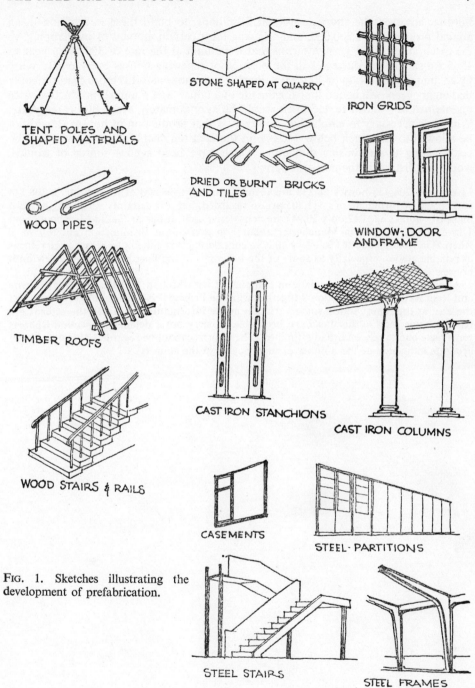

TENT POLES AND SHAPED MATERIALS

STONE SHAPED AT QUARRY

IRON GRIDS

WOOD PIPES

DRIED OR BURNT BRICKS AND TILES

WINDOW; DOOR AND FRAME

TIMBER ROOFS

CAST IRON STANCHIONS

CAST IRON COLUMNS

WOOD STAIRS & RAILS

CASEMENTS

STEEL-PARTITIONS

FIG. 1. Sketches illustrating the development of prefabrication.

STEEL STAIRS

STEEL FRAMES

Putting, however, the shortage now at 2 millions, to build these in addition to an annual production of 200,000, and allowing for a certain amount of overlapping, to the extent of 50,000 a year, it means that if we built at the rate of 350,000 a year to 1965 we should put ourselves in the position of renewing houses every eighty years by an annual production of 200,000.   By that time, however, it is more than probable that eighty years will be too long for the life of a house, and if annual production were maintained at 300,000 replacement would be approximately every fifty-three years. What it is necessary to emphasize, however, is that production of houses should not be allowed to fall much below 350,000 in the next ten years, otherwise we shall be perpetuating those housing difficulties which have been such a source of trouble, worry and distress in the post-war period.

Liverpool's 204,486 houses 88,233 are regarded as unfit, 68,000 of Manchester's 208,144 and 50,250 of Birmingham's 311,805 are so regarded, but it is certainly surprising to learn that of London's 830,017 only 20,947 are considered unfit. It means that in Liverpool about 1 in every $2\frac{1}{2}$ is unfit, in Manchester about 1 in every 3, in Birmingham about 1 in 6, whereas in London about 1 in every 40 is so considered. It is difficult to accept such returns as reliable guides, especially as some of the boroughs in the East End give very few unfit houses.

Although the returns were made in compliance with Section 1 of the Housing Repairs and Rent Act 1954, and Section 9 together with the Principal Act determined the standard there is, as the report states, some variation in the information on which the returns are based: 'some local authorities have been able to carry out a detailed inspection whereas some have had to rely on broad estimates'. The returns cannot be regarded, therefore, as an accurate indication of the number of unfit houses in the country.

CHAPTER III

SPEED, ECONOMY AND METHODS

T HE possibilities of the use of larger prefabricated units as standardized parts should be fully realized.[1] If there is a large number of different designs of houses, all using the same or similar standardized parts manufactured as large units in the factory, then these units can be assembled very quickly on the site, and houses could be built with a speed greater than is possible with older traditional methods. The illustrations give some indication of the development of prefabricated parts used in building from early primitive structures to the fullest modern development. Poles and skins and fabrics sewn together in convenient sizes to form a tent are among the most primitive examples. Then in more durable buildings we have the small units like bricks, tiles, panes of glass (gradually becoming larger), pipes in wood and earthenware and iron grills. Timber has always been a material suitable for the manufacture of large units, and we get early examples in timber doors, window frames, staircases, balustrades and rails, and roof trusses. The advent of iron in building construction opened up fresh possibilities in columns and beams made to standard sizes, roof trusses, steel casements, steel staircases and cast-iron pipes. The next development, involving the introduction of new materials, takes the form of sheet sections of fibreboard, plywood, blockboard, concrete and toughened glass used as wall panels; then it is a logical step to complete wall, floor and roof panels. Complete plumbing units are also made. Then there are the complete prefabricated half-sections of houses, and lastly the complete house which can be transported to the site.

It is worth reflecting on what the great architect-sociologist, Walter Gropius, has to say of the possibility of an increasing use of prefabricated methods. 'Building,' he says, 'hitherto an essentially manual trade, is already in force of transformation into an organized industry. More and more work that used to be done on scaffolding is now carried out under factory conditions far away from the site. The dislocation which the seasonal character of building operations causes employers and employed alike—as, indeed, the community at large—is being gradually overcome. Continuous activity throughout the year will soon become the rule instead of the exception.

'And just as fabricated materials have been evolved which are superior to natural ones in accuracy and uniformity, so modern practice in house construction is increasingly approximating to the successive stages of manufacturing process. We are approaching a state of technical proficiency when it will become possible to rationalize buildings and mass produce them in factories by resolving their structure into a number of component parts. Like boxes of toy bricks, these will be assembled in formal compositions in a dry state; which means that building will definitely cease to be dependent on the weather. Ready-made houses of solid fireproof construction, that can be

[1] The building of the Crystal Palace first pointed the way to the possibilities of the extensive use of standardized parts. There were, for example, 3,300 standard columns, and 2,300 girders of standard lengths. Here was a building covering 773,000 square feet, three times the size of the cathedral of St. Peter's at Rome, and completed in sixteen weeks.

9

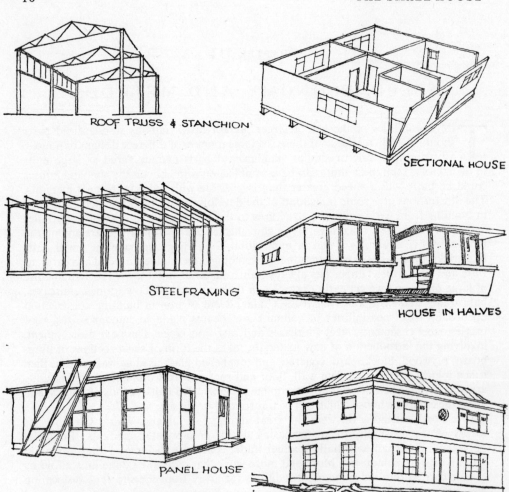

ROOF TRUSS & STANCHION

SECTIONAL HOUSE

STEELFRAMING

HOUSE IN HALVES

PANEL HOUSE

FIG. 2. Sketches illustrating the development of prefabrication.

THE COMPLETE HOUSE

delivered fully equipped from stock, will ultimately become one of the principal products of industry. Before this is practicable, however, every part of the house—floor-beams, wall-slabs, windows, doors, staircases and fittings—will have to be normed. The repetition of standardized parts, and the use of identical materials in different buildings, will have the same sort of co-ordinating and sobering effect on the aspect of our towns as uniformity of type in modern attire has in social life. But that will in no sense restrict the architect's freedom of design. For, although every house and block of flats will bear the unmistakable impress of our age, there will always remain, as in the clothes we wear, sufficient scope for the individual to find expression for his own personality. The net result should be a happy architectonic combination of maximum standardization and maximum variety.

'Dry assembly offers the best prospect because (to take only one of its advantages) moisture in one form or another is the principal obstacle to economy in masonry or brick construction (mortar joints). Moisture is the direct cause of most of the weaknesses of the old methods of building. It leads to badly fitting joints, warping and staining, unforeseen piece-work, and serious loss of time and money through delays in drying. By eliminating this factor and so assuring the perfect interlocking of all component parts, the prefabricated house makes it possible to guarantee a fixed price and a definite period of construction. Moreover the use of reliable modern materials enables the stability and insulation of a building to be increased and its weight and bulk decreased. A prefabricated house can be loaded on to a couple of lorries at the factory—walls, floors, roof, fittings and all—conveyed to the site, and put together in next to no time regardless of the season of the year.

'The outstanding concomitant advantages of rationalized construction are superior economy and an enhanced standard of living. Many of the things that are regarded as luxuries to-day will be standard fitments in the home of to-morrow.' [1]

This was written over twenty years ago, but its truth is more apparent to-day than then. Indeed the prospect of the complete house being made in the factory and delivered to the site by helicopters is not very remote. The only site work would be the foundations.

There is risk, however, that the very strong conservatism of the British people will stand in the way of the ready adoption of many new methods. There are those who want the brick-built house with tile or slate roofs because, they say, it has stood the test of time. They strongly criticize the speedily assembled prefabricated house. Yet other materials, like steel, plastics and wood, lend themselves much better to the manufacture of large prefabricated parts than brick, although, as will be seen in the next chapter, prefabricated brick panels have been employed. But the manufacture of these parts and their assembly is viewed with suspicion as of a slipshod and unreliable character. There is still a strong tendency to regard the modern small house as evolving from the mediaeval cottage, rather than as a product of modern engineering having affinities with the aeroplane and motor-car. When the latter view is more widely accepted there will be a more tolerant attitude to the manufacture of prefabricated parts of a house, and there will be a realization that these parts can be as strong as those of an aeroplane.

One disadvantage, from the standpoint of speedy construction, of the conventional brick-built house with pitched timber roof covered with tiles or slates is that a very large number of small units—in the region of 20,000 for the small house—are put together by hand, and however quickly a bricklayer works, even if he lays 800 bricks a day (and generally it is more like half that number), it is a slow method. If the number of units to be erected on the site were only 100 the house could obviously be built more rapidly. The extent to which labour can be increased on the site is severely restricted because only a certain number of men can operate on a wall at once. If much of the assembly of the units can be done in the factory so that large sections arrive on the site, more labour is available at once, divided between factory and site, thus more people operate on a house, and this greatly assists speed. A further disadvantage

[1] Walter Gropius, *The New Architecture and the Bauhaus* (London, 1935), pp. 28-31.

of the traditional method, emphasized by Gropius, is that the wet method of jointing involves stoppages in frosty and very wet weather and this often causes considerable delay.

The reader may be sceptical of the claims for the new materials of construction used since the war because they have not generally fulfilled their promise and given the results confidently expected of them in the matters of speed and economy. They have generally been a little quicker—one or two very much quicker—but not more economical. But the new methods have not, even now, been given a fair trial. Rarely have they been built in sufficiently large numbers for full speed and economy to be realized. The *Housing Manual 1949* of the Ministry of Health refers to non-traditional systems of house construction and says that 'theoretically, the increase in speed of erection which all approved methods are designed in varying degrees to effect should produce a price below that of the traditional house, and the opposing factor, the initial outlay on plant and equipment which has been responsible for the higher price, should gradually cease to operate'. Mention is made of the economics in time, labour and cost that could be effected by the prefabrication of internal parts and fittings to fit a shell of standard size while the plumbing system can be very largely prefabricated.

In constructing the shell of the house with traditional methods, quantity has very little influence upon cost per house. It is true that the cost is slightly lower if a hundred houses are being built instead of five, but it is improbable that any substantial reductions of cost per house are effected by increasing the quantity required on any particular estate above a hundred. Where mass production is applied, the greater the quantity the less the unit cost, provided always that the quantity is sufficient to justify the necessary machinery and organization.

What has happened with motor-car production could happen with house production. In 1919 a car cost £750. In 1939 a better car could be bought for £150. How was the great reduction in price achieved? By mass production methods, which also put the motor-car within the reach of a far greater number of persons. The same would happen with house production.

If plant in one factory could produce units for five thousand houses a year and this maximum could be maintained, and repeated in twenty factories, then it is clear that the speed of production would be limited only by the speed of assembly, as it is in the case of bricks. The speed of assembly of a house in the case of completely prefabricated walls could be at least ten times that of the brick-built walls, as the building of the Crystal Palace so well demonstrated. And mass production of large units, like the mass production of motor-car parts, would gradually reduce costs and put the house, with accommodation commensurate with a high standard of living, within the reach of an ever-increasing number of families.

This, however, is theory, and is not likely to be realized on more than a limited scale for some years to come. We are not likely quickly to abandon traditional methods—the brick house with pitched roof—for these new methods whereby the house is more a product of modern engineering and mass production methods. If I might venture on a prophecy it is that the two will proceed side by side with a large and increasing number of houses which are a combination of the two methods. The English village traditional type is still in the ascendant, partly as a sentimental reaction against the war dominance of the machine, and partly because of our conservative affection for tradition. But gradually the engineer's house—if I might call it so—will appeal more and more as its excellencies and essentially rational and serviceable character, and its economic potentialities become apparent. It will not have a chance until a very large estate or several adjacent estates are built on these lines, but when that occurs, its popularity will increase, it will take the lead from the English village traditional type and ultimately hold the field almost alone. And later still, when the brick house with pitched roof of tiles or slates is a quaint old relic of the past, we may paint imitation bricks on the prefabricated walls, and disguise the flat roof to look like a pitched roof to give it an old-world appearance, just as we have put wooden boards on the façades of suburban houses in imitation of half-timber work, in our childish efforts to give a London suburb the picturesque character of a Tudor village. We shall probably then look back to the early vigorous pioneer days of the standardized prefabricated house and its culmination, after a period of trial and error, to something like perfection, which, in its appearance was a frank and honest expression of engineering, and, in its simplicity, in its fine fulfilment of purpose, in its logical and unashamed use of materials, in its decorative emphasis emerging from purpose and structure succeeded in being both a work of science and a work of art, like the aeroplane and motor-car that helped to give it birth.

CHAPTER IV

NEW METHODS OF HOUSE CONSTRUCTION

U P to 1939 most small houses were built of brick walls with a pitched timber roof covered with tiles or slates. The walls were generally solid—9 inches thick. The cavity wall had been used for larger houses, often a 9-inch external wall and a $4\frac{1}{2}$-inch internal wall, but this was too expensive for the small house where economy was a paramount consideration. Occasionally we find the 11-inch cavity wall, particularly in the north of England, but it was not until later that this became at all common. Different methods of house construction formed the subjects of experiment from time to time, but few houses were actually built by other methods. In the latter part of the eighteenth century a small house, the lockkeeper's cottage at Tipton Green, Staffordshire, was built with cast-iron vertical wall panels as the external linings with lath and plaster internal linings.[1] An iron-framed house with brick cavity walls was exhibited at the Paris Exhibition of 1867, and, from 1900 to 1914 concrete houses appeared from time to time, either built *in situ* or with pre-cast sections. The house called 'Red Hawthorne', at Letchworth, was built in 1909 of fifteen large pre-cast concrete sections. But such houses before 1918 were rare, and they were rather the exception that proved the rule of conventional brick construction.

The building stoppage during the First World War produced a considerable housing shortage. After the war there was a great increase in the cost of materials and labour, and most countries in Europe were very slow in reviving house building. It was for these reasons that experiments were made with alternative methods of construction on an unprecedented scale. The purpose of these experiments was mainly to build houses with greater speed and economy. As a result a considerable number of new methods of construction were evolved, and many houses were built by these methods, principally in the nineteen-twenties. Some of the methods were good, and they contained promise of being even better, but very few were continuously developed, as they might have been. In the nineteen-thirties there was a general adherence to the conventional traditional methods of house construction. The reason for this was that providing employment was a more urgent question than economy and speed in house construction, which may have saved labour. Also, somewhat too rigid by-laws do not accelerate the adoption of unconventional and non-traditional methods.

These alternative forms of construction used in the inter-war period were reviewed by a Government inter-departmental committee under the chairmanship of Sir George Burt, and its report was published as number one of the Ministry of Works Post-war Building Studies.[2] In this review the methods were classified under Concrete Houses,

---

[1] This cottage is illustrated in *Prefabrication in Building,* by Richard Sheppard (London, 1946), p. 38.

[2] This was published in 1943. In 1946 a second report was issued (P.W.B.S. No. 23) in which a further nine experimental houses, developed since the first report, were reviewed. A third report (P.W.B.S. No. 25) was issued in 1948, in which another ten methods were described.

Framed or Solid Timber Houses, Steel-framed Houses and Metal Clad Houses. Among the many varieties of concrete houses classified were houses with 'no-fines' concrete walls, single leaf walls cast *in situ;* cavity walls cast *in situ;* cavity walls with pre-cast concrete slabs and concrete piers and concrete block construction. These methods were considered with regard to strength and stability, moisture penetration and condensation, thermal and sound insulation, fire hazard, maintenance, durability and vermin infestation. On examination it was found that many, although not all of these alternative forms, compared very favourably with traditional methods of construction. In this examination it was necessary to take some desirable standard of habitability, and although the brick house has long been established in public confidence it could not be taken as a desirable standard. For satisfactory future developments the 11-inch cavity wall is nearer to a desirable standard than is the 9-inch solid wall, mainly because it resists moisture penetration much better, the failure of the 9-inch wall in this respect making it very largely responsible for the great number of damp houses in the country. That is perhaps the main reason for the change of practice from the 9-inch solid wall to the 11-inch cavity wall. But even the 11-inch cavity wall is unsatisfactory in many respects. Both are quite strong enough, but both have poor thermal insulation, while the 9-inch party wall required in many by-laws, has poor sound insulation.

The housing shortage confronting the country in 1945 was far more serious than that of 1919, and the experiments in alternative methods of house construction were revived on a much greater scale than in the nineteen-twenties. But there is now considerable difference. Much progress has been made in building science and building research since the Building Research Station was established in 1921 by the Department of Scientific and Industrial Research, and experiments in new methods of house construction were controlled, guided and tested in a systematic way, in contrast to the somewhat haphazard procedure of the nineteen-twenties. The procedure was that the promoter of a new method of construction submitted his scheme to the Ministry of Works and applied for a licence to erect a prototype or experimental house. The construction was considered by technical experts and, if thought promising, a licence was granted. Then the prototype was examined and subjected to tests. I understand that nearly 1,400 methods of construction were submitted to the Ministry of Works by the end of 1945, and about eighty-three of those for complete houses were considered sufficiently promising for licences to be granted. Of these about twenty were in production at that time. In addition, the architects or engineers of several local authorities have combined with private building contractors to devise new methods.

Alternative methods of construction can contribute to speed in the provision of houses firstly by supplementing the houses built by traditional methods, secondly by increasing the volume of labour and material available for house building by employing labour and materials not used in traditional methods, and thirdly because these methods may be more rapid in themselves than the old. Speed is undoubtedly the main reason for these experiments, but there are others almost as important. The possibility of more economical production of houses is almost as important, for many of these methods allow for standardization and mass production to a high degree, and this means added economy in the long run. And there is the question of improving the construction of the house. We should not be a very progressive people if we were satisfied with the brick house as the best construction we could evolve.

It is useful in noting some of these latest methods of construction to follow some such classification as that given in the Burt Committee's report on house construction. But there are more general classifications which are instructive, and which must be considered first. There is the broad distinction of structures where the walls are load-bearing, and framed structures where the walls are merely screens. With the former the strength of the actual walls is important; with the latter, the walls being mostly screens, strength is a minor question, but moisture penetration, thermal and sound insulation are quite important. The framed structure may thus have this advantage that the material for the walls can be selected not so much for its strength as for its thermal and sound insulation value, and its resistance to moisture penetration. Also framed construction contributes to speedy erection, and the roof can be fixed before the wall cladding commences, so that in case of bad weather the latter operation can proceed with some degree of protection.

Another classification is according to the degree of prefabrication employed. There is the completely prefabricated house where the whole is assembled in the factory and transported to the site. This has been done with bungalows in America. Secondly, cubical sections are made in the factory, as in the aluminium house, the only site work being the assembly of sections. A third type consists of large wall and other sections, as in the Jicwood house. Fourthly, are the frame and panels systems of which numerous examples are given. In some of the last mentioned, and in some concrete frame and pre-cast panel systems, much of the construction is of fair-sized factory-made sections, but with a certain amount of site work associated with traditional building. Lastly are the houses in which only a comparatively small degree of pre-fabrication is employed and the bulk of the work is on the site. This would include concrete houses built *in situ*. The justification of the last from the standpoint of speed is that the walls can be poured and finished with a rapidity greater than is possible with brick construction.

The principal new types of construction can be classified as follows:

A.—CONCRETE HOUSES

1. Solid concrete walls poured *in situ*. This includes 'no-fines' concrete walls.
2. Cavity concrete walls poured *in situ*.
3. Walls, either solid or cavity, constructed of concrete slabs or blocks.
4. Cavity walls constructed of concrete slabs or panels forming external lining, and internal lining of concrete or other materials.
5. Walls built of a combination of pre-cast concrete slabs forming cavity and concrete poured *in situ*.
6. Reinforced concrete frames of post and beam construction with concrete panels forming cavity walls.

B.—STEEL FRAMED HOUSES

7. Walls and roof with steel frame construction and external cladding of asbestos cement, concrete, brick or other suitable material.

C.—METAL CLAD HOUSES

8. Walls and roof constructed of sheet steel sections throughout.
9. Constructed partially of sheet steel sections and partially of other materials.
10. Walls and roof constructed of sheet aluminium.

D.—Timber Houses

11. Timber frame construction with walls of external and internal boarding.
12. Timber frame construction with walls of plywood or other sheet material.
13. Timber walls constructed of timber sections or panels.

E.—Other Panel or Slab Types

14. Panel or slab construction of asbestos cement, plastics, or other suitable material, in which the slab construction is load bearing.
15. Similar panel or slab construction to No. 14, but with framed support.

F.—Prefabricated Brick Houses

16. Walls of prefabricated brick panels of cavity construction either with two brick leaves or internal leaf of other material like concrete or asbestos cement.

There are several examples of various types of houses built by these methods, but it must suffice to mention one or two of each.

A.—*Concrete Houses*

1. The difficulty with solid concrete walls is to secure an effective resistance to moisture penetration. 'No-fines' concrete gives a much better performance in this respect than ordinary solid concrete. It should be explained that 'no-fines' concrete consists of a mixture where the fine material, that is the sand, has been removed. This means that the resulting concrete has a number of air cells, which serve to keep the wall dry, and serve the purpose of a cavity. In a good 'no-fines' concrete wall a damp-proof course is not absolutely necessary. The aggregate can be anything that is sufficiently hard and gives the necessary texture. Clinker and stones or shingle have been most commonly used.

A very good example of the use of 'no-fines' concrete is the Wimpey construction. The 'no-fines' concrete walls are 12 inches thick and are built on conventional brick foundations. The noteworthy feature of the system is the method of erection. The external shuttering consists of large sheets the full size of the walls, and the internal shuttering of large trellis sections, which also serve as scaffolding. The concrete is poured up to eaves level in one operation. The internal scaffolding is removed through the top before the roof, which is of conventional construction, is put on. The advantage of this system over ordinary brick construction, according to the promoters, is that the houses are built more speedily. It is calculated that this method can secure a saving of 293 hours per house, while there is a greater proportion of unskilled labour employed. The calculation is based on a bricklayer laying bricks at the rate of fifty per hour (Plate II, a). About 70,000 Wimpey 'no-fines' concrete houses have been built since the war.

2. Concrete cavity walls built *in situ* have the same advantages as the brick cavity wall, while generally they are built more rapidly. One particularly good system, developed after the 1914-18 war, is the 'Easiform', which consists of cavity walls 9 inches and an internal leaf of clinker concrete $3\frac{1}{2}$ inches thick. Both leaves are reinforced with steel rods, such reinforcement being increased for lintels according to the span. A special system of steel shuttering contributes to speed of erection, and it is claimed

that one set of shutters produces a complete house in a week. One valuable feature of this method is that there is a continuous cavity, a feature which is not obtained very often in the post and panel or framed construction, and it is noteworthy that the party wall is also a cavity wall (Plate II b). About 52,000 'Easiform' houses have been built since the war.

3. Solid or cavity walls built with solid concrete blocks are similar to brickwork, while cost, speed, thermal and sound insulation appear to be about the same. Cavity and hollow concrete blocks have the advantage of lightness, and insulation properties superior to those of solid blocks. One interesting method of which a prototype was made, although not proceeded with, consisted of cavity concrete blocks 4 feet by 2 feet by 11 inches. The bond between blocks consisted of an external horizontal lap of 9 inches and an internal lap of 2 inches, the same shaped block being used the reverse way up in alternate courses. For small houses a framework is unnecessary, but for larger houses, involving bigger spans, the frame should be used. It consists of piers of 6-inch by 3-inch section, built *in situ* at centres of 8 feet.

4. Load-bearing pre-cast concrete slab or panel construction has been the subject of many ingenious systems. This is probably because it is a method that holds out great possibilities for future development. The size of the panel and facility in fixing it are important considerations. Where the panel can be increased in size and swung into position by a moving crane it will probably increase speed of erection. For concrete panels to be lifted into position by hand there must be restrictions of weight, and consequently size. There is, however, the view that to have panels small enough for one man to carry comfortably results in the speediest construction. This view I find difficult to accept. I believe that four or eight panels forming the complete side of a house could be fixed by means of a moving crane more rapidly than thirty panels fixed by hand. There are many examples in which panels are sufficiently small to be lifted by hand, and of the larger type requiring a crane. The Tarran system is an example of the former, and the Wates of the latter. In both, reinforced concrete vertical panels are made to standard widths. In the Wates system the panels are of story height and are normally 3 feet wide. The panels are tray shaped, the side flanges being recessed so that when two panels are placed side by side, a cavity is formed to receive the concrete which joins the panels together on the site. The internal faces of the flanges are provided with timber plugs for fixing the inner lining, which is normally of wood wool slabs. Stringer and eaves courses serve to tie the work together, with the aid of continuity steel reinforcement placed in the joints. The units are erected by a mobile crane, a temporary tubular steel jig being used for accurate positioning (Plate V a). In the Tarran system the concrete panels are smaller, being 1 foot 4 inches wide and in the original system were framed in timber, thus being sufficiently small and light to be lifted by one man. A later Tarran prefabricated wall unit (designed for permanent types of housing) is 1 foot 4 inches wide to the full height of the walls, and constructed of reinforced concrete $1\frac{3}{8}$ inches thick. The wall units are bolted to each other, and to the square reinforced concrete posts at the external angles, by wing nuts. The joints between the wall units are made with a special moisture and weather resisting compound. Although heavier than the prototype plywood framed reinforced concrete panel, from which is was developed, this wall unit is easily handled. Both the Wates and the Tarran systems are flexible, and the sizes of the units can be varied. Erection is speedy; once the foundations are laid the Tarran house can be erected in a day.

In the case of the Wates system, the shell erection of a pair of houses, including site concreting, occupies four men and a crane for four days.

Another noteworthy system in which concrete slabs of ingenious design form the main construction is the Stent. The external walls consist of load-bearing concrete units which are story-height by 12 inches wide, and of pre-cast tee section. To facilitate erection the units are secured to the plinth by holding-down bolts. At window and door openings special L section wall units are provided, the stem of the L forming the reveal to the opening. The wall units are tied at first floor and eaves level by special pre-cast concrete band and eaves units. The vertical joints of the wall units are sunk pointed in cement mortar on the outside and sealed with bitumen-impregnated hessian on the inside V grooves, thus excluding all possibility of moisture penetration. The internal lining is fixed after the outer shell has been completed and may consist of any convenient and available material. Normally, 2-inch standard clinker blocks are recommended (Plate V, c).

5. One of the most interesting of recent systems in which pre-cast concrete and concrete poured *in situ* are employed is the Bryant. This is a combination of those given in classifications 1 and 3. The walls consist of pre-cast twin slabs of foamed slag or clinker concrete on the inner side, the slabs being $2\frac{1}{4}$ inches thick with $1\frac{1}{2}$ inches cavity between, the twin slabs being joined by stout webs of the same material. High-grade concrete is poured *in situ* 4 inches thick on the outer side of the wall, reinforced with high tensile steel bars. The wall is thus 10 inches thick with four distinct sections. It is unnecessarily strong for the small house, but it gives good thermal insulation, 50 per cent. better than the 11-inch cavity wall, while moisture penetration is negligible. The roof of the Bryant house is pitched at an angle of 30 degrees and is constructed of 'Presweld' lattice steel frame made in large sections in the factory. On this framework are timber purlin laths held in position with channel clips, to receive the tiles. Timber roofs can be used if preferred. The floors of this system are of concrete reinforced with trough-shaped steel frames laid on steel beams.

In the erection of the Bryant house 'Kwikform' steel shuttering is employed. This can be rapidly erected and dismantled. The outside shuttering consists of steel sheets linked together with angle iron runners secured by non-detachable wedge clamps and with vertical tubular supports. On the inside the pre-cast slabs act as the inner formwork. A light tubular steel scaffolding is an integral part of the shuttering. As in the Wimpey system speed of erection depends very largely on the shuttering and scaffolding.

A method developed a little later, in 1948, which is perhaps the speediest yet devised is that known as the 'Reema'. In this system the walls are story-height pre-cast concrete hollow panels. *In situ* concrete columns are poured at the junction of the panels, with pre-cast concrete quoins at the corner posts, and pre-cast concrete junction units at the party walls, each of which acts as shuttering to the poured concrete. The tops of the panels form a trough with slots at intervals on the inner side into which pre-cast floor joists are fixed. The trough is then filled with *in situ* concrete, reinforced, forming a beam, and this operation is repeated on the next floor. The construction can take a timber and tile pitched roof or a concrete flat roof. The exterior of the slabs has a fine rock face, and the interior lining is $\frac{1}{2}$-inch insulation board. Following the cavity principle of construction the walls provide excellent thermal insulation. The pre-cast slabs forming the walls can of course be made in a variety of sizes, but for the usual

2

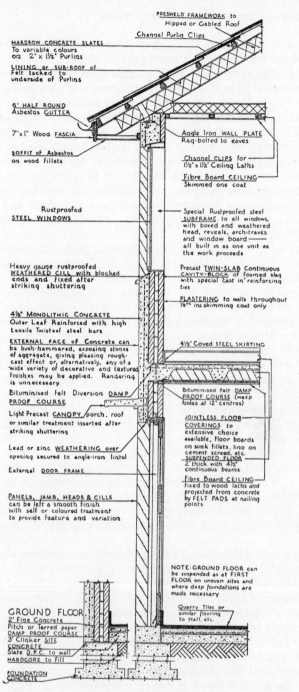

PRESWELD FRAMEWORK to Hipped or Gabled Roof
Channel Purlin Clips

HARDROW CONCRETE SLATES To variable colours on 2" x 1½" Purlins

LINING or SUB-ROOF of Felt tacked to underside of Purlins

6" HALF ROUND Asbestos GUTTER

7"x I" Wood FASCIA

SOFFIT of Asbestos on wood fillets

Rustproofed STEEL WINDOWS

Heavy gauge rustproofed WEATHERED CILL with blocked ends and fixed after striking shuttering

4½" Monolithic CONCRETE Outer Leaf Reinforced with high tensile Twisteel steel bars

EXTERNAL FACE of Concrete can be bush-hammered, exposing stones of aggregate, giving pleasing rough-cast effect or, alternatively, any of a wide variety of decorative and textured finishes may be applied. Rendering is unnecessary

Bituminised felt Diversion DAMP PROOF COURSE

Light Precast CANOPY, porch, roof or similar treatment inserted after striking shuttering

Lead or zinc WEATHERING over opening secured to angle-iron lintol

External DOOR FRAME

PANELS, JAMB, HEADS & CILLS can be left a smooth finish with self or coloured treatment to provide feature and variation

Angle Iron WALL PLATE Rag-bolted to eaves

Channel CLIPS for 1½" x 1½" Ceiling Laths

Fibre Board CEILING Skimmed one coat

Special Rustproofed steel SUBFRAME to all windows, with boxed and weathered head, reveals, architraves and window board — all built in as one unit as the work proceeds

Precast TWIN-SLAB Continuous CAVITY-BLOCK of foamed slag with special cast in reinforcing ties

PLASTERING to walls throughout ⅛ᵗʰ ins skimming coat only

4½" Coved STEEL SKIRTING

Bituminised felt DAMP PROOF COURSE (weep holes at 12" centres)

JOINTLESS FLOOR COVERINGS to extensive choice available, floor boards on sunk fillets, lino on cement screed, etc. SUSPENDED FLOOR 2" thick with 4½" continuous beams

Fibre Board CEILING fixed to wood laths and projected from concrete by FELT PADS at nailing points

NOTE: GROUND FLOOR can be suspended as at FIRST FLOOR on uneven sites and where deep foundations are made necessary

Quarry Tiles or similar flooring to Hall, etc.

GROUND FLOOR
2" Fine Concrete
Pitch or Tarred paper
DAMP PROOF COURSE
3" Clinker SITE CONCRETE
Slate D.P.C. to wall
HARDCORE to Fill

FOUNDATION CONCRETE

FIG. 3. Bryant system. Vertical section showing construction. (See page 19.)

900 to 1,000 square feet three-bedroomed, two-story house, the slabs are of room height by half the width or length of the house. The slabs are transported to the site by a trailer and hoisted in position by means of a mast and jib. The main secret of the success of this method of construction is the large prefabricated unit, because it is this factor which reduces site labour to such a small item.

From the investigations carried out by the Ministry of Works into new methods of house construction the 'Reema' system is shown to have a remarkably high standard of performance. The Ministry of Works report[1] gives the total number of man-hours for the external walls, party walls and partitions as 595 per house compared with 1,100 for the traditional brick house. Of this 595 man-hours 405 are in the factory and about 190 on the site (65 being allowed either way for variations in conditions, etc.) Commenting on the small number of site man-hours, the report speaks of 'the outstanding position of Type 13 (which is the reference given to the 'Reema' system) in which the estimated productive times for walls range around 200 man-hours'. 'It is noteworthy', the report continues, 'that these productive times were achieved on houses which were of the order of 10 per cent. larger than the other types.' About 10,000 houses have been built by this method.

6. The reinforced concrete frame, or post and panel construction has been the subject of a very large number of experiments and variations. Some of the best of the new methods of construction evolved in the nineteen-twenties, like the 'Duo-slab', the Boot, Wright and Underdown houses were variations on this theme. Perhaps the best was the Boot because a continuous cavity was secured. In the other methods the cavity was blocked at the intervals of the upright posts, but in the Boot method the posts were in two sections, held together by steel clips to allow this continuous cavity. I understand that this method is being further developed. Good recent examples of the reinforced concrete frame and panel construction are the Orlit and Airey houses. In the former the concrete framework is cast in convenient lengths for handling, and the connections in the case of the vertical members are effected by steel plates which are cast into the ends of the members and bolted together, while in the horizontal members the connecting ends are so designed that a cavity is left with the steel rods projecting, and into this a small amount of concrete is poured. The wall consists of external slabs about 2 inches thick with a stone aggregate facing, placed on the outside of the frame, a cavity of $5\frac{1}{2}$ inches, and an internal lightweight concrete slab, with plaster as an interior finish. The horizontal joints are tongued and grooved and the vertical joints are grooved for water proofing. Lime mortar is used for the joints, but experiments are being made with a special plaster jointing material so as to eliminate wet operations.

In the Airey system horizontal concrete slabs 3 feet by $9\frac{3}{4}$ inches are fixed to vertical concrete posts spaced at 18-inch centres. The posts are 4 inches by $2\frac{1}{4}$ inches in section and have a timber fillet cast on the inner face to receive linings. The horizontal joints are laid dry while the vertical joints are bedded against the posts with a bitumastic compound. The slabs are secured to the posts by means of copper wire ties connected to copper hooks cast in the backs of the slabs. The internal wall lining is of plasterboard and an insulating material is introduced between the outer slabs and the plasterboard, thus creating a double air-space.

[1] *New Methods of Home Constructions,* National Building Studies Special Report No. 10 (London, 1949).

The roofs of the rural type of house are pitched and are of traditional construction. The urban type of house originally had a flat roof with overhanging eaves. This flat roof is constructed of light lattice steel and timber joists boarded to receive bitumen roofing felt finish. This flat roof is insulated in the same way as the wall. Both the Airey and Orlit are speedily erected, and there is a comparatively small amount of skilled site labour (Plate V, b). About 26,500 houses have been built by the former method and about 8,900 by the latter.

Other systems of a similar type are the 'Woolaway' and 'Unity' in which external and internal wall slabs fit into posts of story height. In the former posts are spaced at $2\frac{1}{2}$-feet centres, they are of 6-inch square section reinforced, with rebates to receive the slabs, which are 4 feet high, thus two to each story, by 2 feet wide and 2 inches thick of aerated concrete reinforced with high-tensile twisted steel of square section. The cavity is 2 inches. The slabs weigh about 90 lb. and can thus be placed in position by hand. The slabs are bolted to the posts, and the walls are rendered externally with rough-cast and internally with plaster. Nearly 6,000 houses have been built by this method.

The 'Unity' system consists of pre-cast reinforced concrete columns 6 inches by $3\frac{1}{2}$ inches section and story height spaced at 3-feet centres, with slabs 3 feet long by 1 foot wide placed horizontally and forming a cavity of 6 inches. The external slabs are $2\frac{1}{2}$ inches thick of concrete coloured by a special process, while the internal slabs are 2 inches thick of clinker concrete. The slabs are held against a vertical damp proof strip on the columns by means of copper ties and clips. About 17,500 houses of this type have been built.

Another similar method which has proved very popular is that known as the 'Cornish Unit' system which consists of pre-cast concrete post and panel construction with cavity walls for the ground floor, and a Mansard roof for the upper story. The aggregate of the concrete is Cornish granite, being the waste silica quartz in the production of China clay which forms the pyramids for which the Cornish landscape in the region of St. Austell is famous. Nearly 30,000 houses have been built by this method (Plate IV, b).

An interesting system falling in the same category is that of the British Cast Concrete Federation. An outer structural shell is provided, consisting of full height reinforced concrete columns and beams as framing, and pre-cast concrete panels as wall infilling. Columns are spaced normally at $5\frac{1}{2}$ or 6-feet centres, permitting of complete freedom of planning. The framing will support a roof of any normal type. Internal wall lining, partitions, finishes, and fittings are independent of the structure, and can be carried out in any suitable available materials. A light mobile hoist may be used for the erection of the pre-cast concrete units, but the work can be undertaken by any competent building contractor without the use of special plant and labour.

B.—Steel Framed Houses

7. Interesting variations of the steel framed house with cladding of various materials have been developed. In the nineteen-twenties several types were built both here and abroad, and since 1944 a number have been built experimentally, and some of these have been erected in various parts of the country. Examples are the Howard, Braithwaite, Hill, Cranwell, 'Unity' and Coventry types, the last named being the design of D. E. E. Gibson who was then the city architect of Coventry.

The Howard house consists of a light steel frame erected on a foundation slab.

(a) Wimpey system. Walls of 'no-fines' concrete 12 in. thick poured from foundation to eaves level in one operation. The wall-size external shuttering is being removed and the internal shuttering, which also serves as scaffolding, can be seen on the left. (*See* p. 17.)

(b) 'Easiform' system. Concrete cavity walls built *in situ*. (The cavity is continuous.) The illustration shows operations up to first-floor level with the first floor joists in position. (*See* p. 17.)

PLATE II. (a) *and* (b). *Methods of House Construction.*

(a) 'Reema' system of construction consisting of story height pre-cast concrete panels. Panel with window being hoisted in position on the first floor.

(b) Panel with door being lowered into position on ground floor.

(c) Panels being transported on trailer. (*See* p. 19.)

PLATE III (a), (b) and (c). 'Reema' Method of House Construction.

(a) 'Unity' system of construction with pre-cast concrete columns and concrete external and internal slabs. Placing the slabs in position. (*See* p. 22.)

(b) Cornish Unit system consisting of pre-cast concrete post and panel construction in the ground floor and mansard roof for the upper floor. Placing the slabs in position. These slabs are made with an aggregate of Cornish granite. (*See* p. 22.)

PLATE IV. (a) *and* (b). *Methods of House Construction.*

(*a*) The Wates system.   The tray-shaped panels are being placed in position by a crane.
(*See* p. 18.)

(*b*) The Airey system. Showing connections between posts and floor and roof units. (*See* p. 21.)

(*c*) The Stent system. The tee section wall units are tied at first-floor level by a pre-cast concrete band. (*See* p. 19.)

PLATE V. (*a*), (*b*) *and* (*c*). *Methods of House Construction.*

The panels forming the walls can be made of a variety of materials framed in creosoted timber. Panels actually used consist of an external cladding of asbestos sheeting $\frac{3}{8}$ inch thick which has on the inside an insulating layer of felt attached by a bituminous solution. The external face of the asbestos sheet is treated with bitumen and pebble dash. The cavity is $2\frac{1}{4}$ inches and the internal lining consists of asbestos wallboard $\frac{1}{4}$ inch thick, backed by compressed woodwool 1 inch thick covered with a sheet of aluminium foil. These panels may not appear to be very substantial for wall lining, but not being load-bearing they do not need to be. They are, of course, sufficiently strong to be rigid, although something a little more substantial than the asbestos sheeting $\frac{3}{8}$ inch thick would be an advantage. Thermal insulation, it is claimed, is better than a 11-inch cavity brick wall. Up to the ground floor window sills is a plinth of pre-cast concrete slabs faced with briquettes or tiles. The Howard house contains a kitchen which is made in the factory, and transported to the site complete, and then placed into position in the steel frame by means of a crane. There is also a completely prefabricated plumbing unit which is dropped into position in a similar way. The house is erected speedily. One team erects the steel framework in a few hours, and passes on to the next pair. The kitchen and plumbing units are then placed in position and the asbestos roof sheets are put on so that the remainder of the work can proceed under some degree of cover. Another team then puts in the wall cladding. This house can be erected in much less time than a brick house of a similar size (Plate VI, a).

The Hill house has a similar light steel frame construction, the cladding in this case consisting of an external lining of vibrated concrete slabs 2 inches thick, laid in bond in cement mortar and attached to the steel stanchions by galvanized iron ties bedded in the joints and insulated from direct contact with the steel by felt strips. The internal lining consists of wallboard fixed to wood-filled metal channel members running horizontally between the stanchions. Bitumen bonded glass fibre is placed under the wallboard for additional thermal insulation.

The Braithwaite method consists of a number of light guage ladder-like frames which for the two-story house are 18 feet high by 3 feet 2 inches wide. The sections can be adapted to a one-, three- or four-story building. The floors and flat roof are suspended steel frame constructions. Timber panels or concrete slabs are placed on these frames, and for the roof they are covered with a two-ply roof felting. In an alternative for the ground floor the timber sections are laid on the concrete foundation slab, which in this case rests on hard core. One ingenious feature of the Braithwaite system is the manner in which the external and internal linings are fixed to the steel frame. One form of external cladding consists of asbestos cement sheets, $\frac{1}{4}$ inch thick by grid width formed with vertical fluting on the exterior face to stiffen the sheet between the supporting horizontals. The sheets are spaced $\frac{1}{4}$ inch apart and butt up to the upstanding leg of extruded aluminium cover clips. These cover clips are firmly constructed and are shaped to fit over the flutes of the cladding sheets. The sheets are firmly held between the weather edges of the cover clip and the steel frame by tension clamps spaced at predetermined intervals ensuring a weathertight joint by intimate contact between cover clip and sheet along their full length. The internal lining which may be plasterboard, fibreboard, plywood or glazed asbestos is clipped into position in a similar way.

The Coventry house represents one of the most advanced exercises in engineering applied to the small house. The construction is of a tubular steel frame. Three tubular steel braced uprights reaching the full height of the house are fixed at the four corners on pre-cast concrete foundation blocks. Horizontal framework for the two floors and roof complete the essential framework. Tubular steel uprights for the attachment of the wall cladding are placed at intervals of 3 feet (Plate VI, b). The ground floor, like the first floor, being suspended, allows for free circulation of air underneath the house, which serves to keep it dry. The ground floor consists of approximately 3 feet square by inch thick pre-cast concrete units laid on an insulating blanket. As there is no timber in the construction of the floor, it is possible to seal the space under the ground floor and so eliminate cold draughts. The external wall cladding of the Coventry house consists of concrete slabs, $1\frac{1}{2}$ inches thick, to the underside of the first floor windows. These are fixed with cruciform plates and with joints finished with cream pointing. Cream asbestos cement ribbed sheets at first floor window level complete the outside cladding. The internal lining consists of panels, which are 3 feet wide by room height of timber framed plaster-board backed by an insulating material and finished with wood veneer, leather, cloth or other suitable material according to the type of room.

The steel framework of the Cranwell house is especially light, consisting of vertical R.S.J. 4 inches by $1\frac{3}{4}$ inches, the complete height of the house, placed at 3-feet centres with horizontal stanchions at the first floor level supplemented by timber joists. The corner stanchions are of special design, consisting of two of angle section with connecting pieces. This system is interesting, however, mainly because of the external cladding which consists of hollow King tiles 3 feet long by 6 inches high by 4 inches thick which are grooved at each end to fix into the steel frame while they are held together by cement mortar joints. The external face is covered with cement rendering and finished with splatter box spray. There is a cavity of 1 inch and an internal lining of plaster-slabs or other material about $1\frac{1}{2}$ inches thick, held in position by special clips which adhere to the vertical stanchions. The wall is thus about 7 inches thick. The party wall consists of two external walls side by side with a cavity of 2 inches between. The thermal insulation of the wall is claimed to be particularly good because in addition to the cavity there is the air space in the hollow tiles of the external cladding. A virtue of this construction is that it is extremely light, being little more than half the weight of a normal brick house, while it can be speedily erected, the hollow tiles being not too heavy (30 lb.) to be lifted by one man (Plate VII, a).

All five houses noted in this section are based on a horizontal grid. That of the Howard construction is 3 feet 6 inches, that of the Hill 3 feet 7 inches, that of the Braithwaite 3 feet 2 inches (which is also the vertical grid), and that of the Coventry and Cranwell 3 feet. It would obviously assist the interchangeability of parts and equipment, and facilitate the production of houses if there could be some agreed module, of which the grid could be a multiple. It would have been better if they had all been designed to a grid of 3 feet, 3 feet 4 inches, or 3 feet 6 inches, which would thus be a multiple of an agreed universal module of 4 inches or 6 inches.

One of the advantages of the steel frame construction in which the floors are suspended is that it makes possible considerable flexibility of planning. The partitions can be placed anywhere and just be attached to the floors.

C.—Metal Clad Houses

8, 9 and 10. The metal clad method has not been developed to the same extent as the two methods previously described. The chief reason is probably that the metal cladding contributes very little to either thermal or sound insulation, and this had to be provided mainly by the addition of some other material. Several methods were developed in the nineteen-twenties like the Weir, Atholl, Cowieson and Telford, and it was found in these that neither thermal nor sound insulation was equal to conventional brick construction. It is a method that allows for a high degree of prefabrication, and that is probably why this type of construction was used to the greatest extent in non-traditional construction in the years immediately following the end of the Second World War.

In this period, some 36,000 steel-framed semi-steel-clad B.I.S.F. Houses were ordered by the Ministry of Health for erection throughout the country, to the requirements of the various local authorities. These houses were based on experimental units built by the British Iron and Steel Federation at Northolt for demonstration purposes. Two were steel-framed structures, one of hot rolled sections and the other of cold formed sections, in which the upper half of the building was entirely clad in steel sheet. The third type was a panel construction, each steel panel two-stories high being erected complete with door frames and window frames as necessary and connected by floor beams of cold rolled sections. The choice made by the Government for mass production was Type 'A' house in which hot rolled sections were used for the main framework with the upper cladding of sheet in a vertical ribbed pattern. Steel was also used for the door frames, window frames and staircase. The steel sheet cladding was treated on the inside with corrosion-inhibiting material and was painted externally. The internal lining was usually in fibreboard and plasterboard. The insulation was a glass-silk quilt between the internal lining and the exterior cladding (Plate VII, b).

In the Spooner system metal cladding is partially used. On the ground floor the walls are of $4\frac{1}{2}$-inch brickwork forming the outer leaf, a cavity of $1\frac{1}{2}$ inches and an inner leaf of 3-inch timber-framed panels lined with bitumen felt on the cavity side and plasterboard on its internal face. On the first floor the inner lining is also of timber-framed panels, but the other lining is of 18 gauge steel sheeting backed by $\frac{1}{2}$-inch fibreboard and nailed to the timber frame. The steel sheeting is prepared for painting by means of a phosphate treatment and is painted both on the external and internal faces with a red lead primer. Over 4,000 houses have been built by this method.

It might be objected that a disadvantage of the steel-clad house is that frequent repainting is necessary to maintain it in good condition, but special methods of painting, such as that used in the Spooner system, would appear to be the answer to such an objection. This matter is dealt with in the review of Metal Clad Houses in the Burt Committee's report on House Construction (paragraph 526). It is stated that in the early life of the Scottish steel-clad houses 'there was considerable corrosion of the outside surfaces of the steel sheets, bolt heads and vertical cover strips, and it was considered that it would be necessary to repaint all the external steelwork every three years. However, in 1933, a method of painting (paint harling) was adopted which has been effective in preventing appreciable rusting since that date. Most of the Scottish steel houses have been tested in this way and the result has been entirely successful. Examination of a number of houses treated in 1938 failed to disclose any appreciable deterioration of the paint, or corrosion of the steel sheets. The only rusting observed was an insignificant amount on some of the rounded heads of the bolts and drive screws used for fixing the sheets. The paint harling is still in such good condition that repainting is likely to be unnecessary for several years.' A specification is given of paint harling (paragraphs 818-23). A thick coat of special lead paint is applied and graded granite chips, coated with the same paint, are then thrown on. This produces a roughcast and quite attractive appearance.

D.—*Timber Houses*

11, 12 and 13. Timber houses are among the oldest types, but a number of new forms of timber construction have been developed, allowing varying degrees of pre-fabrication. A certain number of timber houses were erected in the nineteen-twenties; among these may be mentioned those erected at Watling and Becontree by the London County Council. These were constructed of a timber frame of 4 inch by 2 inch sections covered externally with creosoted weather-boarding on thin bitumen felt, and internally with wood fibreboard. A number of timber houses were also erected in Scotland in the early days of the war. One of the most interesting of these types was erected at Dundee and is described in the Burt Committee's Report on House Construction. The walls consist 'of prefabricated panels of 3-inch tongued and grooved cedar boards set vertically, lined externally with wind-proof paper'. It has an external finish of vertical cedar boards $\frac{3}{4}$ inch thick and corner strips on cedar weather-boarding and an internal lining of plasterboard fixed on battens. The thermal insulation appears to be better than normal brick construction. The houses seem to be strong, but durability depends on resistance to fungal attack which can presumably be effected by periodic painting or creosoting. Western red cedar is a valuable timber for this purpose, as it is immune from fungal attack. One drawback with timber construction is that when once the house is infested with vermin, disinfestation is more difficult than with most other types. This was the experience of the London County Council on the Watling and Becontree estates.

It is with the timber frame and plywood cladding that there appears to be some of the most interesting possibilities for future development. I remember one method of construction designed by J. Cecil Clavering in a housing estate scheme which received first prize in a competition organized by the Incorporated Association of Architects and Surveyors. In this scheme the houses are constructed of timber framed units with stressed plywood membranes on either side, for both walls and floors, with thermal insulating material between the wall membranes. The designs for timber houses submitted in the competition, organized by the Timber Development Association in the winter of 1944-5, showed some, but not extensive, use of plywood; the concentration was rather on prefabricated elements in which framed units and boarding formed the sections. For example, in the design placed first by John P. Tingey the walls consist of units 10 feet $7\frac{1}{2}$ inches wide by 17 feet 11 inches high—that is the full height of the house up to the eaves. These units have 4-inch by 2-inch studs on which are fixed diagonal boards 1 inch thick, then a layer of bituminous paper and then red cedar boarding 1 inch thick fixed vertically. These units ars bolted together. The internal lining consists of plywood or plaster on fibreboard. In the design placed second, by Ralph Erskine, plywood is used to a considerable extent. Here both the external and internal wall linings are of stressed skin plywood panels.

Timber is required for a great variety of purposes and as we normally import the bulk of our consumption it was in very short supply for many years following the war. This is obviously why a large number of experimental houses of this material were not erected, as it clearly lends itself to a high degree of prefabrication. I have little doubt that if timber had been plentiful, large numbers of temporary dwellings would have been built of this material. One interesting house of timber, the Jicwood, was built on the lines of the temporary dwellings. It is probably the first stressed-skin plywood house to be built in England. The whole house—walls, floors, roof and partitions are built of a composite board, called 'Jicwood', of sandwich construction consisting of two sheets of plywood with insulating material between which is either expanded rubber or wood fibre. The boards are $1\frac{5}{8}$ inches thick for external walls and 1 inch thick for partitions. These may appear thin, but it should be emphasized that the stressed-skin construction is very strong, having been adopted for the Mosquito aircraft. It is claimed that both thermal and sound insulation is better than for a 1-inch thick for partitions. These may appear thin, but it should be emphasized that example, the Jicwood bungalow which provides accommodation similar to the standard types—that is, with living room, two bedrooms, kitchen and bathroom, is constructed in eight sections. The house is erected on a concrete platform in a day, although there seems no reason why it should not be erected in half a day.

Another interesting timber construction is that of the Scottwood house. In this the walls consist of two sheets of plywood each $\frac{3}{8}$ inch thick glued to timber studs $2\frac{3}{4}$ inches by $\frac{3}{4}$ inch at 12-inch centres, thus making the wall $3\frac{1}{2}$ inches thick. The cavity is filled with glass wool between bitumen paper moisture barriers. The wall sections used are of considerable size being story height and up to 24 feet long (PlateVIII, a). interlocking joints are employed, with bolts and covering where necessary. The floor and roof are constructed in a similar manner.

There are vast possibilities for further developments in timber construction for houses, especially for plywood, used perhaps in conjunction with other materials.

E.—*Other Panel or Slab Types*

14 and 15. There is probably no limit to the number of materials that could form suitable panels for house construction, some strong enough to be load bearing, others forming a screen and fixed to a frame. These panels might be composed of partly synthetic materials. So far, however, the most noteworthy construction in this category is the Uni-Seco. The panels in this system are of sandwich construction, and consist of an insulating core of wood wool sandwiched between asbestos cement sheets, and enclosed in a timber frame. The thickness of the panel is $1\frac{3}{4}$ inches and the timber frame is $2\frac{3}{4}$ inches projecting a little on either side of the sheets. For ordinary house construction where big spans are not required the panels are strong enough for the necessary load bearing, but for larger building work where bigger spans occur than in the small house, a frame construction is desirable. The beams and columns comprising this are of boxed plywood or light steel construction (Plate VIII, b).

The Seco system was used in buildings for war-time purposes both in England and in Scotland. A large proportion of the temporary houses were built of this system of dry-unit construction.

F.—*Prefabricated Brick Houses*

16. Experiments have been made with pre-fabricated brick panels for house construction and houses have been built by these methods, one of the most interesting

being that of Simplified Brick Construction Ltd. In this system the panels consist of a brick external face 4½ inches, a cavity of 2 inches and an internal sheet of concrete 4 inches thick. The panels are manufactured on a timber frame, mounted on steel channels, into which is fixed a cast-iron brick grid. Standard bricks are placed in position on the grid, steel sides are fitted above the timber frame, the cement is poured into the joints, the cavity shuttering is then placed between the steel sides for the internal concrete sheet, reinforced rods are placed in position, and the concrete is poured and levelled off. The sections include lintels, window and door openings and ventilations. If a large number of houses of the same design, or of various designs based on a suitable module were built by this method then the panels could be standardized and production could be rapid (Fig. 4).

In another system developed by Howard Smith and the British Steel Constructions (Birmingham) Ltd., slabs of foamed slag concrete are faced with bricks 1½ inches thick. The total thickness of the slabs is 8 inches for the ground floor and 6 inches for the first floor, and the majority are 6 feet long by 2 feet high, the slabs at corners and at the sides of doors and windows being of different sizes, while there are special units for lintels. The slabs are rapidly made in steel moulds by the conveyor belt system. On one face of the moulds are slots for the bricks, and when those are placed in position cement is poured in followed by the foamed slag concrete (Plate IX).

Some of the methods indicated in this brief survey are proving to be excellent, and with further development some, I think, will prove to be better than any method of small house construction yet evolved. The greatest possibilities exist with methods like the concrete slab construction forming cavity, the reinforced concrete frame construction with concrete panels, and with steel frame houses with panels of various materials (6 and 7). With concrete the advantages of pre-cast sections are considerable, but it is a further advantage if the sections are thoroughly dry before fixing, so as to avoid movement in the concrete and consequent cracks. In many of the pre-cast concrete houses described, such as the Orlit, 'Reema' and Smith, a quick drying process is employed. The concrete panels are dried in heating chambers in about nine hours, which, it is claimed, is the equivalent of twenty-eight days of ordinary maturing.

When dealing with the steel frame construction mention was made of the desirability of houses being designed on the same grid, or at least on a grid that is a multiple of an agreed universal module of 4 inches or 6 inches.   This would make possible a certain interchangeability of parts among various systems and would thus allow for standardization and mass production on a greater scale. A considerable amount of research has been done in America on this subject, where there appears to be a preference for a module of 4 inches. It is a matter that merits prompt and full consideration in this country, and an agreement regarding a universal module would certainly make a valuable contribution to economical house construction.

The Modular Society was formed in 1952 with this purpose. Later the European Productivity Agency of the Organisation for European Co-operation appointed a committee to study the subject and a first report was published in 1956. Eleven European countries—Austria, Belgium, Denmark, France, Germany, Greece, Italy, the Netherland, Norway, Sweden and the United Kingdom—with Canada and the United States, are taking part. In the second stage of the work a two year programme of experimental building to test theories is being undertaken by each country. The module which is being adopted for this experimental work is 10 cm. for countries

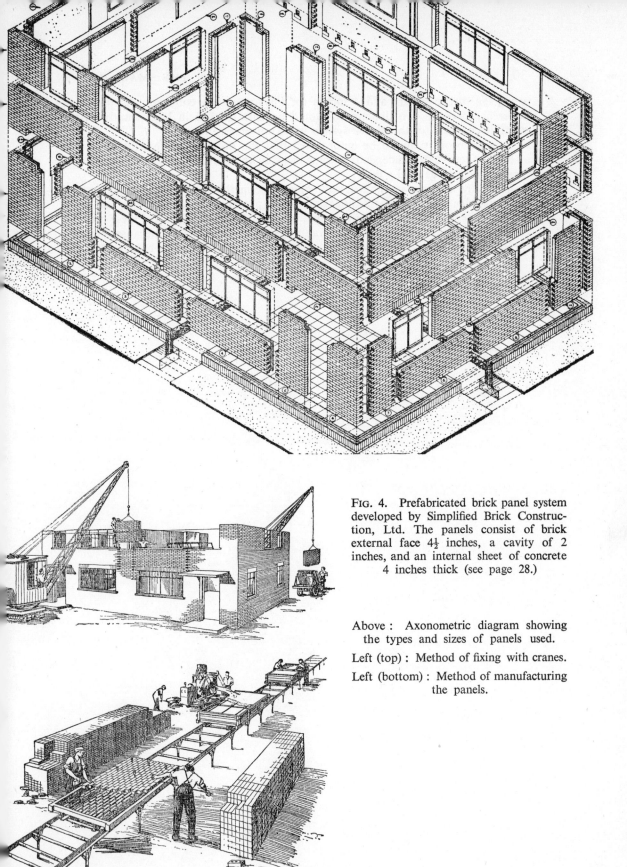

FIG. 4. Prefabricated brick panel system developed by Simplified Brick Construction, Ltd. The panels consist of brick external face $4\frac{1}{2}$ inches, a cavity of 2 inches, and an internal sheet of concrete 4 inches thick (see page 28.)

Above : Axonometric diagram showing the types and sizes of panels used.

Left (top) : Method of fixing with cranes.

Left (bottom) : Method of manufacturing the panels.

using the metric system and 4 inches for the foot-inches countries. As the slight difference in these two dimensions would become marked in large multiples, the sensible course is for the metric system to be universally adopted.

In conclusion it should be emphasized that the progress made with these new methods of construction depends in some measure on the attitude to them of architects, builders and the general public.

There are immense possibilities in many of the methods, and we must go forward with confidence in their possibilities and not be prevented by a deadening and senti-mental conversation. I am confident that, properly developed, many of these methods will challenge the conventional and traditional brick construction, because they may prove to be in the long run speedier to erect, more economical and more serviceable.

(*a*) The Howard system. The wall panels are being fixed to a light-welded frame. (*See* p. 23.)

(*b*) The Coventry system. The tubular steel framework. (*See* p. 23.)

PLATE VI. (*a*) *and* (*b*). *Methods of House Construction.*

(a) The Cranwell system. Steel framework and external wall lining of hollow King tiles. (*See* p. 24.)

(b) The B.I.S.F. system. Framework and steel cladding of upper story with sheets 10 inches wide and story height. (*See* p. 25.)

PLATE VII. (a) and (b). *Methods of House Construction.*

(*a*) The Scottwood system. Plywood wall sections being placed in position. The wall sections consist of two sheets of plywood with cavity filled with glass wool between bitumen paper-moisture barriers. (*See* p. 27.)

(*See* p. 27.)

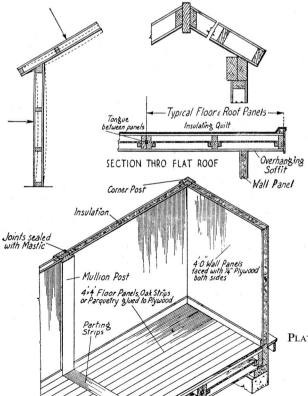

(*b*) Stressed skin plywood construction. Walls of composite board of sandwich construction consisting of two sheets of plywood with insulating material between.

Typical Floor & Roof Panels
Tongue between panels
Insulating Quilt

SECTION THRO FLAT ROOF

Overhanging Soffit
Wall Panel

Corner Post
Insulation
Joints sealed with Mastic
Mullion Post
4'·4' Floor Panels, Oak Strips or Parquetry glued to Plywood
Parting Strips
4'·0' Wall Panels faced with ¼" Plywood both sides

PLATE VIII. (*a*) *and* (*b*). *Houses of Timber Construction.*

PLATE IX. The Smith system. Gantry used for erection of house constructed of brickfaced concrete panels. (*See* p. 28.)

CHAPTER V

A MINIMUM STANDARD OF ACCOMMODATION

ONE of the first questions in considering the small house, that is, the house for at least 90 per cent. of the population, is to ask what is the minimum accommodation for families according to a standard of living at which we in this country should aim. This depends on the financial capacity of the majority and this in turn is dependent on a social and economic system which will make this capacity possible. It means that there should be a workable relation between minimum wages in industry and the cost of living which should include housing to provide a desirable minimum accommodation. How to achieve such a workable relation is outside the scope of this book, but that it should be achieved is an almost unanimous opinion. Difficulties arise in reaching agreement on the best ways and means.

What is the desirable minimum accommodation? That the size of families should be a determining factor is obvious, but this has rarely been so in the past. When Saltaire was built in 1852 to house the employees of Sir Titus Salt it represented a great advance in housing for factory workers. The houses were mainly of the parlour and non-parlour types with three bedrooms, one for the parents, one for the sons, and one for the daughters. This pattern has been largely followed for family houses ever since. In the days of large families it resulted in overcrowding, but in the period between the two wars, owing to the gradual reduction in the size of families, such accommodation has approached nearer to a desirable standard. In 1850 it was common to have ten children in a family, of whom two or three died before reaching adulthood. This meant that in the one-family house cited, eight children occupied two bedrooms, probably from the age of two years (until which age they often slept in their parents' bedroom) to the age of twenty, after which the number was gradually decreased by marriages. If there was a preponderance of one sex the position was aggravated. This was a common way of living in one-family houses from 1850 to the early years of this century, and being one-family houses it represented a much higher standard of living than in areas of industrial overcrowding, where large families living in one or two rooms were not uncommon, Conditions in small one-family houses improved, not so much because of the provision of more adequate accommodation, but because of decreases in the sizes of families; and in the majority of small houses built between the wars accommodation was still of the old mid-Victorian standard of the one-family house, consisting of parlour and non-parlour types with three bedrooms. It has seemed to be the rule that whatever the size of family it must fit into the three-bedroom standard; thus fitting the family to the house rather than building the house round the needs of the family. This is the reverse of organic building which should always be a biological and social aim.

In the Housing Act of 1935 (Section 2) the permitted number of persons occupying dwelling houses is : One room, 2 persons; two rooms, 3 persons; three rooms, 5 persons;

four rooms, 7½ persons; five rooms, 10 persons; with an additional 2 in respect of each room in excess of 5. No account is taken of a child under one year old; and a child over one year old, but under ten, is reckoned as a half a unit. Anything in excess of this is regarded as overcrowding. It is also regarded as overcrowding if persons of opposite sex not being husband and wife sleep in the same room. Also, to accommodate 2 persons a room must be 110 square feet or more, to accommodate 1½ persons (1 adult and 1 child) the room must be 90 square feet or more; to accommodate 1 person it must be 70 square feet or more.[1]

There is nothing in these provisions to prevent overcrowding of bedrooms. If a family of ten occupies a non-parlour house with three bedrooms, or a family of twelve occupies a parlour house with three bedrooms and the sons sleep in one of the bedrooms and daughters in another, which means perhaps five boys or five girls sleeping in one bedroom, there is no indication in the Act that this is overcrowding. Even if some of the children slept downstairs to relieve the congestion there would still be most undesirable and unhealthy sleeping conditions.

Provided each room is 110 square feet or more the average of two persons per room for each of the five rooms does not infringe the overcrowding regulations, as there is no stipulation in the Act that ten persons shall not sleep in three of the five rooms. More satisfactory regulations would make stipulations about the number of persons sleeping in rooms.

The standards provided by the Act are much too low, and it is only the acute shortage of small houses, which has always existed in this country, that has made us acquiesce in such standards. Low as they are, the adherence to them has meant a considerable improvement in living conditions in many overcrowded and slum areas. I take the extreme cases of families of ten and twelve to demonstrate the implications of the permitted standards, but the problem is not likely to be so difficult as the hypothetical cases indicate, as families of this size since the First World War are the exception rather than the rule.

It is clear that the permitted number of persons to a house represents a standard with which we would not for long be satisfied. The Registrar-General for England and Wales in his evidence before the Barlow Commission said that among the factors most important in enhancing the death rates of residents in towns was 'the crowding together of people into houses too small for them'; while the Joint Medical Committee in its evidence suggested that 'overcrowding per room should, as far as possible, be avoided'. It is not avoided by the provisions of the Housing Act of 1935.

To suggest that the standard of living at which we should aim should provide every child over the age of ten with a room of his own cannot surely be regarded as too idealistic. Privacy for the individual as well as privacy for the family is an important requisite for full cultural development. As Lewis Mumford so well says in *The Culture of Cities*: 'The cloister in both its public and private form is a constant element in the life of men in cities. Without formal opportunities for isolation and contemplation, opportunities that require enclosed space, free from prying eyes and extraneous stimuli and secular interruptions, even the most externalized and extraverted life must eventually suffer. The home without such cells is but a barracks; the city that does not possess them is but a camp. In the mediaeval city the spirit had organized shelters and

[1] See the first schedule of the 1935 Act.

accepted forms of escape from worldly importunity. To-day, the degradation of the inner life is symbolized by the fact that the only place sacred from interruption is the private toilet.'[1]

In the small house with only living room, kitchen and bedrooms, to what place can the adolescent son or daughter retire to study, to do homework, or to be at peace and think? The wireless may be on, or the parents may want to talk. Often in the past the child has had to struggle with his work through a din of talk or the wireless, and it is obvious that in such circumstances the child is not having a fair chance. If there were another room on the ground floor, say a dining room, to which he could retire it would be better, and this is often the case; but then if there are many children even with this extra room the studious child may not be able to get that desirable isolation so important for this work. It would be much better if each child could retire to a bedroom of his own where he could work, and that the bedroom were of a size to allow ample space for a fair-sized working table or desk.[2] This provision would also contribute to making the bedroom of an adequate size from the standpoint of health, so that there would be little risk of its falling below the minimum of 100 square feet recommended by the Royal College of Physicians.[3]

This provision is concerned with the growing child who, engaged in homework and other studies, later leaves school, goes to work, and still later gets married and leaves home. What of the parents? Are they not to have a privacy equal to that of the children? As a unit they have, of course, as much privacy as the child with a room of his own; but it can hardly be expected that one or other of the parents shall work and study in their joint bedroom. When they have wanted to do work requiring concentration it has generally been done in the living room, and the rest of the family has had to remain quiet. 'Hush, Daddy is working' is a familiar saying in domestic history. Where there are two rooms, the parent has sometimes gone to the other room. The advent of broadcasting has made these problems of privacy, seclusion and quiet more difficult. Where a man has much work to do requiring quiet, he has generally insisted on a room of his own, and slightly larger houses provide studies. There is also the wife to be considered; she may want periods of quiet when she can read and study, and it is to be hoped that these wants on the part of the wife will greatly increase in the future.

I think the best solution of this problem is the abandonment of the double bedroom for the small house, both for children over ten and parents. Two people sleeping in one room, even if they are man and wife, is neither wholly hygienic nor always aesthetically agreeable. This is particularly so if one has a cold, or is otherwise unwell. Some young married couples may not like the notion of separate rooms at first thought, but after a little reflection they may, I think, realize that it has its advantages. After a few years of married life such an arrangement would be generally appreciated, and is more likely to preserve romantic feeling than when all the processes of going

[1] *The Culture of Cities* (London, 1938), p. 29.

[2] In winter the enjoyment of these facilities depends on the room being adequately heated, and this may mean extra expense. I deal with question in the chapter on Heating and Ventilation.

[3] In a Memorandum prepared in 1942 at the request of the Central Housing Advisory Committee of the Ministry of Health.

to bed and rising in the morning are completely familiar to one's husband or wife. The maintenance of romantic feeling depends a little on the preservation of remoteness about personal habits and intimate ways of life.

From the standpoint of hygiene and from the standpoint of those pursuits which are best followed in solitude, a room of one's own is important, and is an ultimate essential of a standard of living at which a progressive civilization should aim. The psychological value of a room all to oneself, to which one can retire completely from the world cannot be over-estimated. It is, after all, what the well-to-do have always enjoyed as a matter of course.

Following such a recommendation it is more important, therefore, that each member of the family should have a room of his own than that there should be a dining room in addition to the living room or kitchen; but, as will be seen later, this provision for meals can be of a very flexible kind. What a desirable standard requires is a bedroom not less than 100 square feet for each member of the family over ten; a good kitchen, and a fair-sized living room. It might be said as a general principle that in a two-story house the ground floor with kitchen, living room, hall and adequately designed space for meals is the family part of the house; the first floor with bedrooms is the individual part.

If houses are to accommodate families according to a desirable standard it is important to take account of the probable future size of families and it will be seen, I think, that this would make a room for each member of the family not such a remote ideal.

At the 1931 Census the average size of household was 3·8 roughly as follows:

Size of family	Percentage of total
1	3·5
2	19·5
3	27
4	22·5
5	12·5
6	7
7	4
8	2
9	1
10	1

In the 1951 Census 1 per cent. sample tables the average size of household was 3·21 persons divided as follows:

Size of family	Percentage of total
1	10·8
2	27·6
3	24·8
4	19·1
5	9·6
6/7	6·5
8/9	1·3
10 or more	·3

In the last thirty years it will be found that the families of the medium and higher wage groups are smaller than among the lower wage groups. In an estate built since 1930 on the outskirts of London inhabited by medium income groups (pre-war £250-£600) the sizes of families, where the mothers were between thirty-five and fifty years of age, so that future increases are not likely to be great, were as follows:

Size of family	Percentage of whole
2	6
3	18
4	48
5	20
6	8

The average works out at 4·06. With final expansion it is not likely to be more than 4·5, and it would probably take place mainly in the enlargement of families of three to families of four. It is clear that among medium wage groups at the present time the majority of families consist of two children.

In poorer districts such as occur in the east-end boroughs of London, families are larger than among the medium and higher income groups. In the survey of housing conditions in Shoreditch, one of the poorest and most over-crowded districts in the country, made by the Shoreditch Housing Association and published in 1938, the sizes of families based on 377 cases was as follows:

Size of family	Percentage of whole
2	1
3	8
4	14
5	18
6	22
7	16
8	11
9	6
10	3
12	1

The average size of family here is six. But this is considerably smaller than it would have been fifty years earlier, for it is noted that even among the lower income groups families have been getting smaller.

The reason for larger families among the lower income groups is that among such groups birth control is not so widely practised, and there is not such a desire to limit the size of family as among the slightly higher income groups. In the latter the standard of education is higher and parental responsibility stronger. This tends towards limiting the number of children, because the parents want to provide adequately for the children they have, and they want to give them a good education and a fair chance in life. I think it may be said that raising the general standard of education will result in a general limiting of families to an average of two or three children. An average of three children would effect a slight increase in population, while an average of two children would mean a slight decrease, provided marriages continued at their present level, and provided the survival rate is high.

Many have argued that if the population is to maintain a steady increase, there must be social security and people must be well housed. The evidence suggests the reverse.

3

Among the medium income groups, like the black-coated workers, where there has been comparative social security and people have enjoyed comparatively good housing, families are smaller than where housing is of a low standard and there has been less social security. The truth is that with a higher standard of education a sense of parental responsibility increases and there is a stronger desire to limit the size of families. It is a concentration on quality rather than quantity. When this social security with a higher standard of education together with the limitation that a medium income means spreads to what are at present the lower-wage groups, there will be this widespread tendency to limit families to two or three children. To those who are apprehensive about the future of the population it may be replied that it is far better to have a high quality stable population, where the survival rate is high, than to have an increasing population of lower quality. We should think of quality primarily rather than of the mere maintenance of quantity.

The ideal that everyone should have a room of his own, and that we should build houses accordingly may be difficult to accomplish in the immediate future, as it would depend, as before mentioned, on the financial ability of every family to acquire such a house. Until there is that workable relation between minimum wages and a cost of living which includes the standard of housing I have indicated, it cannot be accomplished. It depends on how long we take to achieve that workable relation. There are also the practical difficulties. If we were to embark on a programme based on this standard in the immediate future it would involve ultimately the replacement of most of the existing small houses, and this would mean a housing programme in the region of 12 million houses. If the standard is too high for the immediate future because of economic difficulties until that workable relation between wages and a good standard of living is accomplished, it may be necessary to affect a compromise. Here are some suggested compromises.

Size of family	Desirable number of bedrooms	Compromise 1	Compromise 2
A. 2 (no children)	2	1 : 1 double room	
B. 3 (one child)	3	2 : 1 double, 1 single	
C. 4 (two children)	4	3 : 1 double, 2 single	
D. 5 (three children)	5	4 : 1 double, 3 single	3 : 2 double, 1 single
E. 6 (four children)	6	5 : 1 double, 4 single	4 : 2 double, 2 single

No bedroom should be less than the minimum of 100 square feet recommended by the Royal College of Physicians, and I think no double bedroom should be less than 150 square feet.

It is suggested that the second less satisfactory compromise should form a statutory minimum with as little delay as possible. Even this represents a much higher standard than the minimum of the Housing Act of 1935.

The standards are, of course, higher than those recommended by the Dudley Committee.[1] The latter do not represent sufficient advance on unsatisfactory traditional standards, for the Committee's suggestions mean only comparatively slight improvements. The ideal that I have indicated for a family of five means five bedrooms of not less than 100 square feet each; the first compromise one double bedroom not less than

[1] Report of the Sub-Committee on the Design of Dwellings of the Central Housing Advisory Committee of the Ministry of Health (London, 1944).

150 square feet, and three bedrooms not less than 100 square feet, and a second compromise two bedrooms not less than 150 square feet and one not less than 100 square
feet. The Dudley Committee recommends for a family of five one double bedroom
not less than 135 square feet, a second double bedroom 110 square feet and a single
bedroom 70 square feet.[1] The Ministry of Health had received the recommendation
of the Royal College of Physicians 'that in a dwelling of three bedrooms no room used
for sleeping should be less than 100 square feet, and that the "second" bedroom should
be as large as the first',[2] about eighteen months before the Dudley Committee reported,
and yet the Committee appears largely to have ignored this important suggestion of
the most authoritative medical body in the country.

For the desired standards indicated in a two-story house for a family of five or more
the first floor with bedrooms needs to cover a larger area than the ground floor, in
which the main requisites of kitchen and utility room, dining space and living room
can be included in a smaller area for the family of five or more. One failure of the
Dudley Committee has been to allow what is almost an adequate ground floor to limit
the size of the first floor. This mistake results from the Committee's too close adherence
to traditional methods of planning.

Let us take the more difficult case of a family of six. If the first compromise is
adopted, which gives reasonable accommodation at one double and four single rooms,
this, with bathroom and W.C. will require a much larger area than kitchen, utility
room, dining space and living room. What are sometimes made outbuildings, such as
fuel storage and shed for garden tools, cycles and perhaps a bench could be included
in the ground floor. The problem is more easily solved if a garage is possible for this
could be included in the ground floor and the first floor built over it. But if neither
garage nor shed is included in the ground floor, one solution is to put one of the bedrooms on the ground floor. Another solution for families of five, six and more is to
extend the house vertically by having two floors of bedrooms. It might be useful to
incorporate a basement or semi-basement for storage, utility room and heating plant.
Reference to the advantages of the basement for such purposes and consideration of
its possible revival are discussed in Chapter XX.

These considerations demonstrate how very important it is to plan logically according to family needs based on a fairly high standard of living, rather than on traditional practice. The Dudley Committee was obviously much influenced by traditional
practice. The three alternative ground floor plans suggested by the Committee are
adaptations of what already exists in many small houses throughout the country,
and although they are good as far as they go, they do not represent any important
innovations.[3]

I fully realise that the ideal family accommodation proposed in this chapter may
be difficult to attain for the majority, and may seem to many to be somewhat remote.
But many such ideals of the past have seemed, when proposed, similarly remote, and
many of these are now realities. It is mainly in this way of fixing a goal and moving
resolutely towards it that progress is made.

[1] Op. cit. para. 157.   [2] Op. cit. p. 3.
[3] These three types shown on pages 34, 36, and 38 of the Dudley Report are as follows:
Alternative 1, Dining-Kitchen with Utility Room and Living Room; Alternative 2, Working
Kitchen, and Living Room with Dining Recess; Alternative 3, Kitchen-Living Room,
Scullery and Sitting Room.

CHAPTER VI

PROGRESS AND PEOPLE'S WANTS

NUMEROUS inquiries have been conducted by many institutions and individuals to discover the kind of houses that people like. A great variety of questions have been asked of a large number of people in all conditions of life and in all parts of the country. The questions cover all conceivable kinds of preferences relating to dwellings and their surroundings. The most exhaustive inquiry conducted in this country in recent years is that of Mass Observation, the results of which were published in March 1943, in a book called *People's Homes*. Other inquiries have been conducted by the Townswomen's Guild (results published in *The Townswoman* for June 1943), Society of Women Housing Managers (result published in a Memorandum, May, 1943), the Woman's Advisory Housing Council, the National Council of Women, the National Federation of Women's Institutes, the Standing Joint Committee of Labour Women, the Women's Group on Public Welfare, the Electrical Association for Women, the Women's Gas Council, and many other bodies.

Whilst lecturing on planning and housing to the Forces during the war I conducted similar inquiries, and I give some account in Appendix II of discussions on various questions concerned with preferences in house types and design, and I give the results of voting on these preferences. The National Women Citizens' Association also sent a questionnaire on my behalf in 1955 to its branches and the results are given in Appendix III.

What is the purpose of these inquiries, these questionnaires? Those responsible for them claim that the evidence they provide of people's wants is likely to prove useful to architects, sociologists, politicians, technicians and others who are concerned with building houses, that, they, in brief, should act as a partial guide to the kind of house that should be provided. It is obvious that a very large number of people think that the results of such inquiries should be a guide; there are others, however, who doubt their value. Few who have conducted these inquiries would suggest that they should be an absolute guide, uncritically examined, but they would, I think, assert that the views expressed should in some degree influence the kind of houses built. It may be useful to consider to what extent the opinion of the great majority should determine the kind of houses that are built.

These inquiries are conducted on the democratic assumption that policy should be determined by the will of the people. Democracy is but one form of government, and its chance of survival depends very much on its quality. In other words a democracy based on a fairly high level of general intelligence is more likely to succeed and survive than a democracy based on illiteracy. That is why education is so fundamental in any democratic system. Because it is based on the will of the people, because it is the oneness of the individual and the State, the democratic system demands for its success the co-operation of citizens. It necessarily asks more participation than a dictatorship, because the people are the government, and therefore education is a necessary instrument. Understanding of government and essential social needs is the price that

(*a*) One central ceiling fitting which is unsatisfactory because shadows are cast by the housewife whilst working.

(*b*) Fluorescent lighting eliminates the shadows.

(*c*) Two fittings which in combination give general diffused lighting.

PLATE X. (*a*), (*b*) *and* (*c*). *Examples of lighting in the kitchen.*

PLATE XI. *Efficient linear lighting in a kitchen.*

(*a*) A pull-up-and-down light fitting over the table in the meals' nook.

(*b*) Arrangement with one centre wall light, fixed to pelmet while three spotlights over plants give an attractive decorative effect.

PLATE XII. (*a*), (*b*) and (*c*). *Lighting for meals.*

(*c*) Fluorescent lamp concealed in base of shelves, lights service hatch below, and shelves above.

(*a*) Upward and downward light from the portable standard lamp on left, and from the metal wall fitting, which is pierced to give visual interest. The fluorescent lamp over the bookcase lights the books and the ceiling.

PLATE XIII (*a*), (*b*) and (*c*). *Lighting.*

(*c*) Localized lighting. An adjustable bracket fitting with 180° swing. The shade is fitted in underneath to screen the lamp itself.

(*b*) Diffused pelmet light and localized table lamp.

citizens have to pay for a successful democracy, and few would deny that it is worth while. It is on some such basis that the opinions expressed by people in answer to questionnaires on housing must be respected.

The extent to which these answers should be a guide is the question. If they were taken as an infallible guide, progress would be determined by the thought of the majority rather than by that of the enterprising and gifted few. Progress would thus obviously be slow. Further, there is much in housing which is technical, which the layman, who forms the majority, cannot understand. In the matter of the use of larger prefabricated units, he has but a vague idea of what is meant. He hears a little of these new methods from not always reliable sources, is easily the victim of propaganda from various interests, and it is clear that his opinion is of little value. I think it may be said generally that in housing, technical matters, such as the actual construction of the house, should be left to the experts. But the design, accommodation and surroundings of the home are different matters. Here the voice of the majority is more important. All people have had experience of living in houses, most people have ideas of what they want, and the opinion of the ordinary intelligent man or woman is often just as good as that of the so-called expert, and better, if that so-called expert is just an architect dreaming of the fame he will acquire in building magnificent blocks of flats. What experience is better in determining the design of a house than that of an intelligent housewife keeping house for a family, doing housework and cooking? She knows the sort of house that is inconvenient, and can probably suggest many improvements. It has often been contended that for an achitect to be properly equipped to design houses he should have taken part in the actual construction. It is an antiquated and unsound notion. Is a bricklayer equipped to design a house? Provided an architect knows what various materials will do, that is sufficient. It would be a far more serviceable training for the domestic architect if he did housework, and engaged in the preparation of family meals for a period. That would give him the necessary idea of what is essential in a house, and what not essential, what convenient and what inconvenient.

There is one aspect of the matter which must prompt a critical examination of the stated preferences of the majority. People, especially in their daily habits, are very conservative. It is a tendency born of the liking for security. There is an instinctive dislike of the unknown. People will therefore generally have a bias for the familiar rather than for the unfamiliar. This is less likely with the young and adventurous, who are often willing to try new things, than with older people. I think we can say that where there is reason to believe that if, when anything new becomes familiar, it is likely to be preferred to what already exists, there is sufficient incentive and justification for introducing or adopting it. That evidence is provided by an imaginative understanding of people's requirements, and experience of these innovations in other spheres.

There is a dislike among a very large number of people for the flat roof, and a preference for the pitched roof. I have found that with a few it is based on apprehensions of the structural efficiency of the former, emanating from those who either want to go on building pitched roofs, or who have inadequate knowledge of flat roof construction and have not been very successful with it. But the great majority of those who dislike the flat roof dislike it on the ground of appearance, thinking that it produces monotonous box-like structures. They prefer the more familiar pitched roof. The effect of the flat roof is too exclusively associated in the popular mind with modern architecture. A very large number of Georgian houses have either flat leaded roofs or a parapet hiding a low pitched roof, thus having an appearance from the ground similar to that of a flat-roofed house. Yet there does not seem to be the objection to the Georgian house that there is to modern flat-roofed houses. With this reflection in mind and from experience of some of the beautiful and well designed houses with flat roofs on the Continent harmoniously related to their landscape settings, and in view of their other advantages (enumerated by Walter Gropius in his book, *The New Architecture and the Bauhaus*) one is justified in thinking that in time many people would come to prefer the well-designed flat-roofed house to the traditional pitched-roof house. Here then is sufficient justification for introducing it.

Again, in a large number of houses built within the last twenty years, the functions of kitchen and scullery are combined in the kitchen. It is now the familiar kitchen. The separate scullery and kitchen, not on the old lines, but on scientifically worked out principles, has not been widely experienced. Preference for the familiar in this case is understandable, but from the evidence of those who have experienced the new, it is justifiable to assume that in this case the unfamiliar, becoming familiar, would be preferred.

In contrast, let us take the case of two-story houses and flats. Most people in this country are more accustomed to the former, and they are preferred by a large majority. It is sometimes contended that the opinions expressed have little value because people cannot express preference for things they do not know and cannot imagine. The benefits of a modern block of flats with modern amenities cannot, it is argued, be imagined by the majority accustomed to other modes of life. This may be partially true, although many of the same amenities can be enjoyed in the two-story house. There is evidence that it is for other, deeper reasons that there is the preference for two-story houses. Is there, in fact, any reliable and convincing evidence that if flats became as familiar as two-story houses with gardens they would be preferred? There is not. All the evidence points the other way. For example, many who have lived in flats express their preference for two-story houses, and many who have lived in flats on the Continent all their lives want to live in houses with gardens. Here is a case where the more traditional way of living in this country would still be preferred, however attractive the less familiar flat life were represented, and it is an example where the stated preferences of the people should be a guide in the kind of dwelling that is provided for the majority.

It should be added that in some of the questionnaires conducted by the various bodies mentioned at the beginning of this chapter a certain amount of stimulation of thought on the questions has been given, but more often there has been no such stimulation, and the results suffer in value thereby, It is true that with some persons an intelligent response can be expected because they have had experience of the things with which the questions are concerned and they have thought intelligently about such experience, but in very many cases they have not thought intelligently and have not thought of possible improvements, developments and changes. An expressed preference is more valuable after thought has been stimulated by discussion of each question.

The preferences expressed by men and women in the Forces, recorded in the Appendix, were always given after the various alternatives had been discussed.

CHAPTER VII

SITUATION, SITING AND SUNLIGHT

AMONG the first considerations in thinking of the health of the occupants of a house are the situation and orientation. It is best that the house should not be on a low-lying ground, especially where there is the slightest risk of dampness. The ideal situation for houses in England is on the southern slop of a hill with an easy gradient. In building on undeveloped land, and building new towns this should be borne in mind. Much of the country in England is of an undulating character, and in planning new residential areas it would be a wise course to use the southern slopes of low hills.

In a national planning policy the interests of agriculture and housing must be related, and in planning new residential areas in country districts it is naturally desirable to avoid as far as possible good agricultural land for housing, and to select rather the land of moderate quality. It frequently occurs that the best land for agriculture, which is often low and flat, is not the best land for housing, whereas low hills, the southern slopes of which are perfect for housing, do not frequently provide the best land for agriculture. Yet in the past the builder and housing authority have too often looked for the flat land, whereas they would have served both housing and agriculture better if they had more often looked for sites in undulating country. Much of the flat land to the east and south-east of London is good agricultural land, and a large number of houses were built on this land between the wars in continuation of the vast unplanned urban sprawl. It would have been much better, as most planners realize, if most of these houses had been built on the hills farther out, forming new communities or towns.

After reviewing the various claims on land in this country, Professor Dudley Stamp in an article on 'Where to Build the Houses'[1] speaks of the wisdom of building our new towns and our new housing estates on the medium or poor-quality soils of the country, especially on land which is light and sandy, or on stretches of chalk where the soil is very thin. Although such soils are not good agriculturally, 'what a range', he adds, 'of fascinating garden plants can be cultivated', while fertilizers can easily be imported for the gardens. The advantages of hilly sites are stressed for other reasons. 'In the architect's office,' says Professor Stamp, 'a town plan on a sheet of paper on a drawing board may look intriguing and even exciting. How dull when translated into reality on a flat stretch of land! Yet our town planners and our builders seem to seek far too frequently for flat and gently-rolling farmland and hesitate to use the far better natural sites afforded by comparatively hilly conditions, where almost every house may enjoy a little vista different from that of its neighbour. Where do we find the really attractive old towns in Britain? Nearly always on hilly sites. It is doubtful whether, with the timidity of the present age, anyone would dare to suggest that a town could be built on the site of Durham, or Bath, or any one of the little Cornish villages, which nestle happily in secluded valleys. Yet these are the very sites which avoid using the good land from which we should draw our food.'

[1] *Building Digest*, vol. xii (1952), p. 145. This journal is now *Building Materials*.

It is not always possible to have so favoured a site as the southern slope of a hill; often a northern slope has to be used, when the house should be orientated with its large windows towards the hill. Sometimes there is no easy alternative to low damp ground, in which case it should be thoroughly drained before building, although that has not always been done in the past; indeed houses have sometimes been built on such ground with insufficient damp proof precautions. Where such land has to be used it would be wise to lift the house above ground on piles, so that air circulates underneath the house. Alternatively the ground floor could be used as a workshop or garage, with the living quarters on the first and second floors. There is a house like this in Frognal Way, Hampstead, designed by Maxwell Fry, although this is built on a slope. As is well known, many houses of this type have been built by Le Corbusier in France. Many of the new steel-framed houses, mentioned in Chapter IV, have the ground floor suspended above the ground, and this is certainly a type that might be used on low flat ground.

SUNLIGHT

The health value of introducing a fair measure of sunlight into the house is being increasingly realized. Dark and dusty interiors, unfortunately still very common, harbour germs, like the tuberculosis and typhoid germs, which live in such conditions for years, yet when they are exposed to clear sunlight they quickly die. There are also the valuable health-giving properties of ultra-violet rays in clear sunlight, and it is thus of considerable value if these are admitted to rooms.

These remarks apply generally to sunlight throughout the year, but the penetration of winter sunlight into homes is perhaps the most important aspect of the matter. This is emphasized in the Report on *The Lighting of Buildings,* by the Lighting Committee of the Building Research Board of the Department of Scientific and Industrial Research (Post-War Building Study, No. 12, 1944).[1] People spend far more time in the open in the summer and have far more opportunities outside the house of receiving the benefits of sunlight than in the winter, when a much greater proportion of time is spent indoors. This makes it all the more important in the interests of health to admit sunlight in winter. This circumstance restricts the scope for orientating the house satisfactorily. In summer, rooms will get some sunlight if they face within the circle from N.N.E. to N.N.W. Bedrooms facing N.N.E. will get the early morning sun, and living rooms facing N.N.W. will get the late evening sun; but for winter sunlight the circle is reduced approximately E. to W.[2] With thin walls permitting narrow reveals this could be extended a little either way, but I am assuming cavity walls of 11 inches, and therefore a little would be cut off by the window reveal, while any window facing east-north-east or west-north-west would get a negligible amount of winter sunlight. It is best to have the windows as large as possible with the sunlight unobstructed, which is not easy

[1] In paragraph 67 of *The Lighting of Buildings,* it is stated that 'the horizontal range of the sun in mid-winter is only about 90°, from south-east to south-west. If a window is in a thin wall the extreme limits of orientation which would permit any penetration of sunlight would then be the other 270° from north-east to north-west. In practice some allowance would have to be made for a cut-off due to the depth of window reveal, and this would reduce the limits of orientation to about east-north-east and west-north-west—a range of about 225°.'

[2] Ibid. paras. 137-48.

in areas of high density. But with fairly spaciously planned housing estates that should not prove a difficulty. It may be objected that the large windows may admit too much sunlight in the summer, but this is a matter easily controlled by blinds if desired, or better still by planting a small tree which casts its shadow into the room in the hottest part of the day. It should not be an evergreen because it would then obstruct the winter sunlight, but its leafless boughs would cause comparatively little obstruction.

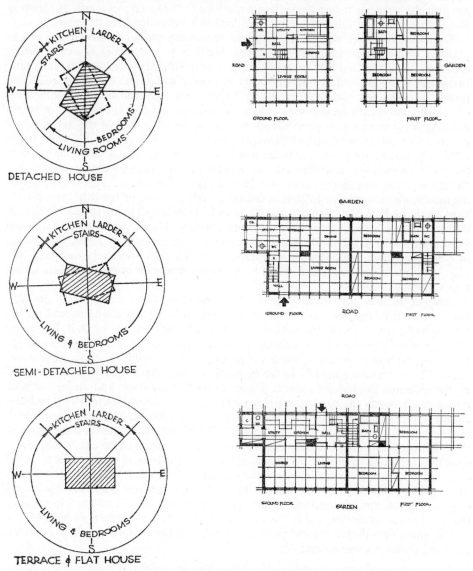

FIG. 5. Diagrams of orientation illustrating the best siting of houses—detached, semi-detached and terrace—according to the sun.

In the past small houses have been chiefly built in rows on either side of streets laid out according to an elongated grid-iron pattern. Thus the houses are orientated according to the geometric pattern of streets. The principal rooms are therefore controlled in the direction they face by this pattern, and it is unavoidable that large numbers have half the rooms facing towards the cold north. In the much admired domestic squares of the late eighteenth and early nineteenth centuries half the rooms on two sides face towards the west-north-east circle. It is a sacrifice to the square as a unit of planning. But in those days the value of sunlight was far less appreciated than it is now.

To orientate houses according to the sun the minor roads in a new estate can be planned, or the house plans can be adapted; but if there is difficulty in accomplishing this, the houses need not face streets or roads. I deal with this question more fully later in discussing the residential unit. The point at present is that both bedrooms and living rooms are pleasanter and healthier places if they are designed to admit a fair measure of sunlight. Bedrooms should get the morning sun, and thus face roughly east or south-east. As the living room is generally most used in the latter half of the day it would be most desirable if this faced south-west or west.[1] In a small detached house it is not difficult to arrange two or three bedrooms to face south-east, and the living room to face both south-east and south-west, the north-south axis running diagonally through the house, as shown in the plans of standard types of dwelling. This would obtain maximum winter sunlight. In some examples, such as those of the dwellings for the workers in the Bata Shoe Factory at Zlin, both bedrooms and living rooms face south, the bedrooms opening on to a balcony with corridor, kitchen, larder and bathroom windows opening to the north. This is an arrangement adopted by J. Cecil Clavering in designing detached houses for an estate. It can be most effectively devised if the plan is long and narrow, and it could be utilized for terrace houses and flats facing roads running east-west.

Many of the new prefabricated houses have the living room and dining room with two bedrooms facing one way, which should obviously be south, and should preferably form the garden front. This is the case with the house designed by D. E. E. Gibson when he was Coventry City Architect, where the living room, dining recess and the two principal bedrooms face towards the garden, which should invariably be towards the south (see plan on page 89). In the Howard House several variations are designed by the architect, Frederick Gibberd, and in all both living room and dining room or recess face towards the garden, while a variation of the Orlit House which includes garage (type 3) has the living room and dining room or recess facing the garden. These are designed for the living room to face south. There can be no question therefore of these houses *facing* on either side of the road. If they are placed on either side of the road then the living rooms on one side would face the garden and on the other the road or street. But it would be much better if they all faced the garden. This could be effected by arranging the houses on one side of the road, the south side only. The road need only be narrow, for light one-way traffic. Such an arrangement is adopted in some of the new towns and can be seen in the plan of a residential area shown on page 167. It will be noted here that at the end of the gardens is a little green strip which could be used as a children's playground.

[1] In paragraph 141 of *The Lighting of Buildings*, op. cit., the Committee cite the evidence of *The War-time Social Survey* 'that 87 per cent of the people want the sun-light in the sitting-room in the afternoon.'

Where it is not always practicable to obtain this arrangement with terrace, semi-detached or detached houses, it is better to plan roads running approximately north and south, so that windows face east and west, and to arrange the living room always on the west. The main consideration is to avoid bedrooms or living rooms facing north. In the spring or autumn, when the sun is shining, the difference in temperature between a south room and a north room is often 10 or 15 degrees.

Provided that the rooms are situated so that they can admit a fair measure of sunlight it is necessary to have windows large enough. It is now possible to have windows of any size, to the extent of complete glass walls if desired. The results of questionnaires on the size of windows among groups in the Forces showed a general preference for large windows. Two hundred and ninety-three preferred large windows to the minority of eighty-two who preferred medium-sized windows, while none wanted them small except on northern walls. The preference is based largely, I think, on the realization of the health value of sunlight, and the consequent desire to admit it into the house.

CHAPTER VIII

LIGHT

THE majority of small houses are inadequately lighted both by day and night. Considerable improvement has been made in recent years, but there is still room for much more. Municipal houses are generally less satisfactory in this respect than those built by private enterprise. This is noted by the Dudley Committee (Report, para. 142), which recommends that 'larger windows should in future be provided in municipal houses subject always to due regard for loss of heat'. The majority of small houses built since 1935 are very much better lighted than those built thirty years earlier, but they are not lighted well enough. But for the stupid window tax there might have been more progress towards better day lighting, but the window tax meant that the houses of the eighteenth century were better lighted than those of the nineteenth century. It is true that the window tax was abolished in 1851, but the deadening tradition of inadequate windows that emerged under this foolish measure continued well beyond that date.

It was pointed out in the previous chapter that the health value of sunlight is being increasingly realized, and that this prompts larger windows. Light and colour are also being more and more closely associated with health. It is realized that the light and simple interior, where dust can be seen, is preferable to the dark and ornamental interior which conceals dust. It is also realized that mental condition has an effect on health and that the bright, cheerful interior has a more salutary effect on the mind than the dark and sombre interior. But one of the principal reasons for the well-lighted interior is, of course, that we should see well and without strain. That simple fact is even now not sufficiently observed, and many people try to work and strain their eyes in badly lighted rooms. When men and women in the Forces expressed a desire for very large windows, provided they face toward the sun's orbit, in preference to medium-sized or small windows, it was not only the health-giving properties of sunlight, but light rooms of which they were thinking.

What is the desirable daylight illumination in the various rooms of the house? The general method of measurement is to determine the requisite daylight factor at a particular distance of penetration from a window. The daylight factor is defined by the Lighting Committee of the Building Research Board as the 'percentage of the total light available outdoors under the unobstructed sky'.[1] It will be clear, therefore, that in a room with one window the area nearest the window has the highest daylight factor, lessening towards the centre of the room. For a room to be adequately lighted it is necessary to determine what area should be above a certain minimum daylight factor (abbreviated d.f.). The Lighting Committee recommends that for a kitchen up to 100 square feet, 50 square feet should be above a minimum of 2 per cent d.f., for a living room up to 150 square feet, 80 square feet should be above 1 per cent d.f., while for a bedroom up to 110 square feet, 60 square feet should be above 0·5 per cent

---

[1] *The Lighting of Buildings*, op. cit. para. 20.

(*a*) Table lamp with degree of indirect lighting
in addition to direct.

(*b*) Concentrated lighting.

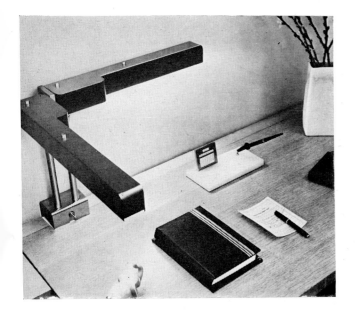

PLATE XIV (*a*) *and* (*b*). *Examples of
concentrated and localized lighting by
means of table lamps.*

(b) Reading or bed lamp.

(a) Tubular lighting for dressing mirror.

PLATE XV (a) and (b). Bedroom lighting.

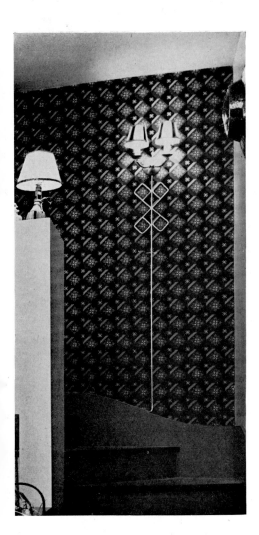

(a) ' Pin-up ' type of wall lighting, in which the flex design harmonizes with the wall-paper pattern.

(b) Soft diffused lighting provided by close ceiling fitting.

PLATE XVI (a) and (b). Stairs lighting.

(a)

(b)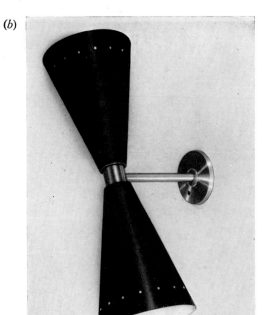

PLATE XVII (a), (b), (c) and (d). *Lighting.*

(a) Wall lamp, (b) wall lamp with upward and downward light.
(c) and (d) Standard lamps, one of which diffuses light to ceiling.

(c)

(d)

d.f. Larger rooms would be adjusted in proportion. Thus for a kitchen 101-120 square feet, the area above 2 per cent d.f. would be 60 square feet; for a living room 151-200 square feet, the area above 1 per cent d.f. would be 100 square feet, and for a bedroom 111-150 square feet the area above 0·5 per cent d.f. would be 80 square feet.

It will be noted that the standard of lighting for the kitchen is highest, and lowest for the bedrooms. It should be explained that these recommended standards are higher than are found in the majority of houses built between the wars, and very much higher than those found in municipal houses. The question is, however, are these suggested standards adequate? Some idea will be afforded by considering the sizes of windows necessary to obtain the suggested illumination. The calculations are based on those prepared by the National Physical Laboratory for the Lighting Committee of the Building Research Board,[1] but I substitute approximate figures for the sake of simplicity. Take a window 5 feet high by 6 feet 6 inches wide, thus a total area of 32·5 square feet with glass area of 25 square feet, 20 per cent being allowed for loss of light through absorption, reflection and dirt. Assuming that there is no obstruction to the light, then about 81 square feet will be above 2 per cent d.f., 138 square feet about 1 per cent, and 226 square feet above 0·5 per cent. But it rarely happens in an estate of small houses that there is no light obstruction. The calculations given by the National Physical Laboratory also take into account various angles of obstruction of 15, 30, 45 and 60 degrees. Assuming an angle of obstruction of 15 degrees for an estate of semi-detached houses built at twelve to the acre, then about 72 square feet would be above 2 per cent d.f., 116 square feet above 1 per cent, and 179 square feet above 0·5 per cent.

If the angle of obstruction is 30 degrees, as it might be in houses built at more than twelve to the acre, then the corresponding figures would be 52, 78 and 110 square feet. It will be seen, therefore, that in relation to the recommended standards, this window with a total area of 32·5 square feet, and a glass area of 25 square feet would be approximately right for a kitchen 100 to 120 square feet, for a living room 150 to 200 square feet, and a bedroom 150 to 200 square feet, provided the obstruction is a little less than 30 degrees.

It would be of advantage, I think, if the daylight area above the specified daylight factor were a greater proportion of each room. In that recommended for the kitchen, about half is above 2 per cent. It is assumed that the equipment requiring most light, like the draining board, sink and cooker should be within this area, but it would allow for more flexibility in the arrangement of this and other equipment if 75 per cent instead of 50 per cent were above 2 per cent d.f. If, therefore, the obstruction is not more than 15 degrees, then for kitchen of 100 square feet a window 4 feet 6 inches high by 7 feet wide, with about 24 square feet glazed area allowing about 25 per cent for bars, would be about right. This is much larger than is provided for the majority of kitchens. If there is a door with a glass panel then the window need not be so large. Also a long narrow horizontal window would be a more convenient shape, and assuming a glass panelled door, a window 7 feet by 3 feet 6 inches might prove adequate. The window would run along the whole wall above the sink and work-table.

I feel that the recommended standards for living room and bedrooms are not sufficiently good. I think 75 per cent of the area above 1 per cent d.f. is desirable, especially if many of the bedrooms are study bedrooms, as recommended in Chapter IV. It must be remembered that anything much less than this 1 per cent d.f. is not good enough

[1] Given on page 20 of *The Lighting of Buildings,* op. cit.

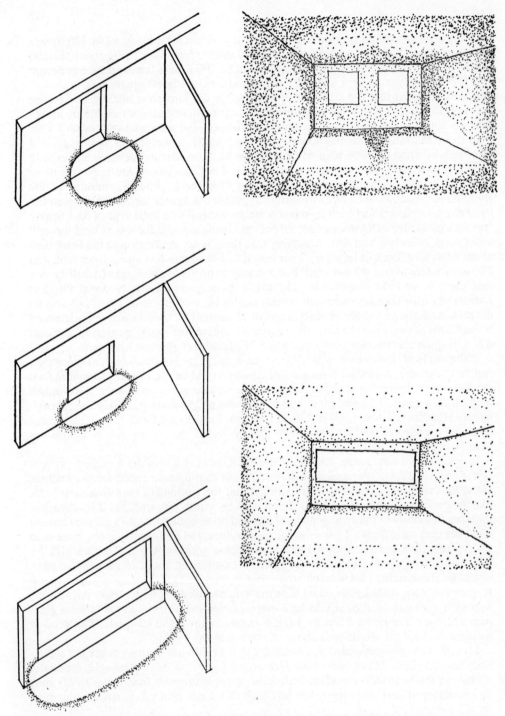

FIG. 6. Diagrams illustrating the amount of light admitted by windows of different shapes and sizes.

for reading.[1] In this case the 25 square feet of glass area with but little obstruction, equivalent to the 15 degrees, would be adequate for a living room or bedroom of about 150 square feet, but anything much less would be inadequate. Thus we may say that for a kitchen a good standard is 25 per cent of glass area in the window to floor area, and in other rooms about 17 per cent. These standards are higher than those recommended in a previous report of the Lighting of Buildings Committee. In these calculations 25 per cent is allowed for glazing bars. In kitchens up to 100 square feet 19 per cent of glazed area is recommended. In a room of 100 square feet this would give a window 4 feet 9 inches wide and 2 feet 9 inches above the floor to a lintel 7 feet 6 inches above floor level. In a living room up to 150 square feet a smaller proportion of 11 per cent is regarded as adequate, and from 150-200 square feet 15 per cent is suggested; in a bedroom up to 110 square feet 10 per cent, and between 110 and 150 square feet 11 per cent is recommended. It will be noted that a slight percentage increase is recommended with the increased size of the rooms. This is due to the circumstance that a small window for a small area gives a little higher illumination at table level than a larger window in a larger area in the same proportion. For example the daylight area above 0·5 per cent d.f. given by a window with glass surface only 4 feet high by 3 feet wide is 90 square feet. For a window double the area 6 feet high by 4 feet wide the daylight area is 142 square feet.

The shape and position of windows are important. Generally the higher the window the better, so that it is above table level. A good position is 3 feet above the floor reaching to near the ceiling. If a room is 8 feet 6 inches high, then a window 5 feet high from a point 3 feet above the floor by as wide as possible is desirable. If it is possible to make it the whole width of the wall the brighter the room. To get the best illumination it is well to keep the window, of whatever height, as high on the wall as possible.[2]

[1] From the calculations made of the relation of window sizes to daylight factors it is not difficult to find by experiment the degree of illumination represented by a d.f. of 1 per cent.

[2] The English Joinery Manufacturers' Association in its booklet on *Daylight Factors for Standard Casement Windows* gives a practical guide in a series of tables for calculating the sizes of its types of windows, to secure the requisite daylight factor in rooms, and these tables are based on the lintel heights of 7 feet 3 inches and 7 feet 9 inches above the floor. It is perhaps interesting to give an example from this serviceable booklet. Suppose the living room for which a window has to be calculated is 15 feet by 12 feet that is 180 square feet. The desirable daylight factor is 1 per cent for an area of not less than 100 square feet. The lintel height is 7 feet 9 inches and the angle of obstruction is 10 degrees. Reference is made to this table and it is found that an area of 102 square feet above 1 per cent daylight factor gives a window 5 feet $11\frac{1}{2}$ inches wide by 3 feet 6 inches high with penetration of 9 feet 6 inches for EJMA type C.K.2. If a narrow horizontal window is required, one 7 feet 10 inches wide by 2 feet 6 inches high will give an area of 109 square feet above a 1 per cent d.f., but if a higher window is required one 5 feet $11\frac{1}{2}$ inches wide and 5 feet 6 inches high will give 107 square feet above the 1 per cent d.f. The penetration in the last two examples mentioned is 9 feet 6 inches and 9 feet 7 inches respectively. It will be noticed that in the former the area is about $19\frac{1}{2}$ square feet (7 feet 10 inches by 2 feet 6 inches) and in the latter about 33 square feet (5 feet $11\frac{1}{2}$ inches by 5 feet 6 inches). Thus the long, narrow, horizontal window of a much smaller area than the large square window gives almost as much light. The only part where it is less is in a small horizontal strip on a table or floor immediately below the window.

One objection I have heard to large windows in bedrooms is that they occupy a whole wall, and with the chimney breast projecting from another, and built-in wardrobes on yet another wall this restricts the placing of furniture. The reply to this is that there should be no chimney breast in the bedroom of a modern house (a question I discuss in Chapter X), and in case it is desired to place furniture against the wall occupied by the window, the sill could be 4 feet above the floor, and a long horizontal window could occupy the whole of the upper part of the wall.

The increase in the size of windows for houses has meant that they have extended horizontally rather than vertically because there is in this way more room for increase. This extension has been made possible often by the use of steel or concrete lintels. Some architects, however, while anxious to provide better lighting, wish to preserve the old vertical window with its Georgian character, and have often preferred to put two vertical windows because of the effect and proportion in relation to wall area, rather than introduce a large horizontal window. The glazed area and the illumination would be less by this method than with a large horizontal window. With a room of 200 square feet and the window wall 12 feet by 8 feet 6 inches two windows 5 feet by 3 feet with 3 feet between would give a glass area of about 22·5 square feet (allowing 25 per cent for window bars) which is inadequate, being very much less than the 17 per cent for living room which I suggested as desirable, although approximately right according to the lower standard recommended by the Lighting of Buildings Committee. If the two windows were made into one 5 feet by 9 feet the glass area would be about 33·75 square feet, which is the 17 per cent. It must be remembered that with the two windows perforating the dark wall area the contrast is likely to be strong and produce glare. By covering a much larger portion of the wall glare is considerably reduced. Indeed the only reasons for having two smaller windows rather than one larger are to preserve an architectural style of the past, and because of loss of heat. The former is mere decadence and is not worthy of serious consideration; the latter can be overcome by double glass. To the objection that the installation of double glass is expensive, the reply is that double glass is a valuable insulator and that the extra cost of installation will probably be met in five years by saving in fuel for heating.

Artificial Lighting

For artificial lighting in the home two principal forms have proved to be the most serviceable: (A) general lighting, where the light which may be regarded as sufficient for general movement about the house, for rest and conversation, is diffused as much as possible over the room; and (B) concentrated or localized lighting, which is additional and is designed to afford a greater degree of illumination over a limited area for work, especially of an intricate kind, reading, dressing and the toilet and other occupations requiring good visibility. Glare should always be avoided, and the diffusion of too much light when concentration on a particular small area is desired is likely to be trying to the eyes. It is often an advantage when using the concentrated lighting to dispense with the general diffused lighting, and the surrounding shadows will often prove to be restful and soothing.

The two principal forms of lighting may be sub-divided as follows:

A.—GENERAL DIFFUSED LIGHTING

1. *Direct* (*a*) central, and (*b*) wall lighting. In this form the lamp is contained generally in a translucent shade, and is fixed in the centre of the ceiling or hangs from the

ceiling or is fixed to the wall. The translucent shade should reduce glare, and should therefore be fairly large as this reduces intensity by spreading the light within the shade.

Although a shade is not generally used with fluorescent and other forms of tubular lighting it would clearly give a softer effect for general illumination.

2. *Indirect Lighting.* In this form the light is projected on to a surface, either the pale ceiling or wall, and reflected back into the room. It is generally a soft, restful kind of lighting, and there is a complete absence of glare. It can take the following forms: (*a*) spot and (*b*) continuous, both of which can be either central or wall lighting. The light is covered by an opaque shade, a bowl form in the former and a trough in the latter, and is projected on to the reflecting surface. Continuous lighting is by means of tubular lamps which could be of the fluorescent electric discharge type, or in a series of bulbs, and one of its advantages is that the trough fitting can be so arranged as to be easily moveable to suit any change of furniture.

3. *Combination of Direct and Indirect Lighting.* This is provided by many fittings, one of which is illustrated, where the shade is designed to diffuse light directly, and also project it on to the reflecting wall or ceiling. The advantage of this is that it gives a fairly powerful light, while the reflected light minimizes the glare of the direct light.

B.—CONCENTRATED OR LOCALIZED LIGHTING

4. This can take the form of (*a*) standard lamp, (*b*) table lamp, (*c*) wall bracket lamp, (*d*) panel lamp. The uses of these will be amplified when discussing the lighting of various rooms.

5. *Combination in one fitting of Diffused and Concentrated Lighting.* The fitting could be either fixed or portable. There are definite advantages for some purposes in having a portable fitting. The diffused lighting could take the form of indirect lighting projected on the ceiling, with the concentrated lighting shining downwards or adjusted at the angle required.

For the living room the two forms of lighting, diffused and concentrated, are essential. Spot diffused lighting can be either direct or indirect. The former can be secured by a central ceiling light covered by a translucent shade, and the latter by means of an opaque bowl with the light projected on to the white or cream ceiling. I think the latter indirect method is the better because direct lighting downwards makes the ceiling lower in tone than the walls and is apt to have an oppressive effect. Continuous lighting by tubular lamps, or a series of bulbs in a trough, is probably the best form of indirect lighting as the diffusion is better. Some people prefer wall lighting, either direct or indirect as this also throws light up to the ceiling. Diffused lighting in the living room should be roughly 150 watts per 100 square feet if tungsten lamps are used, and 75 watts per 100 square feet if fluorescent lamps are used as these these give roughly double the illumination. This would be for direct lighting; a little more would be necessary for indirect.

The amount of light required is partly dependent on whether the room is composed of light or dark surfaces, or whether there is a degree of contrast between the furniture and its background of wall, but I will deal with this later when considering colour. For reading or fine work (needlework, knitting with dark wool, when, by the way, white needles should always be used so that the contrast will assist seeing) the concentrated or localized light is obtained by means of a standard lamp or table lamp. In avoiding glare it is important that a translucent bulb and an adequate shade that

4

hides the lamp should be employed. Anything less than 75 watts is inadequate. A central light over the table in the dining room is usual, but good wall lighting on both sides would I think be more cheerful, although a combination of both is probably best.

For the dining room the light should be over the table whether it is in the centre of the room, when a central drop lamp would be suitable, or abutting a wall, when a wall lamp would probably be quite effectual. It sometimes happens that families like to move the dining table to different positions, and in this case it would be convenient to have the movable trough lighting. The fitting, which is a combination of diffused and concentrated lighting, would be perfect as a table lamp for the dining table or as a hanging lamp over the table. The upper part would project the light on to the ceiling and give a soft diffused light, and when necessary the lower lamp would shine directly down on to the table. It is generally an advantage to have a wall lamp over the sideboard.

If the kitchen and scullery are combined, and the room is of a fair size, then it is desirable to have one diffused light in the centre and one drop lamp over the work table. If the scullery or utility room and kitchen are separate, each requires a separate light, and in the case of the latter it may be adequate to have one lamp over the work table if the kitchen is small. The illumination of 150 watts to 100 square feet should be an absolute minimum for the kitchen. In the case of two lights, they should together be a little more; I would suggest 100 watts diffused light and 75 watts localized light over the work table. A good arrangement for the kitchen is a central flourescent light, 75 watts for 100 square feet. As shown in the illustration this minimises shadows which are a disadvantage of tungsten lamps.

For bedrooms the principle of double or even treble illumination is desirable: the central diffused lighting, and special lighting for the dressing table and for the bed. For the dressing table a single light above or two side lights should be employed, the best form being both combined, with tubular lamps on either side and above the mirror. The side lamps would also be serviceable for the side mirrors. In this way the light comes full on the face with a minimum of shadow.

The bedside lamp is important. One reads in bed by this light when all other lights are turned off, and when one becomes drowsy one just switches off the light and falls asleep. It is one of the best and most pleasurable ways of inducing sleep provided the book is not too exciting. But it is important that the bedside light should be adequate and conviniently placed, without producing awkward shadows, so as to make reading as comfortable as possible. Generally a wall bracket lamp or one on the wall or bedhead immediately above the head is the most suitable place. If this cannot be arranged, a lamp on a bedside table could be used. But it reduces the soothing effect if one tries to read by the central light, especially if it is in front of one.

For the rest of the house lighting has generally been inadequate. Large cupboards and the larder should have small lights. One that is not generally provided is that in the entrance porch. The convenience of this at night both to the occupants of the house and to visitors and callers must be obvious. Usually the hall light has to render the necessary service, but this is not adequate, especially when the door is shut, even if it has translucent glass panels.

It should be unnecessary to emphasize that the stairs should be well lighted, with a switch at top and bottom. Unfortunately this has not been provided sufficiently in the past and the omission has been the cause of many accidents.

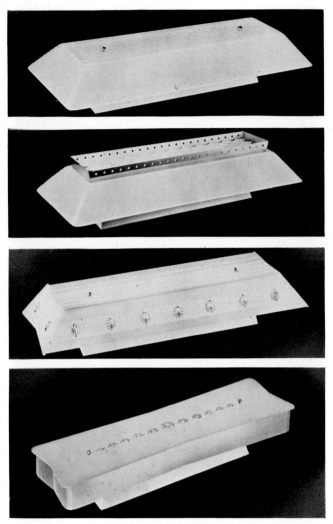

PLATE XVIII. Four fluorescent light fittings for Osram warm white tubes. Each accommodates two 2 ft. 40 W. tubes (equivalent to 100 W. tungsten) and is designed for direct ceiling mounting.

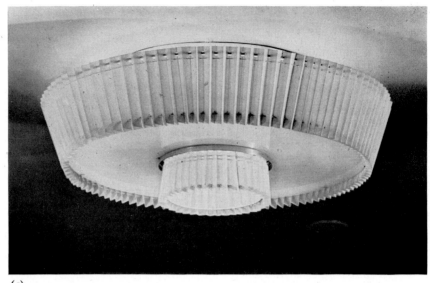

(a)

PLATE XIX (a) *and* (b). Osram circular fluorescent ceiling light fittings
The tubes are 16 in. in diameter.

(b)

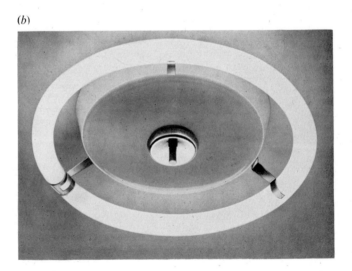

A suggested number of lighting points for the small house is given in Table 8 of the Report of the Lighting of Buildings Committee.[1] This gives two fixed points in the kitchen and one fixed point and three plug points in the living room. In the bedroom where the furniture is fixed, two fixed points and one plug point is recommended, and where the position of the furniture is unknown one fixed point and two plug points. The more points that are provided the greater flexibility is possible in the use of a room. For the large living room it is desirable to have three fixed points, one central ceiling point and two wall points, and three plug points. In bedrooms two fixed points and two plug points placed in relation to likely arrangements of furniture would be most suitable.

[1] No. 12 of Post-War Building Studies, 1944.

CHAPTER IX

COLOUR

C OLOUR in the home cannot be separated from considerations of light and lighting, for colour arises from the light vibrations apparent to the eye produced by the molecular constitution of bodies, which absorb some rays and reject others, the colour of the rejected rays forming the perceived colour of the body. The selection of certain colours can contribute to good lighting and assist in the easy perception of objects. The colouring of a room affects a sense of its size. It creates atmosphere which may conduce to a sense of brightness and cheerfulness or of sombreness, of restlessness or of peace, of general harmony or of discord. It is important, therefore, that if the interior of the house is to form an agreeable background to family activities the colouring should be pleasing, it should be introduced with a sense of light values, of enhancing the sense of space and conduce to those moods which one associates with the idea of home.

To think clearly about the satisfactory use of colour it is of advantage to consider briefly scientific theory and the terms generally employed in denoting colour qualities. In Helmholz's classification, which has met with wide acceptance, three principal qualities are defined: hue, saturation and intensity. Hue is the kind of colour like red, blue or green and is an indication of location in the solar spectrum. The term colour is of general application to all hues. Saturation is the degreee of the colour in its relation to white light. A spectrum colour is a fully saturated colour. When it is paler and mixed with white light it is less saturated. To give an example from pigments: if red is mixed with water in water colour, or white in oil painting, the degree of saturation is reduced. Intensity is the luminosity or brilliance of a colour. Degrees of intensity are from the most brilliant hue, like bright red to faint reddish grey when the particular hue is almost lost. Lowering of intensity results from a mixture of grey with the hue.

It is not always convenient to use these widely accepted scientific terms in speaking of colour in interior decoration, because it is doubtful if they would be as readily understood as more familiar but less precise terms. Terms like tint, shade, tone and neutral colours are often used by artists and others, and it is generally understood what is meant by them, although there is a tendency to use them rather loosely, and in view of this, it is well to indicate what I mean by them. Tint I understand as conveniently used for the lesser degrees of saturation; shade, as the term really indicates, the degree of depth, which may mean on the one hand the amount of light in a hue or the degree of the addition of black. Tone is used in the sense of general intensity. When there are strong contrasts of bright and dark colours in a picture we say it is high in tone, when these contrasts are greyed or paled down it is comparatively low in tone. In a landscape the tones of the distance are lower than those of the foreground. Tone is often employed when speaking of the relative intensity of these in the depth of a picture. A colour is regarded as neutral when a hue is mixed with reflected colours, but for the practical purpose of colouring in the home it may be regarded as a hue of less intensity by the mixture of grey.

Many colourists have followed Newton's classification of pigment primaries as red, yellow and blue, from which the secondaries, orange, green and purple can be mixed, and the tertiaries russet or brown, citrine or sap green, and slate or grey. This has proved very serviceable to colourists. Young and Helmholtz contended that the three primaries are red, green and violet, because it is these three colours which register principally in the retina of the eye, and it is from these three that all other colours can be mixed. Later still it has been the tendency to adopt the seven colours of the spectrum as the primaries, namely, red, orange, yellow, green, blue, indigo and violet, or eight as classified by Oswald, namely, red, orange, yellow, leaf green, sea green, turquoise, blue and purple. But this classification is purely arbitrary; it is just a convenient abstraction of the infinite variety of hues in the spectrum. The actual number of distinct hues in the spectrum that can be perceived by normal vision is probably not more than one hundred, which is probably, therefore, the total number of pure colours, all other variations being degrees of intensity produced by varying degrees of greying down. White and black and the intermediate greys, called acromatic colours, are not regarded as true colours in science, because a white or colourless object does not absorb any of the light rays, but reflects them all back, whereas a black object absorbs all light rays without reflecting any, and thus it may be said that light is not broken up into colour. In pigments, blacks and various tones of grey are useful in reducing the amount of colour in a hue, or reducing its intensity.[1]

From Newton's primaries most other colours can be mixed, which cannot be said of Young and Helmholz's primaries, red, green and violet. It is sometimes argued in criticism of yellow, red and blue as the three primaries, that the mixing to produce most other colours is of pigment and not of light. Pigment and light cannot really be separated in this way. Why does the mixing of yellow and blue produce green? Because yellow pigment absorbs blue, indigo and violet; blue absorbs red, orange and yellow; the only colour, therefore, not absorbed is green, which is reflected from the mixture. It is true that if blue light and yellow light are mixed on a white ground, white light is produced, but if they are mixed before reaching the white ground green light is produced.

The two methods which can be employed as a theoretic basis are the primaries, yellow, red and blue, with secondaries and tertiaries, and the seven or eight spectrum colours. These are generally shown diagrammatically in circles. The opposite colours in the circles are complementaries, which combined produce white light. They are nearly if not quite the same in each circle. In the first, red and green are complementaries,

---

[1] The identification of colours has been made easier by the British Colour Council in their *Dictionary of Colours for Interior Decoration*. This Dictionary illustrates 378 colours each in gloss, matt and pile fabric surfaces to facilitate colour matching to different textures. The Dictionary includes colours for carpets, furnishing fabrics, linoleum, plastics, paint, wallpaper, in fact for all the products that are used in interior decoration. Some of the colours included are: Adam Gold, Arabian Blue, Charcoal Grey, Chartreuse Green, Delft Blue, Georgian Green, Genoese Pink, Flame, Mexican Tan, Majolica Orange, Pimento and many other historical and well-known colours are illustrated. The colours are named and numbered which makes for easy reference by telephone or cable and copies of this work are available in most Public Libraries. Over two thousand firms use this reference. The British Colour Council works closely with industry in the production and co-ordination of colour ranges.

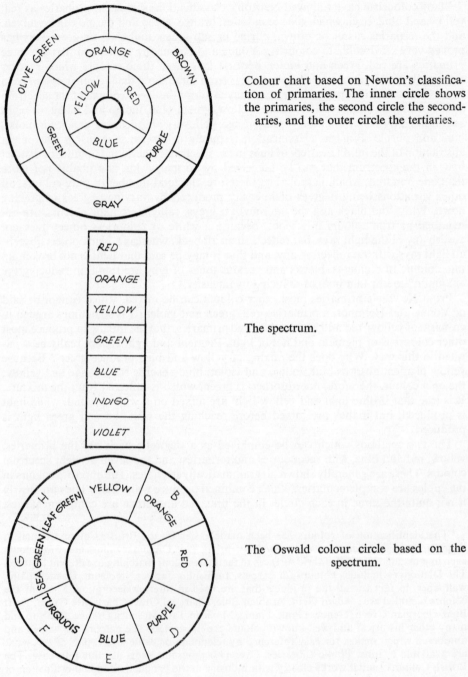

Colour chart based on Newton's classification of primaries. The inner circle shows the primaries, the second circle the secondaries, and the outer circle the tertiaries.

The spectrum.

The Oswald colour circle based on the spectrum.

FIG. 7.

in the true spectrum circle it will be found that green is a little towards blue; in the complementaries blue and orange it will be seen that the orange is a little towards yellow and in the complementaries yellow and purple or violet, it will be found that the violet is a little towards red.

In the colouring of the interior of houses generally spectrum colours with full saturation would rarely be used. The effect would be too rich and over-powering. The colours would either be mixed with white or mixed with grey or black to reduce intensity. Why is this?

If we consider a landscape we shall note that towards the distance the colours weaken in intensity, contrasts are lessened and they become greyer. The purer and more positive colours are in the foreground. Also, it may be noted that foreground colours which appear to come forward are the hues at the red end of the spectrum while the more distant colours are more often at the violet end of the spectrum. A field of ripe corn in the foreground is yellow, orange or gold, in the far distance it is blue or violet, with touches of grey. It is generally felt that the distant hues are associated with and conduce to a sense of space. The softer hues, especially if they have a mixture of grey, are background colours, while the purer more positive colours are foreground colours. It is also apparent in the landscape that the colours of the ground are darker and more fully saturated than the colours of the sky, which have a much greater quantity of white light.

The point of recalling this common visual experience is that it provides the basis of satisfying colour schemes for the home. Natural colouring seems right and beautiful, and it is the general standard of good colour harmonies and contrasts. From the colourings of nature principles for colour schemes can be formulated which give general satisfaction, and it is in this way that Renaissance artists thought of art as an imitation of nature, not in the often misinterpreted and cruder sense of copying the exact forms and colours of nature. Any colour scheme which defies the principles derived from natural colouring is almost always disturbing and ugly to the sensitive percipient.

Thus, it may be contended, the colouring of any ordinary country landscape suggests the satisfying colouring of a room. The tonal relation of floor and ceiling is like that of earth and sky, and the scheme which makes the floor dark or medium shade, the walls slightly lighter and the ceiling lighter still accords with a sense of gravity, for darker shades give a feeling of more weight than lighter shades. The walls are of intermediate tone, they are a background and one must make the most of the limited size of the room, and colour the walls so as to enhance the sense of space. The distant colours of the landscape suggest the most suitable background colours for a room, those which are dimmed by an atmospheric film—pure colours greyed down. Neutral colours which tend to recede rather than come forward, or pale colours of low saturation with a high degree of white light, should be employed. Colours of full saturation should be avoided. Tints of yellow or green, and colours mixed with grey resulting in shades like Bath stone, oatmeal, off white, grey-blue, brown-green, would all conduce to a sense of space and restfulness. Dull wall surfaces recede more than shiny surfaces which often present strong contrasts of light and dark, and thus come forward and often break up form. For a room facing towards the sun between south-east and south-west cool shades or soft pale colours are both suitable, but anything strong or very positive for the walls is unpleasant. The fittings forming part of the walls, like skirting,

Colour diamond based on the Oswald colour circle (Fig. 7). This applies to all complementary colours such as yellow (A) and blue (E), orange (B), and turquoise (F), red (C), and sea-green (G), and purple (D), and leaf-green (H). This forms the basis of satisfactory colour schemes.

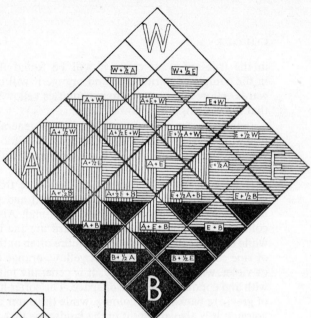

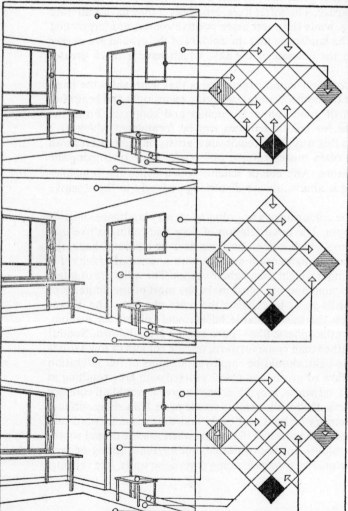

Application of the colour diamond.

An example can be taken with yellow and blue applied to the top diagram. The ceiling would be a very pale warm blue, the walls pale yellow, the curtains yellow, the door a yellow green, the door frame yellow, the skirting and table top yellowish brown (yellow mixed with black), the floor a dark dull green, and the carpet brown. As a note of contrast for the wall the picture frame is blue, but this could be a more harmonious note like yellow-green, yellow or brown.

FIG. 8.

picture rail, doors and window frames, should be a harmonious not a contrasting colour, otherwise the sense of spaciousness and repose is apt to be destroyed by parts of the wall coming forward. Very often a cream or pale yellow wall has fittings like door, skirting and picture rail painted dark brown. This accentuation of these fittings destroys what otherwise might have been a quiet atmosphere, in which a limited space appears to utmost advantage.

Scope for contrast is provided by the objects in a room, and this contrast will help lighting and seeing. Here again we can think of our landscape analogy. The piled sheafs of golden corn of the foreground, seen against the distant grey blue hills, are vivid; or the rich purple-brown earth is strong against the distant grey-blue-green trees; or the tree trunks that pattern the foreground are dark against the pale light beyond the wood. Foreground objects are most vivid when they present a contrast in tone or colour with the distance. In a room a light object against a light wall is less easy to see than a dark object against a light wall. But in having dark furniture care must be taken that it is relieved by light surroundings otherwise there is a risk of an effect of oppressiveness. Brightness in an interior is better obtained by contrasts of colour than by light and dark tones. If, for example, the furniture is of light oak or sycamore the walls should not be dark or of a similar hue, but a mildly contrasting hue like pale green or bluish grey. If the furniture is of a darker wood like mahogany or walnut or stained oak, light walls of a contrasting hue would give a brighter effect than light walls of a similar hue. Brightness and cheerfulness are not inconsistent with harmony and repose, as many modern interiors with grey or cream backgrounds and oak or sycamore furniture and green upholstery can demonstrate. What I have said so far would apply mainly to rooms like the dining room, where the wood predominates in the furniture. But where upholstery predominates, as possibly in the living room, drawing room or lounge, the colour of the upholstery should determine the degree of contrast or harmony with the walls, or vice versa. Upholstery of green of varying intensity contrasts pleasingly with yellow, cream, stone-coloured or grey walls, the measure of the intensity determining the degree of contrast. Red is a difficult colour to treat well, but shades of dull reddish orange sometimes broken by patterns often look well against grey or greenish walls. The floor can add a third note of mild contrast, but if the contrast is violent it will disturb all sense of repose. A powder blue carpet, dull wax-polished light mahogany, and pale bluish grey walls are three mild and effective contrasts. A grey-green floor, with reddish orange upholstery, and stone-coloured walls is another. They are soft and not too stimulating, but if some slightly arresting notes could be introduced by a few pictures with bright colour patterns or by one wall with a highly decorated wall-paper it would add interest to a room.

The degree of contrast that is agreeable is generally found in natural colouring and is often shown in the colourings of plants, the wilder and less cultivated the better the colourings. It will be seen that the foliage of plants with yellow flowers is generally a yellowish green, and that of plants with blue flowers is generally a bluish green. The colours, though a measure of contrast, come towards each other. In determining colour schemes, it is always wise to go continually to natural colourings, especially landscape colourings. An excellent colour scheme, for example, may be derived from a landscape in spring where yellows and greens predominate, with touches of soft blues and browns here and there; or one derived from autumn effects, where browns and russets and greens predominate with touches of purple here and there.

It will be noted that a measure of restrained contrasts is recommended, limited to two or at most three colours, with patches of another bright colour here and there, like vermilion, or bright blue or polished black which should be small in quantity. The element of contrast emphasizes light, and helps seeing, and makes the room more interesting than if it consisted of all shades of one colour, which is apt to be insipid. One reads in novels of the blue room, the green room, and so on. They must have been rather insipid places. It is by a measure of contrast, where one complements another that one's sense of colour is stimulated, and its beauty appreciated. It thus brings a degree of brightness in the home not inconsistent with repose, and contributes very much to making home the lovely place we all like it to be.

CHAPTER X

HEATING

M OST small houses in this country are inadequately and inefficiently heated, and we do not seem to have made very much progress in this matter in the last twenty years. Even now the sole source of heat on a cold winter's evening in the majority of small houses is a coal fire in the living room, round which the family is usually grouped. If the room is of fair size the parts farthest from the fire are cold. There is a reluctance to go into the other rooms of the house, even to get things that are wanted, and at bedtime there is a general reluctance to leave the warm fireside and to go to the cold bedrooms. This crouching round a fire on a winter's evening while all the rest of the house is cold seems primitive, and it demonstrates how backward we are in this matter. Most other countries have far more efficient methods of heating.

In the report on Domestic Fuel Policy by the Fuel and Power Advisory Council (*Simon Report*) published in 1946, a strong criticism was made of domestic heating among the lower income groups. 'Normally', states the report, 'space heating is provided by an open coal fire, which is so inefficient that only one room, or indeed even only part of one room, is heated by a quantity of fuel that could be made to warm the whole house; no heat whatever is used in the bedrooms, though an open fire grate is often provided, involving heavy costs for chimney construction. The result is that though the 4 million houses built in the inter-war period are probably larger than houses in other countries for the corresponding income groups, yet the area of the house properly warmed for comfort during the winter is probably smaller in England than in any other civilized country' (para. 3).

Facilities for water heating are better generally than for space heating, but there is room for much improvement in the more economic provision of these facilities, while they are as yet not widely enough enjoyed. As the *Simon Report* points out, 'only a small proportion of the houses have a proper supply of hot water laid on to the sink and bath. In something like half the smaller houses hot water can only be obtained from a kettle' (para. 3).

Cooking facilities are generally good compared with those for space and water heating.

Before considering satisfactory methods of space heating we should ask what is the desirable condition in a house during the winter months. It should be remembered that the human body is a most efficient heating machine giving off heat by radiation and convection as well as a certain amount by evaporation. In addition the human body is very efficiently thermostatically controlled to within a degree or two, and if we are three or four degrees above our normal temperature we are seriously ill. The problem in heating is to prevent the body losing its heat and, as we lose heat by radiation and convection, it will therefore be easily seen that to be thoroughly comfortable we require a balance of radiation and convection; for example, when we are sitting at rest we require a slightly higher proportion of radiation to convection but, when we are moving around and working a higher proportion of convection than radiation may be more satisfactory. I would suggest that in the daytime, or rather from the time the family rises to the time it retires, the general temperature of the house should be about 55°F. In rooms where persons wish to sit for any length of time, in the living room, or dining room, or study-bedroom then this should be increased to 65°-67°F. At night when the family is in bed the temperature can be allowed to fall to 45°F., but not much lower.[1] The general temperature of 55°F. should be provided by background heating. This general temperature is satisfactory because, assuming good ventilation, it is sifficiently warm to be fairly comfortable, but not so warm as to discourage movement. It is an agreeable temperature for the housewife doing her work about the house. A lower temperature might give a feeling of chill, while a higher temperature is unnecessary.

The temperatures desired would vary a little with circumstances while different persons would have slightly different preferences. These suggested temperatures could be slightly lowered perhaps for young people, and slightly increased for old people. They depend a little upon the amount of clothing worn. If many and thick clothes are worn indoors it is easier to feel comfortable with a lower temperature than if few and light clothes are worn. But it is much healthier to wear few clothes indoors and let the air get to the skin more easily. As a definite example, it is more pleasant to wear few and thin clothes in a well-ventilated room with a temperature of 67°F., than to wear many and thick clothes in a room with a temperature of 57°F. The latter is commoner in England during the winter months, and it has become commoner still with the necessary fuel economies combined with the waste incurred by the domestic open grate.

It is undesirable that the temperature inside the house should fall below 45°F. because this causes condensation on walls, furnishings and clothes. Many people when getting into bed open the widows wide even on a cold winter's night. They do it because they believe it is healthy. They feel warm in bed, because the air inside the bed, being warmed by the body, approaches skin temperature. But the room itself falls to a temperature very little above that outside, which may be 30°F. Clothes left in the room absorb moisture, and it cannot always be healthy when these are put on in the morning.

In the Egerton report it is stated that in a room with windows closed and flue sealed, about 700 to 800 cubic feet of air is changed per hour, due to leakage under the door and through cracks round the opening lights of windows, though on occasion the ventilation may be much less than this (para. 8 1. 1). With a flue the ventilation is greatly increased. The Committee recommended a minimum ventilation for health of 600 cubic feet per hour per person (para. 2. 2. 2). The human organism absorbs less oxygen when sleeping. Thus if one person is sleeping in a room of 800 cubic feet (10 feet by 10 feet by 8 feet) and the air is changed once per hour it is a little above the recommended minimum of the Egerton Committee. With a wall ventilator the change

[1] See report by the Heating and Ventilation (Reconstruction) Committee of the Building Research Board (Egerton Committee) 1945, Chapter 2. The Housing Manual, 1949, following the Egerton report recommends a living room temperature of 65°F. with background heating of 45°-50°F. throughout the house. This standard for background heating is a little low. In Chapter VIII of *Code of Functional Requirements of Buildings—Heating and Ventilation*, 1949, the recommended temperatures for public, dining and sitting rooms in hotels is 65°-67°F. This is also the recommended temperature for libraries and offices.

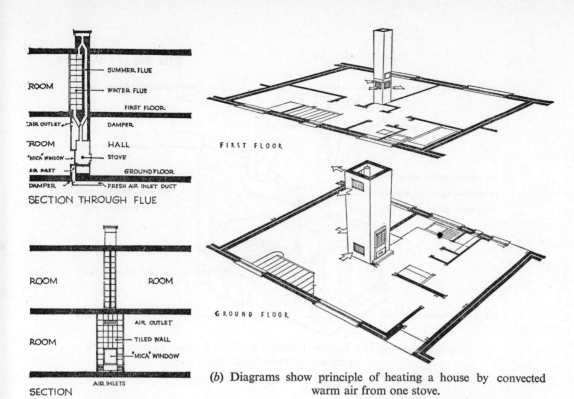

SUMMER FLUE

WINTER FLUE

FIRST FLOOR

AIR OUTLET — DAMPER

ROOM — HALL

"MICA" WINDOW — STOVE

AIR INLET — GROUND FLOOR

DAMPER — FRESH AIR INLET DUCT

SECTION THROUGH FLUE

ROOM — ROOM

ROOM

AIR OUTLET

TILED WALL

"MICA" WINDOW

AIR INLETS

SECTION

FIRST FLOOR

GROUND FLOOR

(b) Diagrams show principle of heating a house by convected warm air from one stove.

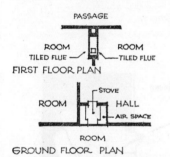

PASSAGE

ROOM — ROOM
TILED FLUE — TILED FLUE

FIRST FLOOR PLAN

STOVE

ROOM — HALL

AIR SPACE

ROOM

GROUND FLOOR PLAN

(a) Stove which heats air circulated in wall duct. (See p. 69.)

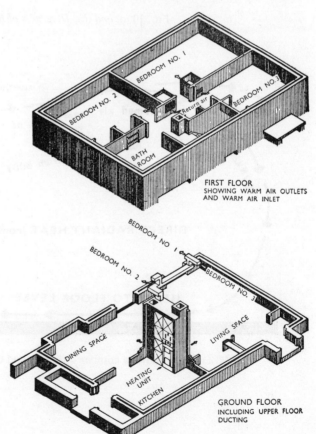

BEDROOM NO. 2

BEDROOM NO. 1

Return air

BEDROOM NO. 3

BATH ROOM

FIRST FLOOR
SHOWING WARM AIR OUTLETS
AND WARM AIR INLET

BEDROOM NO. 1

BEDROOM NO. 2

BEDROOM NO. 3

DINING SPACE

LIVING SPACE

HEATING UNIT

KITCHEN

GROUND FLOOR
INCLUDING UPPER FLOOR
DUCTING

FIG. 9. (a), (b) and (c). Heating appliances.

(c) Isometric diagram of 'Radiation' ducted warm-air system.

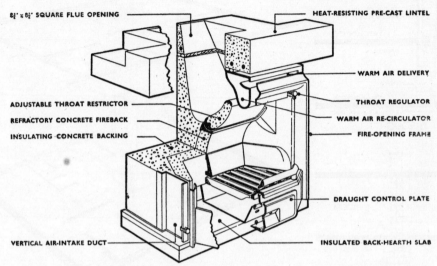

(a) Diagram showing the various features of the insulated open fire which produces increased radiation.

FIG. 10 (a) and (b). Diagrams of heating appliances.

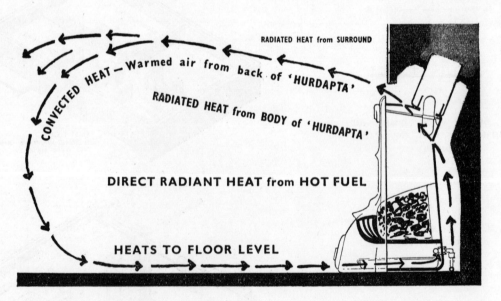

(b) Diagram showing combined radiant and convected heating in open fire.

(b)

PLATE XX (a), (b), (c) and (d). *Background heating.*

(a) Panel radiator in partition wall between living and dining room. This photograph shows the living room side of the radiator. (b) and (c) Heating by means of hot-water pipes incorporated in cast-iron skirting; (b) is the radiant convector type with slotted openings at the top, 9 in. high; (c) is the radiant type 6 in. high. (d) The Evans system of heating floors by means of dumb-bell section hot water units.

(c)

"Granwood" Floor Blocks and Screed

Insulation   Insulation   Insulation
Heat Unit
Concrete Setting Blocks
Sealed Air Spaces
Concrete Sleepers   Reinforced Concrete Panel Slabs

(d)

(a)

(b)

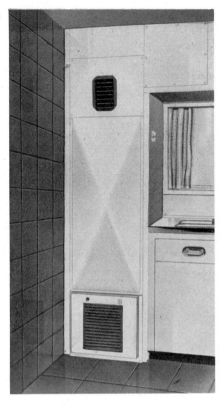

(c)

Radiation whole house warming by ducted air. By (a) solid fuel; (b) gas and (c) oil; the heating plant being installed usually in the kitchen. The solid fuel furnace is on the down-draught principle. (*See* p. 70.)

PLATE XXI (a), (b) and (c). Background heating

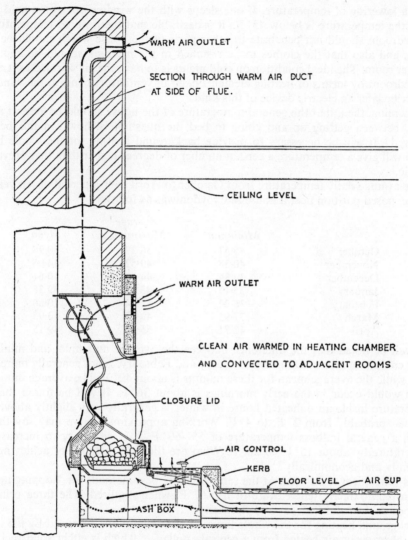

WARM AIR OUTLET

SECTION THROUGH WARM AIR DUCT
AT SIDE OF FLUE.

CEILING LEVEL

WARM AIR OUTLET

CLEAN AIR WARMED IN HEATING CHAMBER
AND CONVECTED TO ADJACENT ROOMS

CLOSURE LID

AIR CONTROL

KERB

FLOOR LEVEL   AIR SUP

ASH BOX

Sectional diagram of coal fire developed by the British Coal Utilization Research Association which provides convected warm air and background heating. (See Plate XXIV and p. 73.)

FIG. 11

of air is increased, but this depends on the direction and velocity of the wind unless
it is of a type which regulates the intake.

When the outside temperature does not fall below 50° F. it is certainly better to
open the window at night, but when it falls well below this to the region of freezing
point, and there is no heating in the bedroom, the disadvantage of sleeping with an
open window probably outweighs the advantages because of the dampness resulting

from a lowering of temperature. If one sleeps with the window open on a cold night when the temperature is below 45° F., it is desirable that the lowered temperature of the bedroom should not penetrate to other parts of the house which should be kept warm, and also that the clothes to be resumed in the morning should be kept in a warmer room. The ideal condition on cold nights is to have the air warmed as it enters the bedroom by means of heating elements fixed in ventilators beneath the windows. I describe later an electric device of this kind.

Assuming, then, that the general temperature of the house should be kept at about 55° F. between getting up and going to bed the question is, how can this be best achieved? It will be necessary to provide background heating for the whole house which will give a temperature a certain number of degrees higher than that prevailing outside.

The average daily temperature from October to April over a period of ten years in an unexposed position near a house in Croydon was as follows:

	Minimum	Average Maximum	Mean
October	45·57	56·39	50·98
November	40·38	49·52	44·95
December	36·84	44·40	40·61
January	35·17	43·59	39·38
February	36·22	45·14	40·68
March	37·95	49·95	43·95
April	42·71	55·59	49·15

It will be noted that the difference between the average maximum and minimum in the coldest months of December, January and February, is not generally more than 9° F., while the average mean for these months is about 40° F. The average minimum which would occur in the early mornings is about 36° F. It will be found that the temperature inside an unheated house in winter is generally very slightly above that outside—probably from 2° F. to 4° F. Working approximately we may say that to obtain a general indoors temperature of 55°-60° F. it is necessary to increase the temperature by about 15° F. to 20° F. What are the best methods of achieving this efficiently and economically?

It is convenient to consider at the same time the best methods for "topping up," to give an approximate temperature of 65°-67°F. when required. The three principal methods are by solid fuel, gas and electricity.

Background heating for the whole house is most commonly provided by the circulation of water or air heated from a central appliance, which is either solid fuel, gas, electricity, or oil. It can also be provided by electric panels and tubes, and oil heated by electrical elements. It will be necessary to consider each in turn.

The chief forms of background central heating by hot water in a house are by means of radiators, wall panels, skirting, floor and ceiling heating, served from a boiler in the basement, utility room or kitchen. The boilers installed in the majority of small houses in the inter-war period have been for the supply of hot water only other than heating the kitchen, although they could have fed one or two radiators to supply a degree of background heating. In the nineteen-fifties numerous houses built by private enterprise and many of the houses built by local authorities have provision for at least one or two hot-water radiators for background heating.

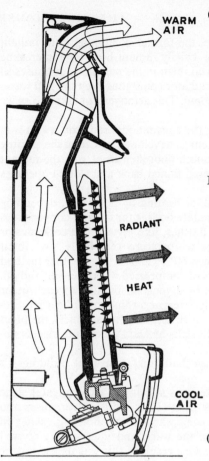

(a) Sectional diagram of the 'GasMiser' fire showing convected and radiant heat.

WARM AIR

RADIANT

HEAT

COOL AIR

FIG. 12 (a) and (b). Diagrams of heating appliances.

(b) Hurseal oil-filled electric radiators with thermostatic control. Column and panel types.

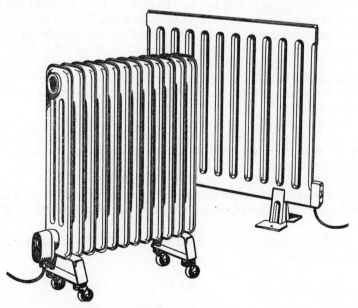

Radiators are of the columnar or panel type, the former combining both radiant and convection heating, whereas the latter gives chiefly radiant heat. One interesting recent use of radiators of the panel type is to instal them in the partitions of houses so that two rooms are heated by one radiator. One radiator could thus keep the hall warm and also give background warmth in the living room. This arrangement takes no space from the room area.

Skirting heating follows the same principle as the conventional radiator, a cast iron skirting covering the hot water pipes. In the system as developed by Crane the skirting is of two types: radiant 6 inches high with a smooth unbroken front, and the radiant convector type 9 inches high which has a staggered finned back and slotted openings at the top (see Plate XX, (b) and (c)).

Different methods have been employed for floor heating by hot water, depending on the type of floor. A common method in a concrete floor is for coils of copper pipes to be embedded in the concrete. Suitable floor finishes, like plywood or cork tiles or some composition tiles should be used and the temperature kept fairly low, about 75° F. which gives a room temperature of between 60° F. and 65° F. Another method used in conjunction with 'granwood' floor blocks of compressed wood, cement and oil, consists of pipes of dumb-bell section 8 inches by 1 inch set parallel to each other under the floor at varying distances from 3 feet to 6 feet according to the heat requirements. The floor is carried on concrete sleepers which form the hot air ducts, the pipes and ducts being insulated below, while concrete slabs are laid across the sleepers to receive the floor finish.

Ceiling heating, although developed for large halls and industrial buildings, is hardly suitable for the small rooms of a house.

District heating by means of hot water or steam is still in the experimental stage in this country. Its first use was in Manchester in 1911 for industrial premises and places of amusement, and its first use for housing was for two housing estates in Dundee in 1920. It was not developed between the wars, and interest was revived only towards the end of the Second World War. One result of this was its use for the Westminster Council flats at Pimlico built in 1946-47. Here hot water is conveyed from the Battersea Power Station under the River Thames to the flats. Many proposals have been made for its use for estates of various sizes, while the use of district heating for new towns was considered in Appendix 4 of the final report of the New Towns Committee published in July 1946. Although District Heating is extensively used in America, and a Mission from the Ministry of Fuel and Power went there in 1947[1] to study American methods, it has still not been developed or used to any great extent in Great Britain.

Background heating by warm air is of two kinds, the gravity system and the forced system. In the gravity system the air is heated by solid fuel, gas or oil and circulated by gravity through ducts of various kinds to the rooms of the house. This was a Roman method of domestic heating known as the 'Hypocaust', in which warm air was circulated under floors from a furnace room built a little lower than the rest of the house and was conducted up ducts in the walls to outlets which warmed the room. The floors were not usually heated, as is sometimes thought, being made of thick material for

[1] National Building Studies Special Report No. 7—District Heating in American Housing (London, 1949).

insulation. A good example of this method of heating is the Roman villa at Brading in the Isle of Wight.

In the forced air system the air is similarly heated and is circulated through ducts by means of an electric fan which is usually placed on the inlet side of the heating chamber. Both systems are used extensively in many European countries and in America,[1] where the heating appliance is often restricted to the basement.

In one method of gravity warm air heating developed from Continental practice, hot air is circulated in a duct in the wall, and part of the surface of the wall is heated. Air is carried to the stove from a duct running underneath the floor boards, and it is heated in the box enclosing the stove. It is then circulated through the flues and passes out through a vent in a stack above the roof. The flues are encased in tubes which are thus heated, and which in turn heat the room. The heat can be shut off by a damper and the hot air passes through an insulated flue. This stove can be in the living room and if it backs on to the dining room part of the wall can be tiled. In the diagram illustrated (p. 63) the stove is shown in the hall backing on to the living room. These fires have an efficiency amounting, it is estimated, to from 35 to 45 per cent, although the vertical ascent of the warm air and its escape through a vent above the roof does suggest a certain waste.

Among the variations of gravity warm air heating is a Danish system recently adopted by an English Company—Glow-Worm Boilers Ltd.—which, it is claimed has a very high heat efficiency.

A solid fuel stove occupies a brick heating shaft centrally situated in the house, with chimney adjoining. Openings to all rooms by means of grilles are placed in this shaft, those for the intake of cold air at the foot of the walls and those for the emission of warm air high up near the ceiling. In the Danish houses, where this system is used, the heating unit is often placed in the basement, but in this country, where basements are not now generally provided, the stove would be on the ground floor. In houses in Denmark without basements the stove is generally fixed in the hall, as this is regarded as the most convenient point for refuelling and de-ashing.

In a typical English house the stove would conveniently be in the corner of the kitchen or utility-room which comes near the centre of the house so that grilles in the heating shaft can be arranged opening to all the rooms. Provided the open fire is eliminated there is scope for the variations in the arrangement of the heating shaft in relation to the rooms. A hot-water supply boiler may be incorporated in the design, which along with a hot-water cylinder equipped with an immersion heater will ensure an all-the-year round water supply economically. The stove and heating exchange unit are finned to offer a large area to the circulating air, and as the brick heating chamber is part of the structure of the house it makes a very efficient heating unit.

In a booklet on the *Gravity Warm Air System* for houses prepared by the Ministry of Fuel and Power (1947) the inset type of heating appliance is recommended as these 'are likely to give the largest supply of warmed air'. Inset closeable fires are also mentioned as suitable. Information sheets are given on six appliances suitable for this system, namely the Courtier 7 A, Esse 'Q', Jupiter No. 3, Neocoke No. 2, Siesta 3 D, and the Sunray (Deep).

[1] See descriptions in *Domestic Heating in America*, Report of a Joint Party from the Ministry of Fuel and Power and the Department of Scientific and Industrial Research, 1946, pp. 10-12 and 47-48.

Two recently developed examples of the forced air systems are the Radiation whole house warming and the 'Weatherfoil' method. Both combine water heating and air heating. In the Radiation system the heating unit is built into an insulated recess and consists of a furnace operated on the down-draught principle, a heat exchanger, a fan and motor, and hot water storage cylinder with a gas circulation for heating water in the summer. In addition to the solid fuel furnace the system can be installed with gas or oil furnaces. The various parts of the house are supplied with warm air from this unit by means of ducts which connect with the various rooms. The cold air is drawn into the unit by a fan, it circulates round the furnace and heat exchanger and then passes through the outlet at the top of the unit into the ducts. (See illustration, p. 63 and Plate XXI.)

In the 'Weatherfoil' system a heating shaft extends the whole height of the house, as in the Danish system. Hot water from an agamatic boiler supplies a coil of copper tubing in the heating unit. Cold air is drawn into the unit near the floor by a fan, and warm air is emitted near ceiling level. In installations which have been made three sides of the unit face kitchen, hall and living room, the cold air intakes being in the hall, with warm air grille above it with another in the living room. It is claimed that by this system the hall, stairs and landing become thoroughly warm, and that merely opening the bedroom doors will give the bedrooms a considerable degree of warmth, although outlets are provided from the heating unit in two bedrooms.

Many years ago, at the end of the war and shortly afterwards, several experiments were made with the all-purpose unit which combines space heating, water heating and cooking. The idea was developed and prototypes were made between 1944 and 1947, but it was only in 1955 that one was actually produced and installed in houses, namely, the 'Heatmaster' produced by Radiation. Among the earlier experiments was one produced by the British Coal Utilisation Research Association in conjunction with the Building Components Producers Association, and that of the Ministry of Works.

The B.C.U.R.A.—B.C.P.A. unit consisted of a framework and casing which extended the whole height of a two-story house. It was like a tall, narrow, rectangular box. The fire was in the living room and was backed by a cooker in the kitchen, the fire providing the heating for the cooker which was insulated. The oven was heated by hot air, while the hot plates were provided with heat conserving cones. The flue in the box warmed the surrounding air, which was admitted under the floor or through a vent in a raised hearth. The warm air was emitted into rooms by means of grilles. At the upper part of the unit were the cold and hot water tanks and water-waste preventer.

The Ministry of Works unit allowed for many variations. The main part was comprised in a steel framework on the ground floor which enclosed a solid fuel appliance with back boiler, an insulated hot-water cylinder of thirty gallon capacity with provision for an electric immersion heater or gas circulator when the solid fuel appliance was not in use. The section on the first floor consisted of a warm air duct with vents that open to the bedrooms, while gas or electric fires could be fixed to the unit. The solid fuel appliance could be an openable stove, an open fire, or a back-to-back unit with a cooker similar to the B.C.U.R.A. unit.

These, however, remained only ideas and models, they were not developed and adopted, leaving the 'Heatmaster' of Radiation as the only all-purpose unit actually produced and installed. It is most satisfactorily installed in the partition between the kitchen and living room or living-dining room. It consists of a free-standing insulated (*a*) Radiation 'Heatmaster' solid fuel appliance which provides the three services of cooking, house heating by ducted warm air and water heating. This appliance can be adapted to burn either bituminous coal or smokeless fuel. It burns the latter on the normal up-draught principle but for the former it is converted to down-draught burning which eliminates most of the smoke. (*See* p. 70.)

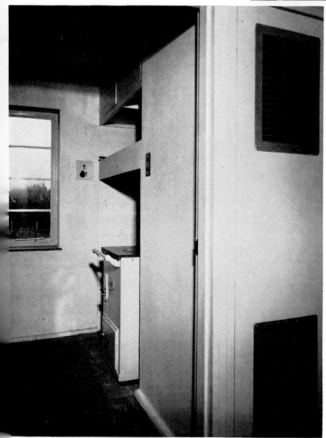

(*b*) Combined hot water and space heating Weatherfoil system by means of a central shaft which holds warm-air heater unit and the hot-water service cylinder, with linen cupboard on first floor. The boiler is situated near the shaft preferably in the kitchen. Warm air is circulated by means of warm air outlets and cold air intakes in the shaft. (*See* p. 70.)

PLATE XXII (*a*) *and* (*b*). *Solid fuel heating.*

(*a*) Tubular heating in bedroom of house in Hampstead. *Architects: Connell, Ward and Lucas, A.F.F.R.I.B.A.*

PLATE XXIII (*a*) *and* (*b*). *Heating.*

(*b*) Electric bathroom heater and towel rail.

(*a*) Coal fire developed by the British Coal Utilization Research Association. It is designed with a draught for combustion drawn from underneath the floorboards which is regulated from the hearth. It will be seen that above the fire is an outlet for convected warm air. Similar outlets are in bedrooms above.

The fire can burn continuously.

(*b*) Camelon fire with underfloor draught.

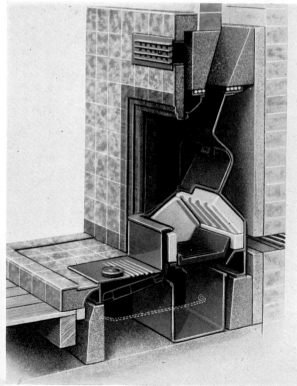

PLATE XXIV (*a*) *and* (*b*). *Fires with underfloor draught.*

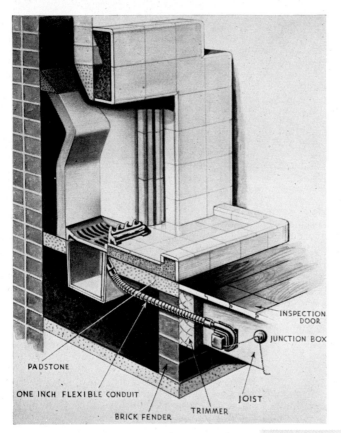

(a) Section of Fandair fire, showing the underfloor controls.

INSPECTION DOOR

JUNCTION BOX

PADSTONE

ONE INCH FLEXIBLE CONDUIT

JOIST

BRICK FENDER

TRIMMER

(b) Section through the Summit fire showing the underfloor air control pipe which provides both primary and secondary air supplies.

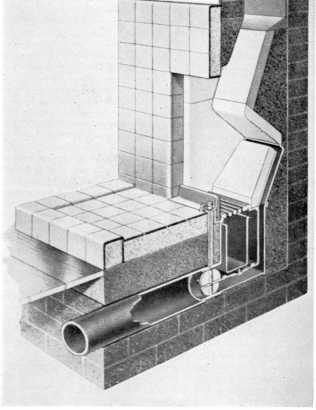

PLATE XXV (a) and (b). Fires with under-floor draught.

(a) 'Hurdapta' fire.

(b) 'Projector' convector fire.

(d) Marvec fire with back boiler and trivet extension.

(c) Rayburn fire.

PLATE XXVI (a), (b), (c) and (d). *Continuous-burning open fires with restrictable throats,*
giving both radiant and convection heating.

(a) 'Parkray' 1.

(b) 'Parkray' 2A (2 is the same but with back boiler).

(c) 'Parkray' 3.

PLATE XXVII (a), (b) and (c). *Open fires with radiant and convection heat and restrictable throat.* 2, 2A and 3 are all downdraught smoke consuming fires. (*See* p. 75.)

(*a*) Yorkdale back-to-back range (No. 4) consisting of a fireplace in the living room, connected to cooker in the kitchen. The living room open fire can be closed down for continuous burning.

(*b*) Sofono 'Sunray' convector fire with guard which slides down from behind the ribbed panel.

PLATE XXVIII (*a*) *and* (*b*).

(*a*) Siesta 4AX.

(*b*) Otto.

(*c*) Panda.

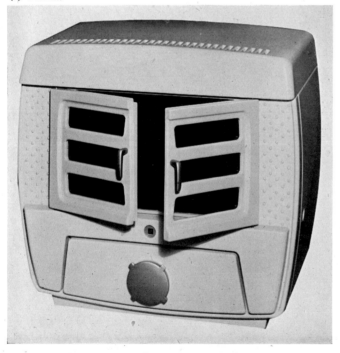

PLATE XXIX (*a*), (*b*) and (*c*). *Solid fuel, continuous-burning openable stoves.*

solid fuel cooker and water heater connected to a heat exchanger which is joined by a short length of flue to the main back flue. When burning suitable fuel the fire box operates by the usual up-draught method, but for bituminous coal it can be converted to the downdraught method which, it is claimed, consumes about 75 per cent of the smoke. Water is heated in an L-shaped boiler which is in direct contact with the fuel bed. Heat is conducted by means of a transfer plate to a convection chamber surrounding the main oven, and the flue gases pass to the heat exchanger. The warm air is circulated through ducts and is emitted to the various rooms through grilles a little above floor level, the whole operation being controlled by thermostats. If, for example, a room requires more heat a fan is automatically switched on and draws air from an inlet, say, on the landing of the upper floor and drives down and round the flue. Some air passes directly through into a mixing chamber (see diagram) and some circulates through the convection chamber round the oven. The two streams of air then mix and pass into the ducts to the room, and this continues until the required temperature is reached, when the fan is switched off automatically. (Plate XXII, (a))

Background heating can also be suitably provided by gas or electricity, especially in older existing houses, where structural adaptation for central water or air heating might be difficult. Background heating by gas is most conveniently provided by heaters with low thermal capacity. There can be either gas radiators or convectors which are manufactured in a variety of designs to stand on the floor against the wall.

Background heating by electricity compares favourably with other methods, while there is considerable promise of further developments. The principal forms are the oil filled radiator, the panel, convector and tubular. Oil filled electric radiators are made in column or panel type and can be thermostatically controlled. The sizes most suitable for the small house are the $\frac{1}{2}$ kilowatt and 1 kilowatt. If one of the former were placed in each room in a small house it would provide adequate background heating. They are completely self-contained yet produce a complete electric heating system. The heating surface can be varied as required from 80° to 170° and can function similarly to the hot water central heating radiator. The panels which should have a controlled surface heat can be placed in the wall, can be free standing, and can act as a firescreen. Among the varieties recently introduced is the glass panel heater with frame, which is designed for fixing to a wall. Convectors, which are produced in a variety of attractive designs, and which have an air vent or grille on the face and sometimes at the top, can be portable or fixed to a wall. Electric tubular heating can be fixed unobstrusively in any position desired. By careful calculation the tubes can be fixed at points in the house so as to ensure an even temperature of about 55° F. throughout in cold weather. Along the skirting underneath windows is a satisfactory position, because if the windows are a little open the warm air from the tubes counteracts the flow of cold air and also produces a desirable movement of air. Tubes of any length, single, double or treble can be fixed in rooms, in the hall, landing and bathroom. For the kitchen it is desirable to have one tube underneath the sink so that it is fairly warm for the housewife when she is working there. An excellent form of background heating of a similar kind is that provided in conjunction with ventilators underneath windows. The air from outside enters through a louvre into a box under the window in which are the heating units which could be tubular or other similar type. The air then passes through the vent in the surface of the window ledge and a film of warm air thus rises in front of the window. The passage of air can be controlled by a regulator.

The whole system of electrical background heating in the house can be thermostatically controlled, and the heating can be automatically switched on half an hour before the family rises in the morning, and switched off half an hour after it has retired.

If background heating throughout the house is in the region of 55° F., topping-up would be required mainly in the living room, dining room, study and occasionally in the bedrooms. In the large number of new small houses the living room has a dining recess and it is mainly a question of topping up in one room, which means merely increasing the temperature by about 10° to 15° F. This can be done by solid fuel fire, gas or electric fire or oil heater. In the case of solid fuel fire, this is more closely connected with the provision of background heating than the other methods and involves numerous considerations.

The ordinary grate installed in the majority of houses before the war in which bituminous coal is burnt provides heat for only one room, while it is inefficient, wasteful, dirty and pollutes the atmosphere. It is calculated that its working efficiency is about 20 per cent which means that 80 per cent of the heat in the coal is wasted.[1] Recent developments, however, in the design of the open grate have increased this efficiency to as much as 40 to 45 per cent.

One should bear in mind that, as the cost of fuels tends to increase, the need for greater control over these fuels becomes increasingly obvious. Furthermore, the tendency will probably be to use various fuels intermittently. One should therefore have in mind, when considering the various methods of heating, the importance of ease of control, flexibility of heat output and whether the appliance can be used intermittently or otherwise. Coal is one of the chief sources of our national wealth; it is rich in by-products, and the sources of supply are not inexhaustible. In 1938, of the 178 million tons consumed in Great Britain, 62 million tons were used for domestic purposes, of which 49 millions tons were burnt in houses as raw bituminous coal. And of the heat which that 49 million tons could produce only about 20 per cent was utilized. Thus 80 per cent and all the valuable by-products were lost. Further, the domestic fire is one of the chief causes of the air pollution which is injurious to health and causes considerable damage to buildings. It was estimated by the Beaver Committee on Air Pollution that the cost to the nation of air pollution is in the region of £250 million a year. As an example of the valuable by-products from coal, it is estimated that 40 million tons of coal produce 400 thousand million cubic feet of gas, 25 million tons of coke, 300 thousand tons of sulphate of ammonia, and 450 million gallons of tar from which innumerable valuable chemical substances are produced. In view of these facts there is every reason why the burning of bituminous coal in houses and the manufacture of grates for such purpose should be discouraged. The only thing to be said in its favour is that a coal fire is cheerful on a cold winter's evening. The general liking for it is based on pleasant associations, but these considerations are unimportant compared with the tremendous disadvantages. Smokeless fuel like coke, coalite and anthracite have not the economic disadvantages of bituminous coal, while the fire from them can be almost as agreeable and cheerful.

Most smokeless fuels are suitable for continuous burning. Some are difficult to ignite like coke and anthracite, while some manufactured smokeless fuels, such as coalite, have the enormous advantage of being very easy to ignite, and they are equally easy to control, providing a bright glow similar to that of bituminous coal.

[1] See *Simon Report*, Chapter III, para. 1.

In the first edition of this book I wrote: 'In most houses of six rooms an open grate is provided in four, two of which are bedrooms.' In most houses built since the war, in fact in 95 per cent of them, there is only one open fire, and in most of the houses built under private enterprise there is also a boiler in the kitchen. Generally speaking, in local authority housing the tendency has been to continue to instal fire-back boilers. Fire-back boilers have been in use in this country since 1908, but there is a strong move throughout the country to replace them with the two-flue house, namely, a small boiler in a recess in the kitchen and a free-standing fire in a recess in the living room—the two flues adjoining. Alternatively, local authorities are experimenting with the use of the free-standing fire in the living room and either a separate gas or electric water heater fitted near the main draw off point, that is, the sink.

In background heating provided by hot water and warm air the best source is either an open fire, closed or openable stove in the living room, or a boiler in the kitchen, utility room or basement. If it is provided by a closed or openable stove in the living room, then all that is necessary for topping up in that room is a little more fuel and increasing the under draught. Experiments have been made with open fires to provide background heating as well as heating the living room, but it is very doubtful if they are adequate. If the source for the background heating is the boiler in the kitchen or utility room, then the living room might call for an open fire, although this topping up could be more conveniently effected by electric or gas fire, but not so economically as by the coal fire, especially in the very cold weather sometimes experienced in December, January and February. Also there is always the cheerful and ornamental effect of the open fire which the Englishman—not quite so much the Englishwoman—is reluctant to forgo. Even in U.S.A. where they rarely depend on the open fire for heating, it is sometimes introduced for its attractive and cheerful appearance.

If then the open fire is installed in the living room for topping up it should be as efficient as possible. A common type is the continuous burning resulting from the more efficient control of the under draught sometimes combined with a cover plate. This fire has the advantage of eliminating a certain amount of labour since it can be used continuously. A further development is the under floor draught which better conserves the heat in the room. This fire is sometimes combined with convected air heating, not only in the living room, but in two bedrooms above, but it is doubtful whether it is adequate to heat the two bedrooms. The first of this type was designed by the British Coal Utilisation Research Association. In this model the air from underneath the floor not only provides the draught for the fire, but passes up behind the fire into a chamber which is warmed by the flue in the centre, and the warm air is emitted through a vent in the living room above the fire, and also through a vent in the bedroom above. The fire can burn continuously, for the grate can be closed by means of a lid which fits into the back of the fire when not in use. An ash pan is placed below the grate and this can be removed through the space in the hearth in front of the fire. The whole device is made clear by the diagram illustrated (p. 65). Several appliances have been produced following this under-floor draught principle, among which may be mentioned the Camelon, the Summit and the Fandair (Plates XXIV, (b) and XXV (a) and (b)).

The greatest progress towards efficiency is the fire which combines under-draught control with the restricted throat, and in addition to radiant heat gives also convected heat by air circulating round the back of the fire and flowing back into the room through grilles. Several have been developed of which a few are illustrated. They include the

'Hurdapta' made by Hurseal, the 'Parkray' made by Radiation and the 'Projector' type made by Allied Ironfounders.

The 'Hurdapta' can be described as a combination of the open fire and the openable stove, the fire opening being less than the former and greater than the latter. This effective control of the air flow below and above the fire throws the heat out into the room and an overall efficiency of over 40 per cent is secured. In addition, a sealed space between the appliance and the fire-back provides a supply of convected warm air. Although the flue is greatly reduced compared with the traditional type, it can be further reduced for slow burning by an adjustable throat restrictor. A cover plate is provided for overnight burning. The appliance is particularly suitable for smokeless fuels, it is inexpensive and can be fixed by the layman if instructions are carefully followed. Its great value is that it burns comparatively little fuel in relation to the heat produced. Indeed a questionnaire to hundreds of users elicited the interesting information that a fuel saving of between a third and a half was obtained while the standard of heat comfort was improved.

A brief indication of the method of fixing will serve to to emphasize some of the special features of the appliance. Combined with the appliance is a flue register plate which consists of a sheet of expanded metal with an oval hole to take the flue connector. This register plate is wedged into the flue. In doing this it is generally necessary to bend or cut the expanded metal at the edge to secure a good fit. The flue connector is drawn through the oval hole of the register plate over the throat of the fire. This first stage is experimental to get the appliance in the right place in relation to the flue. The appliance should be fixed to leave a clear inch from the face of the surround.

Once the right position has been found and marked, the flue connector and the fire should be removed, care being taken not to disturb the register plate. This should then be cemented in with fire cement. It is well to be liberal with this cement—6 lb. should be available—completely to seal the register plate without air leaks. This secures the supply of convected warm air, and an air leak would mean the escape of warm air into the chimney instead of into the room. Having allowed the cement to dry, and at least twenty-four hours should be given for this, the operation of placing the fire in position is repeated. It is essentially a simple operation.

The 'Parkray' Fire has been made in six models, Nos. 1, 2, 2A, 3, 4 and 4A. 'Parkray' No. 1 follows similar principles to the 'Hurdapta' fire, providing convected heating, an adjustable restricted throat and in addition a built-in gas burner. The 'Parkray' 2 is a development which include a back boiler and this provides radiant and convected heat, but also hot water adequate for domestic requirements, and in addition a heated towel rail or radiator in the bathroom. An interesting feature of this fire is that it has a down-draught fire box, which means that a large proportion of the volatiles drawn down through the hot fuel bed is burned by mixing with pre-heated secondary air, which reduces smoke emission by as much, it is claimed, as 80 per cent. The 'Parkray' 2A is similar, but without the boiler. The 'Parkray' 3 also incorporates the down-draught method of combustion which has been developed by Radiation for domestic installations, and which has a considerable bearing upon performance. The very rapid recovery of the 'Parkray' after periods of slow burning is attributable to this method as is the accurate control of all burning rates. The introduction of pre-heated secondary air at the bottom of the fuel bed at the point where the gaseous products leave the firebox (because the primary air is down-draught) ensures that the volatiles are ignited and burned in the secondary combustion chamber at the back of the fire. With normal up-draught combustion these products would pass to waste up the flue and be discharged into the air. The heat from the volatiles in the secondary combustion chamber is passed to the fins at the back of the fire which are in turn 'scrubbed' of their heat by the convected air.

The 'Parkray' 3 which has a neat and attractive appearance, was designed to provide an efficient convector fire which can simply and quickly be installed in conventional 16-inch and 18-inch fireplace openings fitted with standard Milner type firebacks, without alteration to the surround. It has also been designed as a self-contained appliance to eliminate fixing faults and to obviate the need for preparation of convection chambers and air inlet and outlet ducts in the brickwork. 'Parkray' 4 is similar in appearance to 'Parkray' 3, but larger. It incorporates a down-draught firebox, and a back boiler is included as in 'Parkray' 2, 'Parkray' 4A is similar to 4 but without the boiler (Plate XXVII).

This type of appliance illustrates the trend towards factory made, self-contained, solid fuel heating appliances, which is in line with the move towards the prefabrication of most household equipment.

In the projector type of fire, which provides both radiant and convected heat, the air inlets and warm air outlets are incorporated in the casing of the fire (Plate XXVI (b)). There are several variations of these, some of which are illustrated.

The type of fire of which the 'Hurdapta' and 'Parkray' are outstanding examples, which gives both radiant and convected heat and operates with restricted throat is very efficient compared with the traditional open fire, the efficiency being at least 40 per cent. But more efficient is the closed stove or openable stove, either free standing or inset, which similarly provides both radiant and convection heating. A large number of types have been produced since the war, and a few are illustrated. They represent the highest efficiency of solid fuel appliances, the free-standing types reaching an efficiency for both radiant and convected heating of 50 to 60 per cent, and in some cases even more.

With these developments the appearance of stoves has greatly improved (see Plate XXX) and it can be said today that stoves are being installed much more frequently then ever before. On the other hand the open fire is part of British family life and, furthermore, the radiation from the fire may have a beneficial effect. Thus the free-standing open fire with restricted throat, providing radiation as well as convection, would seem to meet the needs and wishes of the majority as well as any solid fuel appliance. These fires are just as free-standing as an ordinary stove, and they provide radiation at a lower level, while the restricted throat reduces the room air change, eliminates room draughts and improves conditions for comfort throughout the room.

This type of appliance is being continually developed and it is anticipated that a number of different models will be available by the time this book is in print. Many of the manufacturers are developing versions of this free-standing fire for use in new houses either standing proudly in front of the wall or, alternatively, installed in a recess or hole in the wall. The advantage of such arrangements is that a free-standing fire can be used at any time, and replaced with some other heating appliance. Indeed the tendency may well be in local authority housing to provide a space or recess for a fire, leaving the householder to purchase, hire or hire-purchase a fire—either gas, electric, or one of the free-standing fires, or stove. Many years ago both the estate developer and local authorities used to provide solid fuel cookers built into the houses. This gave way to the provision of space for either a gas or electric cooker, and the householder was given a free choice of the type of cooking appliance he wished to use. In the future householders should have a similar choice in the type of space heating appliance.

A wide variety of gas and electric fires for 'topping up' are available, and improvements are continually being made. Some are illustrated (Plates XXXI-XXXVII). They may be broadly classified as the small portable types suitable for topping up in the bedroom for short periods, and the larger, more substantial type for the living room, where the family is often seated for the evening. For the larger gas fires a flue is necessary, but this need only be small and can be built into the ordinary thickness of the wall. The Nautilus flue is an example. This is built of flue bricks, each with external dimensions of 1 foot $2\frac{1}{2}$ inches by $4\frac{1}{2}$ inches, thus fitting into the 9-inch brick wall, or one leaf of an 11-inch cavity wall. As in the solid fuel fire, the most efficient type of gas fire is the combined radiant inlet beam type and convector which emits warm air from a vent above the fire.

Electric and gas fires and oil heaters must now be provided with adequate guards, because there have been many cases of people being burnt from an inadequately guarded appliance. The Heating Appliances (Fireguards) Act of 1952 empowers the Secretary of State 'to make regulations requiring gas fires, electric fires and oil heaters of such descriptions as may be specified in the regulations to be fitted with guards and presenting for such guards such standards of construction and fitting as are in his opinion appropriate to reduce or prevent the risk of fire or injury resulting from accidental contact with or proximity to, flames or heating elements'.

I have tried to be impartial in assessing the respective merits of heating by gas, solid fuel and electricity, but I might be allowed the luxury of expressing a personal conviction, which is that electricity holds the greatest promise for future development. Even now it might be claimed that the 'all electric house' is the most efficient, the cleanest and the most convenient; but it is costly and is probably beyond the means of the majority.[1] In these circumstances the best form of heating is probably a combination of two fuels. One may expect to see the continuation of the open fire, preferably the new free-standing variety, with possibly oil-filled electric radiators, or electrically heated panels providing the equivalent of central heating as background warmth. On the other hand the two-flue house is in many ways attractive, one flue being used for a free-standing fire and the second flue for an efficient domestic boiler for hot water and central heating, and it should be remembered that efficiencies of over 75 per cent are claimed for some of the latest boilers. These domestic boilers may require the ash emptied only once a week, and with the introduction of the new small bore pipe system developed by the British Coal Utilisation Research Association and the provision of a small pump to circulate the hot water through lightweight steel panel radiators, the installation can be as flexible and easy to control as the electric heating system, whilst being cheaper in operation. The emphasis must be on ease of control and flexibility and the use of fuel with the utmost efficiency.

[1] With the generation of electricity by nuclear energy it is not impossible that before the end of the century electricity for domestic purposes may be so cheap that the maintenance of a temperature of 55°F. in the house would represent an insignificant proportion of the family budget. While we have to depend mainly on coal for electricity it will be costly.

CHAPTER XI

INSULATION AND VENTILATION

A HOUSE is designed primarily for shelter and one of the main functions in its construction is to protect the occupants from wet and cold, and in a tropical climate also from heat. Although this is obvious, the protection in the traditional house consisting of floorboards on joists, a 9-inch brick wall and a pitched timber roof covered with tiles and slates, is not very efficient, for in the cold weather there is generally considerable heat lost through the floors, walls and roof and spaces round the doors and windows.

The sense of waste with this loss of heat is more apparent with the realization that coal, which provides nearly all the heating in the house, is becoming more costly and precious, while output is hardly adequate for the country's needs. These considerations have prompted much study of various insulation materials and their application in the last fifteen years, which has made it possible for a house to be much better insulated. There is also the consideration that the cost of heating is less in a well insulated house than in a house of the normal traditional construction represented by the majority built between the wars. There may be a little extra cost when the house is being built, but that cost will be repaid in a few years by the saving of fuel. This also applies to older houses where insulation can to a large measure be introduced.

The basis of measurement for the insulation value of materials is the British Thermal Unit which is the amount of heat absorbed by 1 lb. of water when its temperature is raised by 1° F. Thermal conductivity is the heat flow through a material when there is a difference between the temperatures of its surfaces; and the unit of measurement, k, is the amount of heat expressed in British Thermal Units transmitted per hour through a square foot of the material 1-inch in thickness, when the surface temperatures on the opposite sides differ by 1° F. Thermal resistivity is a reciprocal calculation and the unit 1 k is the number of hours taken in the transmission of one British Thermal Unit in the same conditions as those stated for thermal conductivity. Thus it will be appreciated that materials of low conductivity, k, have a high thermal resistivity, 1 k, but the value is usually expressed by a k.[1]

Following are some of the principal insulating materials used in building, with their insulating values based on tests carried out by the Building Research Station.

	Thermal Conductivity	Thermal Resistivity
Asbestos—		
Blanket	0·38	2·63
Insulating Board	0·75	1·33
Fibre: loose	0·40 to 0·45	2·50 to 2·22
Fibre: Spray	0·32	3·12

[1] These definitions are based on those given in *The Thermal Insulation of Buildings* by G. D. Nash, J. Comrie and H. F. Broughton (D.S.I.R. 1955). Much of the information given in this chapter is derived from that valuable guide to the insulation of buildings, to which the reader is referred for a more thorough and detailed study of the subject.

	Thermal Conductivity Varies from	*Thermal Resistivity* Varies from
Concrete—		
Aerated	0·60 to 4·50	1·67 to 0·22
Clinker	2·30 to 2·80	0·44 to 0·36
Vermiculite	0·70 to 1·00	1·43 to 1·00
Expanded clay	1·70 to 3·20	0·59 to 0·31
Foamed slag	1·70 to 2·35	0·59 to 0·43
'No-fines' gravel	5·80 to 6·50	0·17 to 0·15
'No-fines' clinker	3·20 to 3·90	0·31 to 0·26
Pumice	1·30 to 2·00	0·77 to 0·50
Corkboard	0·27 to 0·30	3·70 to 3·33
Cork—		
Granulated	0·32 to 0·36	3·13 to 2·78
Regranulated	0·25 to 0·27	4·00 to 3·70
Eel grass: Quilt	0·27	3·70
Expanded ebonite	0·20 to 0·32	5·00 to 3·00
Felt of wool or jute fibres	0·27	3·70
Fibre insulating board	0·37 to 0·45	2·70 to 2·22
Foamed slag	0·68 to 0·90	1·47 to 1·11
Glass wool or silk—		
Bitumen quilt	0·25	4·00
Loose	0·25 to 0·28	4·00 to 3·60
Mats plain	0·29 and 0·23	3·45 and 4·35
	0·25	4·00
Mattresses	0·26 to 0·29	3·84 to 3·50
Quilts	0·25	4·00
Slabs	0·24 to 0·27	4·17 to 3·70
Gypsum: Loose	0·43	2·32
Lightweight plaster and rendering		
mixed with Vermiculite or aerated	0·75 to 1·8	1·33 to 0·56
Mineral or Rock Wool—		
Loose	0·25	4·00
Mattresses or Mats	0·25 to 0·30	4·00 to 3·33
Quilts	0·25	4·0
Semi-rigid slabs or felt	0·23 to 0·30	4·35 to 3·33
Vermiculite	0·45	2·22
Wood wool slabs	0·57 to 0·80	1·75 to 1·25

J. Comrie, G. D. Nash and H. F. Broughton in Part III of *The Thermal Insulation of Buildings*[1] give several examples of the application of insulating materials to various forms of construction and I propose to select a few examples from the insulation of floors, walls and roof most applicable to domestic building.

FLOORS

The example is taken of a normal 'suspended timber ground floor constructed of 4-inch by 2-inch timber joists spaced at 18-inch centres supported on 4-inch by 2-inch timber plates bedded on sleeper walls and covered with 1-inch tongued and grooved floorboards' of two-story semi-detached houses of 950 square feet. The *U*

[1] Op. cit. p. 70-139.

(*a*) Alicon continuous-burning closed stove.

PLATE XXX (*a*) *and* (*b*). *Continuous-burning stoves.*

(*b*) Redfyre continuous-burning closed stove. In this stove one lever operates three dampers.

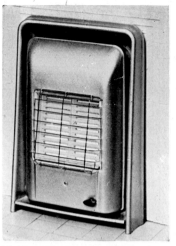

(a) New World 'Vecta Beam' gas fire.

(b) 'Hadrian' New World 'Silent Beam' gas fire.

(c) Portans gas fire.

(d) Lutello panel fire.

(e) Paraglow.

PLATE XXXI (a), (b), (c), (d) and (e). *Gas fires*. All these fires have guards conforming to the Heating Appliances (Fireguards) Regulations.

(*a*) Cannon 'GasMiser', incorporating Multyjet hot-air convector.

(*b*) Port Royal.

(*c*) Bamburgh.

(*d*) Crawley.

(*e*) Conray—for grate fitting or building into wall.

PLATE XXXII (*a*), (*b*), (*c*), (*d*) *and* (*e*). *Combined radiant and convection gas fires.*

(a) C.P. 'Windsor' heater.

(b) Merlin heater.

(c) Cannon radiation and convector heater.

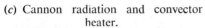

(d) Paravector heater.

PLATE XXXIII (a), (b), (c) and (d). Convector gas heaters.

(a) Safera fire. A safety device automatically disconnects the supply of electricity immediately the fire is lifted by the handle, tilted, or knocked over.

(b) Low level fire designed to fit flush into the wall.

(c) Cosyglo portable reflector fire.

PLATE XXXIV (a), (b) and (c). Electric fires.

(a) Radialt portable screen heater.

(b) Davey Diamond portable reflector fire.

(c) Cosyglo screen fire with glass side panels illuminated by a 60 W. amber-sprayed lamp; this fire is thus suitable for television circles.

PLATE XXXV (a), (b) and (c). Electric fires.

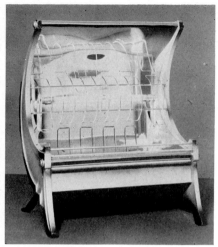

(a) Minera fire.

(b) Memray swivel reflector. 1 KW.

(c) Swan brand 'Waldorf'.

PLATE XXXVI (a), (b), (c) and (d). Electric fires.

(d) Saferod high level reflecting safety heater for wall mounting 25 in. long, embedded rod-type element.

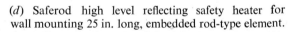

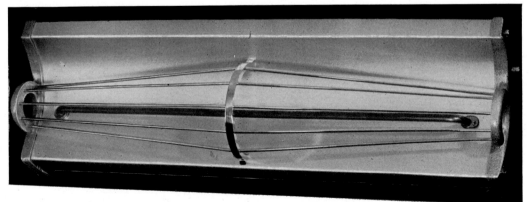

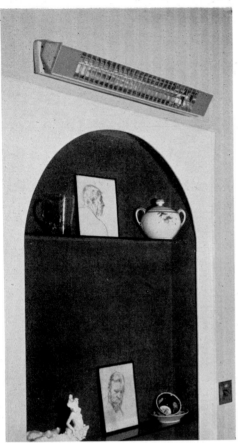

(a) 'Radisil' radiant heater can be fixed in any horizontal position on wall or ceiling. It is claimed to be very safe.

(b) Thermovent radiant glass thermopanel.

(c) Wafer convector heater, designed for wall mounting. Projection from wall is $5\frac{3}{8}$ in., of which $1\frac{1}{2}$ in. is airspace between heater and wall.

PLATE XXXVII (a), (b) and (c). *Electric space heaters.*

value of the floor structure without special insulation is 0·40. The insulation can be improved by:

	U value	1 k
(a) 1-inch cork board laid on joists prior to laying floor boards, which gives	0·17	3·50
or laid (b) between joists and supported on fillets nailed to the sides of joists. This provides an air space between floor and moulding sheet and gives	0·14	3·50
1-inch insulating fibreboard of two ½-inch sheets laid by a method	0·19	2·86
or 1 sheet of ½-inch insulating fibreboard laid by b method	0·20	2·86
2-inch compressed straw slab laid by b method	0·15	1·67
Another method applicable to different materials like mineral or rock wool, eel grass, glass wool or glass silk is to drape the sheets, quilts or mats over the top of joists covered by fillets to which the floor boards are nailed		
Eel grass—		
½-inch thick quilt	0·23	3·70
1-inch thick quilt	0·16	3·70
Glass wool or silk, bitumen bonded, ¾-inch thick quilt	0·18	4·00
Glass wool or silk, bitumen bonded, 1-inch thick quilt	0·15	4·00
Mineral or rock wool, 1-inch thick quilt	0·15	4·00
Aluminium foil double side laid without the fillet	0·25	
If plain and corrugated sheets are combined	0·22	

WALLS

The ordinary 9-inch brick wall externally rendered, with ½-inch internal rendering has a U value of about 0·42, which is not good insulation. The insulation value is improved if ½-inch plasterboard is placed on ¾-inch battens, thus providing a ¾-inch air space. The U value is then about 0·30. If 1-inch wood wool is placed behind the internal finish it is still better, having a U value of about 0·24. Improvements in insulation are still further effected by the cavity wall of two 4½-inch brick leaves and a 2-inch cavity. Without external rendering but with ½-inch plaster internal finish the U value is about 0·30; if lightweight concrete of a conductivity of 1·7 forms the inner leaf instead of brick the U value is 0·20 and if this becomes foamed slag with fibreboard on ¾-inch battens as internal lining, the U value is as low a 0·15.

Framed structures with panels of quite thin sheets of materials with good insulation values give good results. Thus an external sheet of ⅜-inch asbestos cement, an air space of 4 inches and internal sheet of ½-inch insulating fibreboard gives a U value of 0·28, but in selecting materials other considerations, like fire risk have to be taken into account. Three-eighths-inch asbestos cement external lining, a 3-inch air space with ⅜-inch plasterboard backed on to 1-inch slag wool quilt gives good insulation U value of 0·17. If the wool quilt is placed in the centre of the cavity the U value becomes 0·15.

The examples of insulation for external walling given by Comrie, Nash and Broughton,[1] are 11-inch cavity brick wall plastered internally; 11-inch cavity wall with outer leaf brick and inner leaf lightweight concrete; with both leaves of lightweight concrete; walls of concrete blocks, and walls of *in situ* lightweight concrete.

[1] *The Thermal Insulation of Buildings* (D.S.I.R. 1955).

They also give examples of steel framed construction which are more applicable to other types of building.

The U value of the 11-inch cavity wall with $\frac{1}{2}$-inch internal plaster is calculated as 0·30. Where suitable insulation material is placed on the internal face of the brickwork to receive plaster the values are:

Insulating Material	U value	1 k
1-inch cork board	0·15	3·50
$\frac{1}{2}$-inch insulating fibreboard	0·21	2·86
1-inch insulating fibreboard (two $\frac{1}{2}$-inch sheets)	0·16	2·86
1-inch wood wool slabs	1·19	1·67
2-inch wood wool slabs	0·15	1·67
$\frac{5}{8}$-inch vermiculate plaster	0·26	1·00

If insulating material of boards or slabs is fixed to 1-inch by 2-inch battens thus leaving an air space between material and wall, the U values are:

Insulating Material	U value	1 k
$\frac{1}{2}$-inch asbestos insulating board	0·21	2·86
$\frac{1}{2}$-inch insulating fibreboard	0·17	2·86
$\frac{3}{8}$-inch insulating gypsum plasterboard	0·19	—
2-inch compressed straw slabs	0·13	1·67

If aluminium foil is used as a corrugated sheet and fixed to battens by further battens and then covered by $\frac{3}{8}$-inch plasterboard, the U value is 0·15, and if single sided aluminium foil is used the value is 0·19. The U values of other materials employed in the same way are:

Insulating Material	U value	1 k
Eel grass	0·12	3·70
Glass wool or silk $\frac{3}{4}$-inch quilts	0·13	4·00
Glass wool or silk 1-inch quilts	0·12	4·00
Slag mineral or rock wool $\frac{3}{4}$-inch quilts	0·13	4·00
Slag mineral or rock wool 1-inch quilts	0·12	4·00

If the internal leaf of the wall is lightweight concrete blocks (the external leaf remaining $4\frac{1}{2}$-inch brick) plastered internally the improved insulation over the two $4\frac{1}{2}$-inch brick leaves with 2-inch cavity with U value of 0·30, is as follows:

Insulating Material	U value	1 k
Aerated concrete 3 inches thick	0·20 to 0·25 according to density	
Aerated concrete 4 inches thick	0·17 to 0·23 according to density	0·67
Clinker concrete 3 inches thick	0·25 to 0·27	0·33 to 0·44
Clinker concrete 4 inches thick	0·22	0·44
Expanded clay concrete 3 inches thick	0·24	0·46
Expanded clay concrete 4 inches thick	0·22	0·46
Foamed slag concrete 3 inches thick	0·22 to 0·25	0·59 to 0·43
Foamed slag concrete 4 inches thick	0·20 to 0·23	0·59 to 0·43

If both leaves are of lightweight concrete blocks 4 inches thick with 2-inch cavity externally rendered with internal face plastered the values are:

Insulating Material	U value	1 k
Aerated concrete	0·21	0·33
Clinker concrete	0·17 to 0·21	0·44 to 0·33
Expanded clay concrete	0·17	0·46
Foamed slag concrete	0·14 to 0·18	0·59 to 0·43

Other examples given by Comrie, Nash and Broughton are walls of lightweight hollow concrete blocks which give *U* values between 0·25 and 0·30 according to the type of concrete, and lightweight concrete walling 8 inches thick poured *in situ* which has *U* values from 0·18 to 0·27.

Roofs

Among the examples of insulation of roofs given by Comrie, Nash and Broughton applicable to domestic buildings is the pitched roof with tiles on battens and felt with plasterboard ceiling, and a flat roof of timber joist construction, boarded and covered with bitumen felt and chippings and with plasterboard ceiling, and reinforced concrete slab construction covered with bitumen felt and finished on underside with plaster.

The *U* value of the pitched roof construction is calculated as 0·43, and the improvements effected by various insulating materials are given below. In the first list the insulating material is substituted for the plasterboard and plastered on the underside:

Insulating Material	U value	1 k
1-inch cork board	0·17	3·50
1-inch insulating fibreboard (two ½-inch sheets)	0·20	2·86
¾-inch insulating gypsum plasterboard	0·31	—
2-inch compressed straw slabs	0·18	1·67
2-inch wood wool slabs	0·18	1·67
Fillings between joists can be—		
Aluminium foil, corrugated and plain combined	0·21	—
Glass wool or silk—		
4-inch mat	0·08	4·00
1-inch mat	0·16	4·00
Loose gypsum granules—		
2 inches thick	0·14	2·33
4 inches thick	0·10	2·33
Slag mineral or rock wool—		
1-inch quilt	0·16	4·00
2 inches thick	0·10	4·00
Vermiculite (exfoliated)—		
3 inches thick	0·11	2·22
2 inches thick	0·15	2·22
1-inch thick	0·22	2·22
Sheets, mats or quilts draped loosely over the joists to which they are tacked:		
Aluminium foil—		
double sided	0·23	
plain and corrugated combined	0·21	

Insulating Material	U value	1 k
Eel grass, 1-inch quilt	0·14	3·70
Glass wool or silk—		
1-inch thick mat	0·14	4·00
¾-inch thick quilt	0·16	4·00
Slag mineral or rock wool—		
1-inch thick quilt	0·14	4·00
¾-inch thick quilt		
If insulating boards or slabs are nailed above the ceiling joists the values are—		
1-inch cork board	0·15	3·50
½-inch insulating fibreboard	0·21	2·86
1-inch insulating fibreboard	0·16	2·86
⅜-inch insulating gypsum plasterboard	0·23	—
2-inch compressed strawboards	0·15	1·67
2-inch wood wool slabs	0·15	1·67

In the case of the flat roof of timber joist construction, where the basic *U* value is given as 0·32, one method of introducing the insulating sheets is between the boarding on top of the joists and the roofing felt:

Insulating Material	U value	1 k
1-inch cork board	0·15	3·50
½-inch insulating fibreboard	0·22	2·86
1-inch insulating fibreboard	0·17	2·86
2-inch compressed straw slabs	0·16	1·67
1-inch wood wool slabs	0·21	1·67
1½-inch wood wool slabs	0·18	1·67
2-inch wood wool slabs	0·16	1·67
3-inch aerated concrete slabs	0·20	0·67
2-inch vermiculite concrete slabs	0·23	0·67
Frames slag concrete 4 to 2 inches thick	0·20	0·59

An alternative given is to drape the joists with sheets, quilts or mats and then cover with boarding and roofing felt:

Insulating Material	U value	1 k
Aluminium foil, corrugated and plain combined	0·16	
Eel grass—		
¾-inch quilt	0·15	3·70
1-inch quilt	0·13	3·70
Glass wool or silk		
¾-inch quilt	0·14	4·00
1-inch mat	0·13	4·00
Slag mineral or rock wool—		
¾-inch quilt	0·14	4·00
1-inch quilt	0·13	4·00

If the insulating board is used instead of plasterboard on the underside of the joists and plastered, the values are:

Insulating Material	U value	1 k
1-inch cork board	0·15	3·50
1-inch insulating fibreboard	0·18	2·86
⅜-inch insulating gypsum plasterboard	0·24	—

Insulating Material	U value	1 k
¼-inch asbestos insulating board	0·32	1·33
2-inch compressed straw slabs	0·16	1·67
1-inch wood wool slabs	0·21	1·67
1½-inch wood wool slabs	0·18	1·67
2-inch wood wool slabs	0·16	1·67

Another method of roof insulation given is to fix the sheets or quilts of the insulating material to the underside of the joists and resting on a cavity of insulating fibreboard, plasterboard, asbestos, cement sheet on asbestos insulating board. The insulating materials used in this method are aluminium foil, eel grass, glass wool or silk, and slag mineral or rock wool. The insulation value varies according to the thickness and application of the material and the material used for the ceiling, but the range of value in these numerous variations is not great, extending from 0·12 to 0·17 with the exception of the single sided aluminium foil, which is 0·19.

With the flat roof of reinforced concrete slab construction the basic U value is estimated at 0·59. The slab is 4 inches thick. In one case the insulating boards or slabs are laid between the screed and the felt.

Insulating Material	U value	1 k
1-inch cork	0·19	3·50
1-inch insulating fibreboard	0·22	2·86
2-inch compressed straw slabs	0·20	1·67
1-inch wood wool slabs	0·30	1·67
1½-inch wood wool slabs	0·24	1·67
2-inch wood wool slabs	0·20	1·67
3-inch wood wool slabs	0·15	1·67

If lightweight cement is used instead of the screed the values are as follows:

Insulating Material	U value	1 k
Aerated concrete filling from 5 inches thick in the centre to 3 inches at the eaves	0·24	0·67
Foamed slag—		
4 inches to 2 inches	0·31	0·59
5 inches to 3 inches	0·26	0·59
6 inches to 4 inches	0·22	0·59
Vermiculite concrete 4 inches to 2 inches	0·22	1·00 [1]

The insulation of a house is greatly improved by double glazing for the windows, which thus permits having them a good size without serious heat loss. The extra cost of double glazing would be paid for in less than three years by saving of fuel. The Egerton Committee said that if double glazing were used 'the heat loss through the windows would be reduced by half, i.e. from 3·29 to 1·65 million B.Thu.U. per annum for the whole house and from 2·01 to 1 million B.Thu.U. per annum for the living room only; and an increased initial cost of 2s. 6d. per square foot for the living room windows. or of 1s. 3d. per square foot for all the windows of the house could be justified' (para. 4. 2. 4). The costs would be more, of course, in 1956, but not proportionately more.

[1] These lists are only brief abstracts from the far more detailed information given in the D.S.I.R. publication on *Thermal Insulation of Buildings,* to which the reader is referred. Included in the information is a precise indication of the method of application, price and standard sizes.

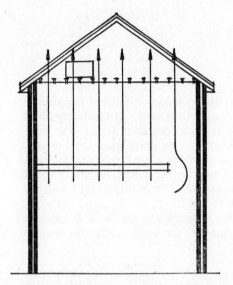

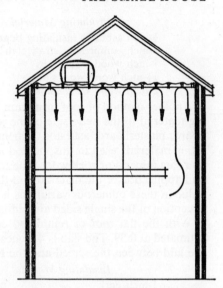

Fig. 13. *Insulation*. Diagrams illustrating the escape of heat through the ceiling and roof, and the conservation of heat when the ceiling is properly insulated. When the ceiling is insulated care should be taken always to insulate the water tank. Below are shown some typical pipe insulating coverings, the first two being of mineral wool and the third of calico strips.

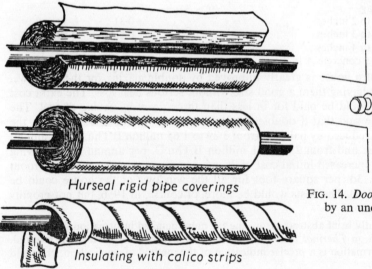

Hurseal rigid pipe coverings

Insulating with calico strips

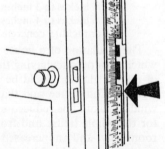

Fig. 14. *Door rendered draught-proof by an unobtrusive metal strip.*

For efficient insulation it is also important that the doors and windows should fit well so that there should be no draughts in the spaces between windows or doors and frames. With a new house in which well seasoned timber is used for the windows and doors and metal windows fit well, there should be no spaces for draughts, but even in these cases some movement takes place resulting from vibrations caused by traffic, while older houses, built before the war, were often so shaken by bombing that doors and windows became less effective seals against infiltration of cold air. Also in building houses since the war insufficiently seasoned wood was often used.

To seal doors and windows and thus complete the proper insulation of the house, weather stripping can be used. Many methods are available. One comprises specially formed inter-locking sections of bronze or zinc which are fitted into grooves formed in window sashes and door stiles. Another consists of a flat strip of high-grade resilient phosphor-bronze which is fitted between the doors or windows and the frames. The strip is applied flat to one surface and then strung away to meet and press gently against the other surface. The strip-type can be satisfactorily applied to existing doors and windows. Another type called 'Stick-a-seal' consists of a strip of self-adhesive plastic foam which can be applied against the stop rebate in a few minutes. It is inexpensive but may have to be renewed every two years (Plate XL).

VENTILATION

Although it is important to reduce the heat loss of a house to a minimum by efficient insulation, it is important at the same time to pay due regard to adequate ventilation in the interests of health. The desirable condition is to obtain a controlled balance of heat retention and ventilation, but in the past there has generally been an uncontrolled heat loss and often ventilation of an uncomfortable kind.

Ventilation is the change of air in a room. It is essential because it removes the air vitiated by the products of respiration, bacteria and all objectionable or unpleasant odours. The minimum air change adopted by the Egerton Committee (para. 2. 2. 2), is 600 cubic feet per hour per person, and the example is given of four persons in a living room of 1,500 cubic feet capacity requiring $1\frac{1}{2}$ air changes per hour (para. 2. 2. 3). It is pointed out that this air change would be obtained with a normal flue of 50 square inches. If there is a fire the air change is slightly increased. This means that a room 15 feet by 12 feet by 8 feet 4 inches high, occupied by four persons, with a normal flue of 50 square inches and with all windows closed would have adequate ventilation. If it is not very cold outside, no lower than, say 45° F., I would personally prefer one window slightly open, and this would increase the air change considerably. If a window and door are both wide open the air change is every two or three minutes. For the kitchen, especially when the housewife is cooking, the air change should be more than in the living room, and 1,000 cubic feet per hour per person is recommended by the Egerton Committee.

The value of the flue in effecting air change is considerable. Where fires are used which do not require a flue, a wall ventilator, generally in the form of an air brick, is employed, but this is not so satisfactory as a flue, especially when a fire is burning. The efficiency of the wall ventilator is not very much increased by the fire.

Several wall ventilators have been produced of recent years. These are designed to regulate the flow of air when the wind velocity is high. When there is little or no wind it is doubtful if the ventilation that they afford is sufficient, because for this to be satisfactory there should be an outlet to draw the air in the form of a flue as well as an inlet. Wall ventilators might usefully be a little larger.

These considerations suggest the wisdom of having a flue in every room even if it is intended to use electric fires. There are no fumes with the electric fire, but it often produces a feeling of stuffiness due to the operation of the rays on the skin, and this is obviated by air movement. A flue of the Nautilus type is fairly economical and effects the desired air change better than the wall ventilator. The Egerton Committee recommends that 'provision should be made for ventilation irrespective of the method of heating, and one way of effecting such provision is by flues' (para. 82), which are suggested in the living room, kitchen and bedrooms. I am doubtful if a flue of 50 square inches is necessary in a kitchen, as the Egerton Committee recommends, especially if the kitchen is small, provided that a ventilated hood with a fan to draw off steam is installed over the cooker, as is suggested in the standard kitchen unit in Chapter XVI. A flue of 30 square inches built into the wall should be sufficient. A happy balance is desirable between insulation and ventilation. Generally in England ventilation has been good, but often improperly controlled, while we have cherished superstitions about cold bedrooms being healthy. It is time that we gave more attention to adequate insulation. It will be forced on us if we do not.

(a) Hurseal 2KW convector heater.

PLATE XXXVIII (a) and (b). Electric convector heaters.

(b) Morphy Richards combined radiant and convection
heating.

(a) Laying fibre-glass bitumen bonded matting over the ceiling joists of a house.

(b) Insulation of hot-water cylinder with mineral wool.

(c) Insulation, by fibre-glass, of water tank in loft.

PLATE XXXIX (a), (b) and (c). Insulation.

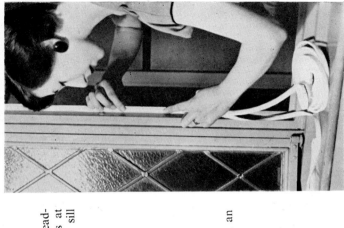

(a) Chamberlain 'Weatherstrips' method. (1) tongue of head-strip mates with groove in sash; (2) interlocking strips at meeting rails; (3) vertical tongue similar to (1); (4) sill strip and groove in bottom rail.

PLATE XL (a), (b) and (c). *Weatherstripping.*

(b) 'Stick-a-seal' self adhesive plastic foam weatherstrip, an economical method.

(c) 'Auto-seal' automatic draught excluder; the flexible blade is adjustable to various degrees of gap.

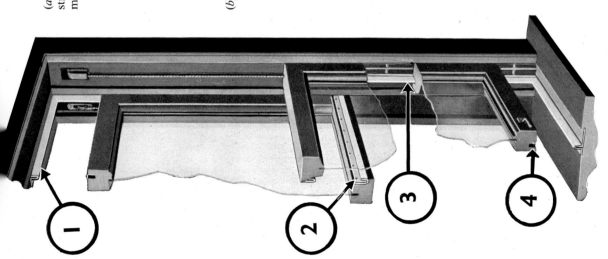

(*a*) New Carlton boiler fitted with an automatic regulator for hot water supply and central heating.

(*b*) ' Agamatic ' 30/80 boiler.

PLATE XLI (*a*), (*b*) *and* (*c*). *Solid fuel water heaters.* Both (*b*) and (*c*) in addition to providing domestic hot water, are adequate for space heating by means of radiators.

(*c*) Rayburn automatic boiler.

(a) Ewart multi-point instantaneous water heater.

(b) 'Newlyn' S. 12/2 sink storage water heater.

(c) 'Speedlyn' S. 30 water heater with push-button Regulo.

(d) Ascot balanced-flue multi-point water heater which takes the form of a wall panel with only a 5 in. projection.

PLATE XLII (a), (b), (c) and (d). Gas water heaters.

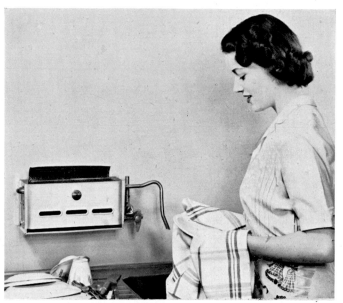

(a) 'Minimain' 60.

(b) Parkinson.

(c) 'Thermain.'

(d) Flavel.

PLATE XLIII (a), (b), (c) and (d). Instantaneous gas water heaters for kitchen sink or wash basin.

(*a*) Creda 'Contour' 2½ gallons.

(*b*) Sadia sink heater 1½ gallons.

(*c*) Creda multipoint heater 5 and 12 gallons capacity.

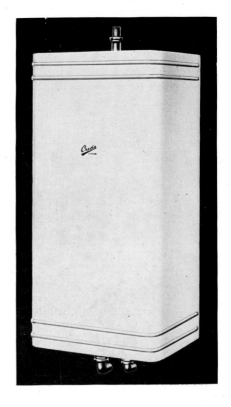

PLATE XLIV (*a*), (*b*) *and* (*c*). *Electric water heaters.*

(a) Cut-away model of Charlton electric twin heater showing internal arrangement.

PLATE XLV (a), and (b). Large gas and electric water heaters and circulators.

(b) The Diplomat domestic gas boiler, manufactured in five different coloured finishes.

CHAPTER XII

FOOD

I T is doubtful if there are many types of small house where facilities for storage, preparation and agreeable consumption of food have given widespread satisfaction. Some housewives are critical and exacting, while others are easy-going and easily satisfied, but it will be found generally, I think, that the former are the more intelligent and cultured and have other things to do in life, or want to do other things, as well as prepare meals, wash up, do housework, mending and shopping, and want, therefore, to reduce these labours to a minimum. They are quick to realize where labour might have been saved with closer adaptation of design to requirements. One of the main purposes, then, is to reduce work to the minimum consistent with efficiency and amenity.

It is questionable if the efforts to improve facilities and make adjustments to changing habits and material progress always succeed, and whether they are not sometimes too drastic, so that a certain retraction is desirable. In this matter of food storage, preparation and consumption, the soundest course is to think hard about family needs and habits, food supply and the machinery of storage and preparation, and having thought about the matter in all its aspects to design logically from the conclusions formed.

Storage, preparation and consumption of food should be considered separately.

STORAGE

The storage of food falls naturally under the heads of perishable goods and dry goods. The former are stored in a larder and refrigerator, the latter partly in the larder, in a kitchen cabinet and in store cupboards.

Considerable change has occurred in the larder since 1860. In the small country house built between 1860 and 1910, of about 3 or 4 reception rooms and 4 or 5 bedrooms, such as was designed by architects in the mediaeval tradition, like Philip Webb, Voysey, and their followers, a larder often opened from a corridor or from the kitchen, and a fair-sized pantry connected the kitchen with the dining room. In the smaller types the larder was sometimes combined with the pantry. In the ordinary 5 or 6 roomed standard houses of the period, that is in most houses for the lower income groups, the larders were of considerable size, and were either in the kitchen or in the scullery. They were often called pantries. A common size was about 4 feet 6 inches by 4 feet, with shelves about 1 foot 3 inches deep on three sides, so that one could stand in the larder. Often, being in the scullery, it was inconveniently placed in relation to the kitchen table where meals were prepared. This separation of scullery and kitchen, with the sink in the former and table in the latter, meant tiring movement from one to the other. The inconveniences of the arrangement prompted the combination of kitchen and scullery, which was introduced in the majority of houses built in the twenty years between the wars. It was variously called kitchen, kitchenette and

scullery. The disadvantages of this imagined improvement have prompted a movement back again, but now we speak of kitchen and utility room, but utility room means
something similar to the scullery. The combination of kitchen and scullery did not
mean a larger room, but everything was more compact, and more conveniently
related.

With this change the larder became very small. From the comparatively spacious
18 square feet it often became a cupboard of about 2 square feet, that is with shelves
often as small as 1 foot 6 inches wide by 1 foot 3 inches deep. This drastic reduction in
size is not due only to the attempt to pack everything in a very limited space for the
purpose of convenience; it had a stronger justification. With the increase in the number
of provision shops, the improvements in supply and distribution of food, and more
widespread and frequent deliveries of goods to houses, there was no longer the necessity to store goods on the same scale as previously; therefore a smaller larder would
suffice. That is true, but designs went to the extreme of providing only a small cupboard. Some have even argued that frequent deliveries of goods would render the
larder superfluous, and that a small cupboard is adequate. Anthony Bertram, in his
book *The House: A Machine for Living In* (1935), would appear to take this view.
'The younger housewife of today', he says, 'has other interests [than preparing meals]:
she sees no reason why, when there is a whole industry producing the things she needs
and delivering them to her door, she should make herself the slave of her or her husband's stomach. Of course, if cooking happens to be her hobby, well and good, This is a
case of a special need; but to supply the mechanism for such activities is no more part of
the house-designer's routine than to supply a carpenter's shop or photographic dark
room. Even a larder should not be necessary in towns where deliveries are frequent.
The refrigerator is quite sufficient. Unfortunately, refrigerators are still luxuries in
England, and in most houses a small larder is substituted. It need only be a cupboard,
preferably to the north, and it can be built projecting from the kitchen wall with slats
on both sides to allow a free passage of air.' Yet there is a widespread complaint among
housewives living in houses built between 1924 and 1939 that the larders are too small.
They do not require them as large as they were once, but as they are built now they
are too small to store the few goods they generally want in the house. It is important
to have a variety of things available in the house, even though there are frequent deliveries of goods. A happy medium is likely to give most widespread satisfaction and be
most serviceable, something between 18 square feet and 2 square feet. A larder 4 feet
3 inches wide by 2 feet 6 inches deep, that is about 10 square feet, with shelves 1-foot
3 inches deep on three sides, thus allowing a space to stand, is likely to prove generally
acceptable. I do not anticipate that there would be many complaints that it is too large.
It should have an adequate ventilator with gauze, opening to the north or north-east.
In so many houses of one type built on either side of roads, larders are placed according to such lay-out, and face in all directions—north, south, east or west. This involves
the whole question of site planning which is dealt with in Chapters VII, XVII and XXI.

The larder is for perishable goods like cheese, meat, fish, vegetables, and for a
certain number of dry goods like dried fruit. It should have shelves with cool surfaces.
Marble or slate is heavy and difficult to combine in standard units. It is better to have
stiffened steel shelves, preferably perforated to allow good air circulation. If there is
no refrigerator, milk and butter would also be kept there. A good alternative to one
larder is to have two smaller larders, one in the kitchen and one forming part of a porch

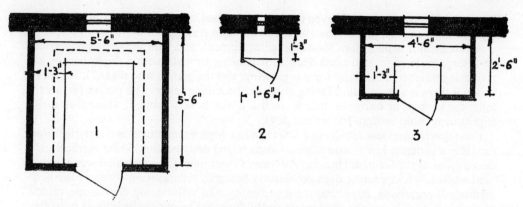

1. Old type of large larder in the small house of sixty years ago. 2. The size to which the larder has dwindled in many houses of 1925-40. 3. Size which is likely to prove generally acceptable.

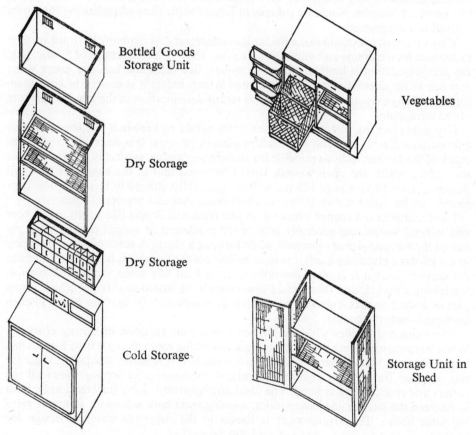

Bottled Goods
Storage Unit

Dry Storage

Dry Storage

Cold Storage

Vegetables

Storage Unit in
Shed

FIG. 15. *Food storage units.*

for the back entrance. It could even form part of a shed, and would be mainly for potatoes, turnips, carrots, green vegetables, and cooking fruit.

A refrigerator is important food-storage equipment, and with the mass production on a large scale of standardized designs, it is being brought within the means of an increasing number. The desire for it is growing, and the people who regard it is superfluous if there is a good larder facing north are becoming fewer. The period for which milk can be kept in warm weather in such a larder is very limited, whereas in a refrigerator it could be kept for several days.

Food deteriorates less rapidly in a low than in a high temperature, and a refrigerator provides a constant low temperature so as to retard deterioration. From medical evidence given to the Scottish Housing Advisory Committee, the conclusion was formed 'that while low temperature does not destroy bacteria, refrigeration is one of the best methods of preserving, improving the digestibility, and maintaining the vitamin values of various foods'. It must be used intelligently. It should be opened as little as possible, be kept clean, and be defrosted frequently. For family use, and I am thinking of families from three to six, it should not be too small. Five cubic feet is much better than three. If the ice-making apparatus were dispensed with, then it could be smaller, but few people, I imagine, would be content to forgo the pleasure of producing their own ice and ices in summer.

That a refrigerator would make the larder unnecessary, as Anthony Bertram appears to suggest, is an extreme and unpracticable view. Even in a refrigerator of 5 cubic feet, the accommodation is limited. But some things, like meat and fish, are better when exposed to the circulating air in a ventilated larder, unless it is desired to keep them for several days, when it would be wise to retard deterioration in the low temperature of the refrigerator.

Dry goods like tea, coffee, flour, dried fruits would be kept in a kitchen cabinet or cupboard preferably in transparent jars of glass or perspex. It is desirable to utilize as much of the kitchen walls as possible for storage cupboards, especially the spaces near the ceiling, which are often wasted. It will be noted that in the suggested standard design of a kitchen on page 122 the wall space is fully utilized in this way. The cupboards can be used for such things as home-made jam and preserved fruits.

Food that does not require preparation like fruit, and drinks like spirits, wine, beer and mineral waters, are generally kept in the sideboard or special cabinet when required for use, and stored elsewhere when forming a stock. A stock of wines maturing in a cool, dark place like a cellar is of little interest to the modest household and need not concern us, but it is often desirable to keep fruit like some varieties of English apples for a period, and these could conveniently be stored in a larder which forms part of a shed or back-entrance porch already mentioned, or in some of the kitchen cupboards near the ceiling.

The sideboard divides with the kitchen cabinet the function of storing crockery. When it is a massive piece of furniture in a large dining room its top is used for serving, but in the small house where the sideboard is smaller, it is hardly adequate in size for this purpose. But there is obviously a certain convenience in serving where all the cutlery and crockery are at hand. The ideal arrangement is for a sideboard to be built in between the kitchen and eating room, opening from both sides with an ample serving table above. The arrangement is shown in the suggested standard design for kitchen.

PREPARATION

The preparation of food in the kitchen is obviously most conveniently done at a table between the cooker and sink, with the larder and refrigerator quite close, say just beyond the sink. To get that convenient relationship is one of the main reasons for the extensive changes in kitchen design from the old kitchen-living-room with sink in the scullery. The equipment for preparing meals and the design of the kitchen should be approached in the same way as the design and equipment of a scientific laboratory. It is best to have a wall table for work, below an adequately sized window, which should have gauze over it, so as to keep flies out when the window is open in summer. Cupboards for storing tools and utensils should be above and below the table. Its surface should be fine textured and cool, preferably white vitreous enamel, or one of the plastic surfaces like formica, warerite or hornitex.

Great strides have been made with cooking apparatus since about 1923, and new developments are continually being made. During the thirties, before the increased efficiency of solid fuel heating had been made, the solid fuel cooker seemed rapidly becoming a thing of the past. But since the Second World War there has been a revival. To the objection: what happens in summer? it can be replied that the cooker is heavily insulated. But whatever recommendations can be advanced for solid fuel cooking, I think the advantages and convenience of gas and electric cooking are widely realized, and there is not, I think, likely to be much rejection of them in favour of solid fuel cooking.

Of the relative merits of cooking by gas and electricity I cannot express an opinion as I have very little experience of cooking on either. The champions of both are numerous. One of the familiar arguments in favour of gas cooking is that the heat can be regulated better, while it is argued that electric cooking is a little cleaner. Be that as it may. I do not think it can be denied that the latest types of both are extremely efficient, and I do not think in this particular sphere we need fear comparison with any country in the world.

CONSUMPTION OF FOOD

That the eating space should be as near as possible to the kitchen consistent with comfort and pleasant appearance is obvious, yet this obvious requirement has rarely been completely satisfied in the small standard house. In some of the larger houses in the Renaissance tradition, and thus planned on classical symmetrical lines, the kitchen and dining room were often well apart. It was common in Victorian houses for the kitchen to be in the basement, and, as there was not always a service lift, the food in such cases was brought up the stairs to the dining room by servants. If there had not been servants to do this it is doubtful whether it would have been tolerated for so long. With the houses of Webb, Voysey and their followers, already mentioned, the various parts of the house, including the kitchen and dining room, were brought into more convenient relationship. A study of some of these plans would be profitable to designers of small houses. One particularly good example is Hirst, Four Oaks, by W. R. Lethaby, where there is convenient access from the kitchen, through the small pantry to the dining room.

The small standard houses built between 1875 and 1915, although of varied design, had considerable similarity in the planning of the rooms. There were the two main

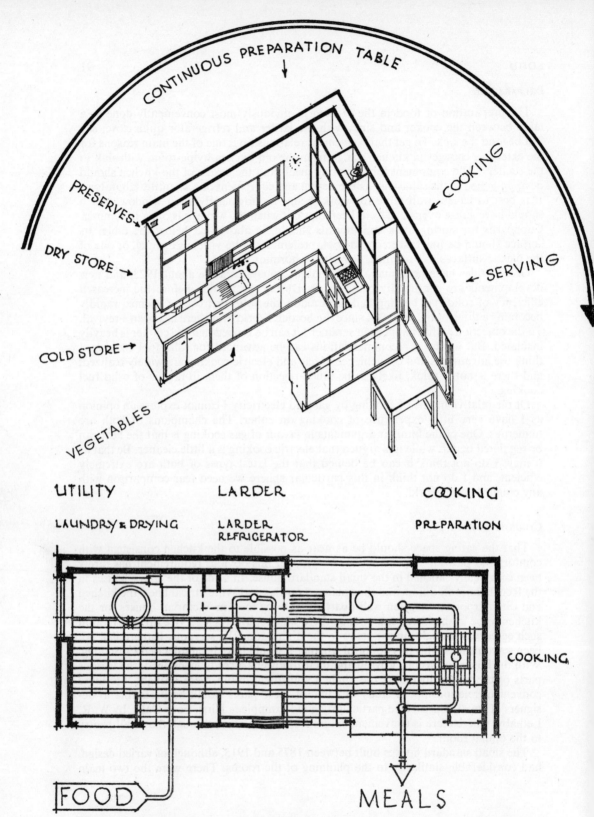

CONTINUOUS PREPARATION TABLE

COOKING

PRESERVES

SERVING

DRY STORE

COLD STORE

VEGETABLES

UTILITY   LARDER   COOKING

LAUNDRY & DRYING   LARDER   PREPARATION
                   REFRIGERATOR

COOKING

FOOD   MEALS

FIG. 16. *Axonometric drawing and plan of kitchen*. The design of the kitchen is based on the sequence of operations in preparing a meal. (*See* p. 122.)

types, the parlour and non-parlour. In the parlour type the kitchen was generally the same size as the parlour and dining room or living room, and there was generally a small scullery opening from the kitchen. In the non-parlour type, the living room was generally larger than the kitchen. The kitchen was usually large enough for meals, and most families had breakfast and the hurried midday meal there. Other meals, in the evenings and weekends, were often taken in the dining or living room. With the development combining the kitchen with the scullery, while not making it any larger, but rather a little smaller, there was no longer space for meals there. The purpose of the development was to make the kitchen a more efficient labour-saving workroom with the machinery compactly and conveniently related; but at the same time there was a feeling in the minds of many social progressives that it was not good for people to have meals in the kitchen where the food is cooked; they should have meals in more congenial surroundings. 'To eat and live in the atmosphere of cooking, and probably washing-up and laundry, is disgusting',[1] says Anthony Bertram. That is a typical atti-tude of many, but not a very realistic one. With the small kitchen and scullery combined in so many small houses, there is no room for meals in the kitchen, nor is an eating space provided adjoining the kitchen, but food has to be taken through a passage into the living and dining room. Some have a small hatch from kitchen to dining room. This is better, but in most cases the hatch is far too small to be of great service. Most people, I am convinced, would like to have some of their meals in or near the kitchen, but the eating space must not interfere with the kitchen as an efficient workroom. In response to a question which I put to men and women in the Forces asking whether they would like such provision, 259 said that they would, while only 35 wanted all meals well away from the kitchen.

There are consequently two possible satisfactory arrangements, each capable of variations, for the eating space in the small house. One is to have a dining room or recess adjoining the kitchen and separated by a moveable partition, so that it can be either part of the kitchen or shut off, as it is often desired to be free of cooking smells; or better still the separation could be by the method, mentioned when dealing with food storage, of a shutter above a sideboard, included in the suggested standard kitchen (p. 122). In this plan the dining room could be separated from the living room by a mov-able partition. The other is to have two eating rooms, the small recess off the kitchen in the manner suggested, with a separate dining room, between the kitchen recess and living room; or the dining room could be recess of the the living room, with a movable partition to shut it off when desired. The second type would be for the slightly larger house, but all these differences are variations on a theme. The relation of the kitchen, eating space and living room should be to provide the family with an arrangement based on the sequence of the operations of storing, preparing and consuming food so that there will be a sense of natural movement or flow, thus conducing to more easy and congenial living, and to reducing the work of the housewife and all those who help her, to a minimum.

In this chapter I have tried to consider the triple questions of the storage, prepara-tion and consumption of food from the standpoint of family needs, these needs being based on family habits derived from a study of a cross-section of the population. It is only in this way, after all, that design can be truly functional.

[1] *The House: A Machine for Living In* (London, 1935), p. 52.

CHAPTER XIII

CLEANLINESS AND REFUSE DISPOSAL

C LEANLINESS being one of the vital contributions to health, a house should be planned and furnished so that it can easily be kept clean. It should also provide hygienic methods for the disposal of refuse, and adequate facilities for personal cleanliness. I propose to divide this subject of cleanliness under the heads of (A) assistance to cleanliness that can be afforded by planning and furnishing; (B) refuse disposal; (C) facilities for washing clothes; and (D) facilities for personal cleanliness.

(A) Cleanliness, depending partially on the ease with which the house can be kept clean, should influence interior design and furnishing. Dust traps in the form of ornaments and mouldings, so common in Victorian interiors, should be reduced to a minimum. Ledges, such as are provided by picture rails and skirtings collect dust and attract germs; but it would generally be contended that the convenience of the picture rail for hanging pictures outweighs its disadvantages as a dust collector, while many people like it as a decorative motif, as forming a frieze-like termination to the wall. The only thing is to apply the vacuum cleaner along the picture rail when cleaning the room.

The ledge of the skirting is not a serious dust collector, and it can be very much modified if the top of the skirting is rounded or bevelled. The corner between the floor and skirting is disliked as harbouring dust, and rounded internal corners should be employed wherever possible, as they make an interior easier to keep clean. They are more likely to be satisfactory if synthetic materials are used where the floor and skirting is in one continuous piece, than if a concave or convex timber strip is put at the corner, as this might warp and produce cracks.

The ordinary soft-wood floorboarding collects dust, and often harbours vermin. The joints between the boards are likely to widen when shrinkage occurs after a few years. This is especially so if straight joints or even dowelled joints are employed, for it is found that with the latter the joints remain flush only at the dowels. The cracks thus formed admit dirt, vermin and draughts. Hard-wood boards like teak, oak, maple, jarrah, karri, and gurgur are much better; and better still are parquet or wood-block floors, but these are hardly an economical proposition for the small house. It is probable that synthetic materials like those with a calcined magnesite basis, and varieties of rubber and cork flooring will be increasingly used. A good finish is 'granwood' which is often laid on concrete as in many houses built during the war. Cork carpet and linoleum are similarly fixed to concrete with suitable waterproof adhesive.[1] Rubber and cork flooring and some varieties of plastic tiles are suitable for the hall, kitchen and bathroom.

A close-grained polished surface is easier to keep clean than a matt surface but it is not so safe. Linoleum is easier to keep clean than cork although the latter is a good finish and a pleasant surface. If rugs are placed on polished linoleum, as is often done,

---

[1] An example is provided by some Coventry Municipal houses built during the war. In these the ground floor consists of 'granwood' on concrete built on hollow bricks, while the first floor consists of cork carpet on pre-cast concrete.

PLATE XLVI (*a*), (*b*), (*c*) and (*d*).
Gas and electric wash boilers.

(*a*) Dean gas wash boiler No. 101/1.

(*b*) Morley 55 wash boiler.

(*c*) Howarth 'Coronet' gas wash boiler.

(*d*) Burco electric wash boiler.

(b) Bendix electric washing machine.

(a) Dean A1 gas-electric washing machine. Gas is used to heat the water and clothes are electrically agitated. The wringer handle can be fitted to either side of the machine.

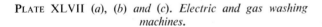

PLATE XLVII (a), (b) and (c). Electric and gas washing machines.

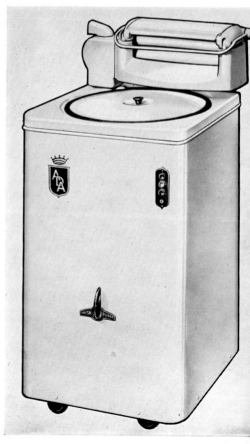

(c) ADA 'Coronation' Mark VI model electric washing machine with push button control power-driven wringer and self-emptying pump.

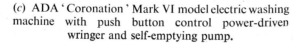

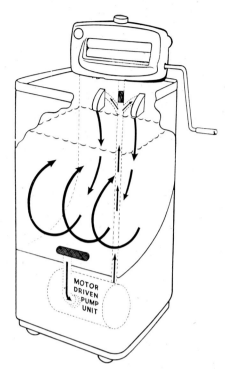

DIAGRAMMATIC DRAWING SHOWING WATER CIRCULATION

(*a*) Parkinson ' Live Water ' washing machine. Gas heated, electrically agitated washing machine, with a new method of agitation. Instead of a mechanical agitator situated inside the tube, the movement of the clothes being washed is caused entirely by jets of water. The machine is easily filled and automatically emptied by a rubber hose. The wringer has 10 in. adjustable rollers and when not in use folds away inside the pan.

(*b*) Diagram of the ' Live Water ' machine.

PLATE XLVIII (*a*), (*b*) *and* (*c*). *Washing machines.*

(*c*) Hotpoint with wringer. Electrically heated and agitated with power wringer.

(*a*) Drying cloths within a trellis box in garden of a house at Lillehammer, Norway. Several lines are suspended from one end to the other. It is less unsightly than the clothes lines of most English gardens. Devices similar to that shown are sometimes seen in England. One device consists of rods radiating from a pole.

(*b*) Interior of drying cupboard with electric heater.

Another method of drying that greatly speeds the process is by means of a spin-dryer. In this machine clothes are spun round 1000 or more times a minute. Dryers can be wheeled to any convenient position. This method is convenient where there is limited space.

PLATE XLIX (*a*) *and* (*b*). *Drying clothes.*

(a) 'Ritemp' rotary ironer.

(b) Hotpoint press iron.

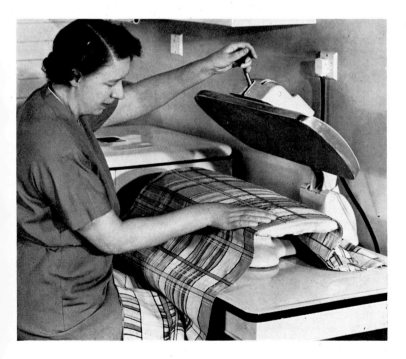

PLATE L (a) and (b). Electric Ironing.

(a) AGA cooker and water heater, model CB.

(b) Sofono open fire cooker and water heater.

PLATE LI (a), (b), (c) and (d). Solid fuel cookers.

(c) No. 3 Rayburn insulated cooker and water heater.

(d) Yorkseal heat retention open fire cooker and water heater, continuous-burning.

(a) New World with four boiling burners, griddle, grill, large oven, warming chamber and storage drawer.

(b) Cannon A125 with foldaway eye level grill, four burners and storage or warming drawer below oven. The high level grill can be fitted as a separate wall unit over a cabinet.

PLATE LII (a) and (b). Gas cookers.

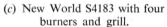

(a) New World four burners and grill, capacious oven and regulo control.

(b) Crusader with four burners and grill.

(c) New World S4183 with four burners and grill.

(d) Warwick. The extra width of 9 in. gives a large oven, five boiling burners and grill.

PLATE LIII (a), (b), (c) and (d). Gas cookers.

then the floor is dangerous, as the rug is apt to slip when a person treads on it. Numerous serious accidents have been caused in this way, and it should be accepted as a general rule that rugs, especially if they are small, should not be on linoleum unless it has a matt surface. The matt surface of cork carpet is good for this purpose.[1]

Generally, in planning the interior of a house and in furnishing there is a sensible tendency to move away from the dark ornamental effects of Victorian days, towards light plain surfaces for walls and furniture. The use of plain surfaces in furniture is made possible to a greater extent by laminated wood, which is now generally used instead of the panel and frame construction in which mouldings are conspicuous.

Cleanliness in the kitchen, where food is prepared, is of primary importance; yet the presence of a boiler fire burning coal, anthracite or coke and often refuse, hardly conduces to cleanliness. Most kitchens of small houses built in the last twenty years have the kitchen and scullery combined, and a boiler fire is often in the kitchen. Whatever is burned, it is impossible to avoid ash and dust, and to prevent this spreading. To heat water by electricity or gas is cleaner, it saves work and is much less trouble, but there is at present the economic objection to this in the winter, which was considered in Chapter X.

Most housewives like their floors to remain clean with as little labour as possible. They naturally do not like the family making the floors dirty by walking into rooms with muddy shoes during wet or muddy weather. In a well-disciplined family shoes should be changed in the hall after being scraped outside, and wiped on the mat inside. When father has been working in the garden, or the children playing there in the winter, or when the ground is none too dry, it is desirable to have some place under cover where garden shoes can be changed before entering the house. It is a serious disadvantage in this respect to have direct access from the garden to the kitchen, as is the case with a very large number of small houses built in the last twenty years, where the kitchen and scullery are combined often in a very small space. Those working or playing in the garden come in with muddy shoes, and although they may change them in the kitchen, there are generally no proper facilities for doing so, and it makes the kitchen floor very dirty. It is much better to have the utility room between the kitchen and the garden, as in the suggested small house, W type (p. 114). It will be noted that in this plan there is also an entrance unit between the utility room and garden.

(B) Most methods of refuse disposal are still primitive and dirty, and it is to be hoped that we shall introduce more hygienic and efficient methods in future housing estates. We put our garbage in an iron bin, which is emptied once or twice a week into a cart moving slowly through a residential area, which in windy weather loses some of its load. The lid to the iron bin may fit tight when it is new, but later is easily removed by prying cats and dogs of the neighbourhood. In the summer numerous insects are attracted to the putrefying garbage. This is more likely to occur with the cheap bins that are too often used. It is much better to use the standard bins, but even these wear out in time and are not always replaced when they should be.

To dispose of all refuse in an aperture in the kitchen or scullery sink, whence it is conveyed to a destructor without being exposed above ground is obviously a more hygienic and efficient method. One method is known as the Evier-Vidoir or Garchey system and has been used in flats in France since the early thirties. It was installed in the Quarry Hill flats in Leeds, which were built between 1936 and 1939, for an

[1] See Chapter XVI on safety.

extension of these flats since the war, in the new flats in Rosebery Avenue, Finsbury, in blocks of flats at Duddeston and Nechells and Aston at Birmingham, and at Queens Court flats at Newcastle-upon-Tyne. It is surely not beyond practical possibility that a similar, perhaps improved method on the same lines could be used for estates of small houses.

The Garchey system was proposed in the 'village green' system of planning developed by Sir Charles Reilly (see *The Reilly Plan* by Lawrence Wolfe, London 1945, p. 15), but I am not aware that it has ever been used for small two-story houses.

Allowing an aperture in the sink of about 7 inches diameter, and a pipe through which the refuse passes about 6 inches in diameter, this would mean that anything larger would have to be broken. The pipe connects with the bath and the W.C. and with the main drainage, and what forms the refuse bin beneath the aperture is constantly flushed with soapy water. Miss Elizabeth Denby mentions in her book *Europe Rehoused*[1] that she visited many flats at Bagneux in which this system is installed, and she says there was no smell from the sinks, nor had the tenants any criticisms although the system had been in use for six years. I visited the flats in Rosebery Avenue some years after the system was installed and my experience was the same as Miss Denby's at Bagneux.

The pipes from the flats connect below ground, and the refuse is drawn by powerful suction to the disposal station where dehydration is effected and the solid refuse is burned. The method is illustrated in the diagram. The heat from the furnace is generally utilized for various purposes. The suggestion has been made that it might supply houses with hot water or steam heating, but it is doubtful whether it would be adequate for the purpose.

The Garchey system is not regarded as the ideal method of refuse disposal by all experts in this country; it is regarded rather as a very important step in the right direction. It is argued that it would be more efficient if crushing machinery were installed in each block of flats, and that it would be more economical if it were connected with the main sewer. For an estate of houses, a crusher could be used for groups of a certain number. It is to be hoped that experiments will be made along these or similar lines as they are in the U.S.A.

(C) Facilities for washing clothes in the modern kitchen are generally inadequate. It has been argued by some that the housewife will send more and more clothe to a laundry or make use of other external facilities like the laundrette, but the increasing use of the washing machine on the other hand means that a great deal will still be done at home, especially clothes that require very careful handling. Also there is always the question of economy. A selection of washing machines is illustrated. The discussion among men and women in the Forces whether there should be a separate scullery or utility room principally for laundry operations showed an almost equal division of opinion. But most women, I find, when thinking of the kitchen and scullery, as separate visualize the older type, where the sink is provided only in the scullery, and where the kitchen is very much a kitchen-living room; but when shown a design where the separation is effected so as to increase the convenience for the housewife, and where sinks are provided both in the scullery or utility room and kitchen, the overwhelming preference is for these to be separate. The fundamental point is that as some laundry operations take place in the small house adequate space should be provided. This is

[1] London, 1938, p. 240.

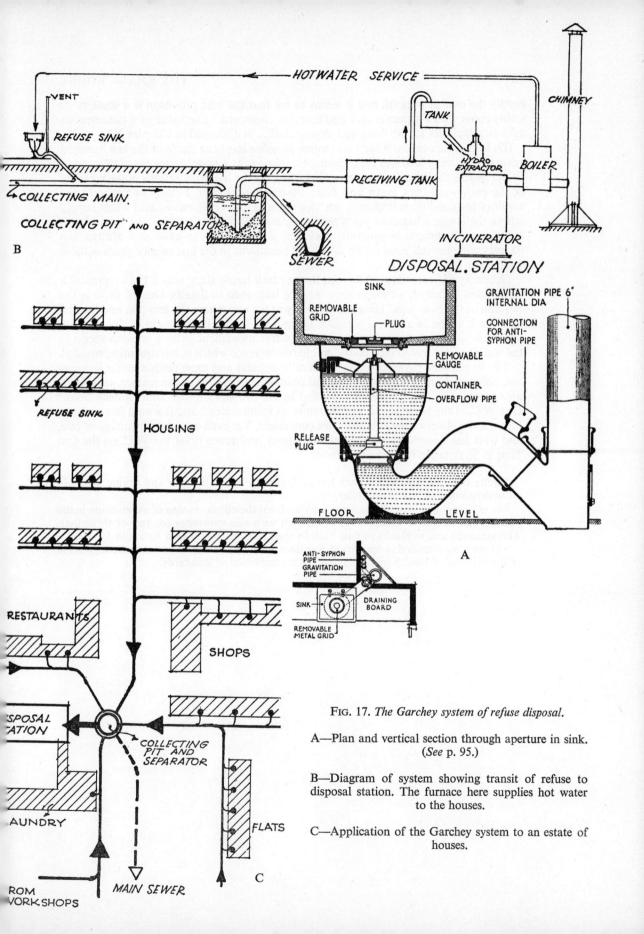

HOTWATER SERVICE

CHIMNEY

VENT

REFUSE SINK

TANK

HYDRO EXTRACTOR

BOILER

COLLECTING MAIN

RECEIVING TANK

COLLECTING PIT AND SEPARATOR

SEWER

INCINERATOR

DISPOSAL. STATION

B

SINK

REMOVABLE GRID

PLUG

GRAVITATION PIPE 6" INTERNAL DIA

CONNECTION FOR ANTI-SYPHON PIPE

REMOVABLE GAUGE

CONTAINER

OVERFLOW PIPE

RELEASE PLUG

FLOOR LEVEL

A

REFUSE SINK

HOUSING

RESTAURANTS

SHOPS

SPOSAL TATION

COLLECTING PIT AND SEPARATOR

AUNDRY

FLATS

ROM VORKSHOPS

MAIN SEWER

C

ANTI-SYPHON PIPE
GRAVITATION PIPE
SINK
DRAINING BOARD
REMOVABLE METAL GRID

FIG. 17. *The Garchey system of refuse disposal.*

A—Plan and vertical section through aperture in sink. (*See* p. 95.)

B—Diagram of system showing transit of refuse to disposal station. The furnace here supplies hot water to the houses.

C—Application of the Garchey system to an estate of houses.

hardly the case at present, and it seems to me that the best provision is a scullery or utility room with a separate sink and a drying cupboard.[1] The value of a basement as affording facilities for washing and drying clothes is discussed in Chapter XX.

(D) It must be acknowledged that much progress has been made in the last hundred years in providing facilities for personal cleanliness. It is largely because in this and in overcrowding that housing was most backward, for the living conditions of the majority of the poor were then mean and filthy beyond description. Family habits were the result of the conditions imposed, not vice versa. To have plumbing and water supply within the house a hundred years ago was the exception rather than the rule. Now a fairly good bathroom is generally included. I would like to have said always, but country cottages and even urban flats have been built in the last twenty years without bathrooms.[2]

Generally the bathrooms provided in the small house since about 1935 represent a fairly good standard, although they may be improved in details. One of these is the position of the bath taps. They are generally at the end where the feet are, and beyond easy reach whilst in a sitting position. It would be better if they were at the side, but not projecting so that they get in the way of free movement. Also a copious recess in the wall for soap would be a considerable convenience which is infrequently provided.

The W.C. in the bathroom is not generally popular and most people prefer it separate, although I understand that medical opinion is in favour of the former. It is desirable that two W.C.'s should be provided in the two-story house, one on each floor.[3] One W.C. in the bathroom is not therefore so inconvenient, and it would have advantages in cleanliness where children are concerned. Yet even with the advantage of two, and with due thought for cleanliness, the usual preference is for the W.C. on the first floor to be separate from the bathroom.

[1] Quite small houses in Denmark have a laundry—boiler, wringer and drying lines—in an underground or basement cellar.

[2] In the simplified type of dwelling resulting from the official axeing of expenditure in the years 1921-5 tenement blocks were often built with one bathroom for two or three flats. This occurred also in blocks of flats built by the L.C.C. at Honor Oak Estate in 1933-37.

[3] These were provided in many post-war houses built by local authorities at the suggestion of the Minister of Health up to 1951 before the reduction of standards.

CHAPTER XIV

QUIET AND SECLUSION

MOST people's idea of home is a quiet and secluded place to which they can retire from the world. Not that they always want to be quiet in their home, but they like to have some control over noise and privacy. There are times when they want to create their own noise, and there are times when they want to be quiet; when they want to mingle with friends, and when they want to be alone. Never do they want the intrusion of outside noise. Generally they want to be secluded from neighbours. A large number of people, liking that seclusion, like, at the same time, to feel that neighbours are near if wanted at any time, and it apparently satisfies a gregarious instinct for people to obtain occasional glimpses of their neighbours.

The chief disturbance of quiet in the home is outside noise. The chief sources of noise are transport, industry, sport and loud wireless sets. If houses are on a main road the noise is much greater than on a local road, and is greatly aggravated if the houses are near a crossing, or on a hill where starting and acceleration of motor vehicles takes place. Railways may be a disturbing source of noise, though generally not so unpleasant as road traffic. If it is a branch line the disturbance is rare; it is more troublesome near a main line, but worst of all near a goods yard.

The noise of air traffic will almost certainly be an increasing source of disturbance, which is likely to be the more acute because of the association of the sound with air raids. So many noises depend for their degree of unpleasantness on associations.

The noise of machinery is the chief source of disturbance from industry, but loading and unloading of goods, especially of cans in a milk distribution centre in the early morning, are often causes of annoyance.

Sport offends less; probably the shouting of children in streets is the worst; but it is doubtful if any noise is more objectionable than other people's loud wireless sets. Some people can work quite well in a room when their own set is on, although, if it is work requiring concentration, they generally forget all about the wireless; but if the harsh tones (and the sound at a little distance of a loud wireless set is generally harsh) of somebody else's wireless penetrates rather loudly, then it seems to be a disturbing influence to most people. Speaking for myself, I prefer any noise, road or rail transport, industry, the shouting of children to the noise of a neighbour's wireless set, and I know from what many others have said that I am by no means alone in this revulsion. It is worst of all in summer when windows are open. To those who can catch the dialogue in say, 'Take it from here' it is very entertaining and amusing, but when the words are indistinguishable, but can still be heard very loudly, it is mere noise. Also, if one wants to be quiet in one's own garden on a summer's evening, the sounds that are in harmony are the wind in the trees and the twittering of birds, not the raucous noise of a wireless set. The B.B.C. constantly reminds people during warm summer weather not to have their sets too loud. During the war announcers used to do this occasionally, giving as the reason that night workers had to get sleep during the day, as if that were the only reason. People want to be quiet, and they want to read and think and work. There are sections of the population who do not seem to mind noise on all occasions—in fact the more noise and excitement they have the better they seem to like it—but these are mostly young, and are generally either empty-headed or neurotic products of our civilization. Some, on the other hand, are condemned to live near constant sources of noise and after a time they get used to them, but this is rarely from choice and many would willingly change to a quieter place if they could.

Noises that emerge from inside the house are wireless, the playing of musical instruments, chiefly the piano, and conversation. These are only 'noise' if you are in another room, or in the same room but do not want to listen, and should thus really be classified with wireless noise coming from another house. Sanitary fittings in kitchen and bathroom, the shutting of doors and other incidental noises of this character are other common sources of disturbance in the house. The wireless and the playing of musical instruments, which often means practice by indifferent performers, are perhaps the most irritating noises to persons in other rooms, although persons who habitually talk in loud voices can also be exceedingly irritating. The other sounds mentioned, being natural to the structure of the houses and not arresting attentions so much, do not seem to be so disturbing unless they occur at night.

The Acoustics' Committee (Sharples Committee) of the Building Research Board in its Report on Sound Insulation and Acoustics,[1] classifies the degrees of loudness of typical noises (paras. 20 and 78). The threshold of painful sound is stated as 130 phons. Twenty feet from an aero engine is given as 120 phons; in an arterial road, standing on the kerb, 100 phons; in a local road in a residential area 40 phons; in a quiet suburban garden 30 phons; loud, average and soft wireless 80—90, 65—80, 50—65 phons respectively; and quiet or normal conversation from 45 to 65 phons respectively.

The question is how to reduce these noises to a minimum in the small house. More can be done by good planning than by anything else. The principles that constitute good planning have scarcely been observed in the haphazard growth of our towns, and this question of planning for quiet has only been sufficiently considered in the few good examples of residential planning like the garden cities of Letchworth and Welwyn, in the Manchester satellite of Wythenshawe, in many of the new towns like Stevenage, Crawley, Harlow, Hemel Hempstead and a few other places. It is necessary to state some of the principles of planning for seclusion and quiet, and for this purpose the example of the neighbourhood unit as a part of a new town such as is described in Chapter XXI may be taken.

Perhaps it is well to begin with a few negatives. Houses should not be built on arterial or main roads, near railways or factories, near any large market or distributing centre, near any large professional sports ground or greyhound track. In planning a residential area according to good principles due account is taken of these questions of noise, and although there are numerous other considerations in planning, equally important, it will be found in studying the example of the neighbourhood unit given in Chapter XXI that the area succeeds in being a fairly quiet precinct. The neighbourhood is bounded by main roads, but no main roads go through the neighbourhood so that the roads actually in the area are all quiet local roads. All through traffic should be denied access to the area. It will be noted, too, that although the area is bounded by main roads, no houses face on to these roads, but the houses nearest face on the inner local road with the gardens backing to a green verge which separates them from the main road. There

[1] *Post-war Building—Study No. 14*, London, 1944.

are no sources of industrial noise like factories, while the shopping centre is concentrated in one part in the form of a square near the main road.

The second consideration in reducing noise is to resist or minimize its penetration into the house and rooms by insulation. This is much simpler with detached houses well separated from each other and well set back from the road at densities of six or eight to the acre than with semi-detached houses at about ten or twelve to the acre, or terrace houses at twelve or fourteen to the acre. It is necessary to concentrate, therefore, mainly on the semi-detached and terrace houses.

It is an unfortunate circumstance that as the sources of noise increase—the motor-car and aeroplane, modern industry and the wireless—the tendency is to have lighter methods of construction which offer less resistance to sound penetration than heavier structures. Much can be done in planning the house and designing the structure to minimise noise. In planning terrace houses it is better to have the noisy parts of adjoining houses together; that is, those parts that contain the sanitary fittings, and where the work is done, in short, the service units consisting of kitchen, utility room and bathroom, and the quieter parts together. This also applies to semi-detached houses. An excellent example of this is the plan of the Howard House designed by Frederick Gibberd. Each house has a service unit consisting of kitchen and utility room on the ground floor and bathroom and W.C. on first floor with the noisy sanitary fittings separate from the living and sleeping sections of the house (see plans). These houses can be either terrace or semi-detached. If semi-detached the service units should adjoin, with the living quarters separate. In the majority of semi-detached houses the reverse has been the case, with the noisy parts, like the kitchen and bathroom on the outside, and the living rooms and bedrooms on the inners side near the party wall. In this arrangement the neighbours' wireless and often the hum of conversation is heard through the inadequate sound-insulating 9-inch solid brick party wall. It would be much better if the kitchens and bathrooms came together and then the living rooms and bedrooms would not be disturbed by noises from next door, although at the same time a party wall giving better sound insulation should be adopted.

Noise can be minimized by construction which breaks the transmission of sound, and by the use of sound-absorbent materials. It should be stated that what is good thermal insulation is not necessarily good sound insulation. They have some relationship, but it is not consistent. A noise produces vibrations in a wall, and if it is of solid material the sound will be transmitted until it is spent. If the wall is brick $4\frac{1}{2}$ inches thick the volume of sound will be reduced by the time it is transmitted through that thickness. but if it is a sound, say, of loud wireless of 80 phons one foot from the wall, the sound will be clearly heard on the other side. If it is a 9-inch brick wall the sound would still be heard but much less, but if it is an 18-inch brick wall the sound would have spent itself before reaching the other side. If, however, there is a continuous break in the path of sound, like a cavity, the sound would not be transmitted over the gap. Thus, a party wall of two $4\frac{1}{2}$-inch brick leaves with a 2-inch continuous cavity gives much better sound insulation. Cavity walls have thus better sound insulation than solid walls, unless the latter are very thick, but this would be neither economical nor practicable. It is better if the cavity is continuous. This should be essential for the party wall, and it is satisfactory to note that in many houses of new construction this is being done. The Airey, Stent and Cranwell houses are examples. The cavity in the party wall is continuous merely being covered at the ends.

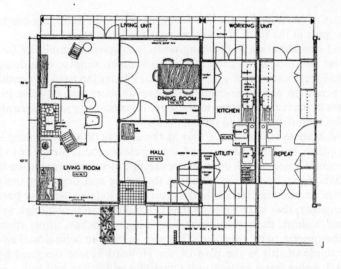

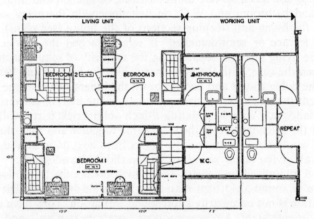

FIG. 18. *Ground and first-floor plans of the A type of Howard House*. Architect: Frederick Gibberd, F.R.I.B.A. In this plan the noisy part with sanitary fittings—the service unit consisting of kitchen and utility room on the ground floor and bathroom and W.C. on first floor—is kept separate from the living and sleeping sections. In semi-detached and terrace houses these service units adjoin.

In most new house constructions the cavity is not continuous for the other walls. In steel-frame and reinforced concrete frame construction the cavity is made only between the vertical members of the frame. This is a disadvantage as far as sound insulation is concerned. There are a few methods, however, where a continuous cavity is secured. One is the Boot method, where the cavity is continued through the concrete piers which are held together by steel clips. Another is the 'Easiform' which consists of

(a) Creda 'Star' cooker with storage drawer.

(b) Creda 'Comet' cooker. The extra width provides for separate grill at side and warming or storage drawer beneath.

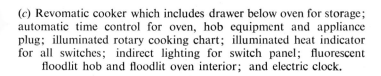

PLATE LIV (a), (b) and (c). Electric cookers.

(c) Revomatic cooker which includes drawer below oven for storage; automatic time control for oven, hob equipment and appliance plug; illuminated rotary cooking chart; illuminated heat indicator for all switches; indirect lighting for switch panel; fluorescent floodlit hob and floodlit oven interior; and electric clock.

(a) Tricity ' Queen '.

(b) Cameo with bracket for kettle.

(c) Jackson with inner glass door.

(d) Falco 'Royal' with thermostatically controlled oven.

PLATE LV (a), (b), (c) and (d). Electric cookers.

(a) The new Astral 1½ cu. ft. and (b) with dry-goods cupboard open below.

PLATE LVI (a), (b), (c) and (d). Refrigerators.

(c) Electrolux 1½ cu. ft. with dry storage drawer above and below.

(d) English Electric small table top refrigerator. This is made with door hinged on right or left.

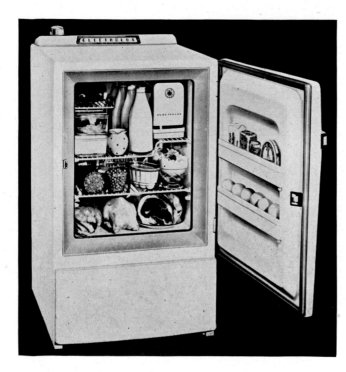

(a) Electrolux gas refrigerator, 2½ cu. ft.

PLATE LVII (a), (b) and (c). *Refrigerators.*

(b) Main 32 gas refrigerator, 3.2 cu. ft. capacity.

(c) Fridge-heater for installation in the larder. This cools and drys the air in the larder and also provides a supply of hot water for domestic use.

two concrete leaves poured *in situ*. But even in these sound would be transmitted through the windows and window frames. To make the sound insulation complete it would be necessary to have unconnected double windows. This would also provide superior thermal insulation. But this is less important than a good sound insulating party wall.

For insulation between rooms, structure and materials with sound absorbent properties should be used as far as possible. In Chapter V I emphasized the value of the study bedroom, especially for the younger members of the family when doing homework, studying for a career or engaged in some cultural pursuit. It is desirable that they should not hear the wireless or conversation from the living room. This sound is less likely to come through the floor and partitions than through doors. The experiment can be made in any house. If the wireless is loud in the living room and the living room and bedroom doors are both slightly open the sound appears loud in the bedroom. If one door is shut it is lessened, if both doors are shut it is lessened still more, but whether it is obliterated entirely depends on whether the doors fit well, and the nature of their construction. If they are of frame and panel construction, and the panels are of thin wood the sound insulation is less satisfactory than if the whole door is of laminated wood about $1\frac{1}{4}$ inches thick.

Generally soft materials like felt and fabrics are good sound absorbents, while hard materials like steel or concrete are good sound conductors. Thus sound insulation is improved if soft materials of a fibrous character are inserted at the joints between hard sound conducting materials to break the path of sound. Also a well-carpeted room with velour curtains, upholstered furniture and tapestried walls absorbs sound, while a room with hard wood furniture, linoleum floor, distempered walls and linen curtains represents the other extreme. The former is excellent for quiet conversation and the wireless, although it might be unsatisfactory as a music room, as the sound would be rather deadened.

The chief reason why the semi-detached house is preferred to the terrace house is that is gives greater seclusion. It provides access from the front of the house to the back without going through, and it provides a sideway for goods. To have one side of the house free gives a far greater feeling of privacy and seclusion than to be in the middle of a block with neighbours on either side. The house set back at least 12 feet from the footway with a small front garden also affords more retreat from prying eyes than having the house on the footway, and that is one reason why it is generally liked. The tendency to have shrubs, a privet hedge and trees in the front garden in addition to being decorative, also adds to seclusion. Most English people like to have their garden front and back fenced or walled round because privacy is dear to them. There has been a movement of late to have the front gardens undivided and one open space, as is done in many other countries, but it does not seem popular here, because it seems an infringement on privacy and seclusion. I think the Englishman is wise in his preference. We are not secluded and alone enough. Privacy and quiet are precious things, they are necessities to full cultural development, and the tendency in modern life is to deprive us more and more of these valued conditions. Most men and women value them at heart—that explains the common dislike of flats and flat life, where quiet and seclusion are far more difficult to obtain.

CHAPTER XV

LEISURE

THERE is every prospect that the gradual increase of leisure during the present century will continue. Before the war there was advocacy of a forty-hour and five day week in industry, and although this has not been realized in all industries during the period of reconstruction, there is a strong prospect that if we are fortunate in preserving peace, the forty-hour week will become fairly general. The tendency of offices will be to reduce the hours of work. Even now many firms have a five-day week, with office hours from 9.30 a.m. to 5.30 p.m., which is less than a forty-hour week.

This means considerably more leisure than the majority were able to enjoy before, say, the First World War. This brings its own problems, the chief of which is the best way of employing that leisure. It is realized that one of the principal functions of education in the future will be to equip people to use their leisure well.

The use of leisure can be broadly classified as relaxation and entertainment, games and sport, and pleasurable activity of a creative, constructive or inquisitive character. To most people one or more is desirable, but I think the last mentioned is the most important. Many people like visiting the cinema, theatre, concerts, watching cricket and football and other games, watching television and listening to the radio. This is entertainment and often valuable relaxation for people who work hard, but if one is fortunate in having much leisure, such as a thirty-five-hour working week would give, and has few household duties, then to spend all one's leisure in entertainment hardly conduces to a very full or satisfying life. A large number of younger people mix such entertainment with the more or less serious pursuit of sport and games. But again it is questionable if entertainment, sport and games represent the most satisfactory use of leisure. It may for a time, for the period of youth, but even then I am doubtful. I feel that one condition of a satisfactory use of leisure is that part of it should be devoted to some creative, constructive or inquisitive activity, unless one's work is of that kind, and then it will probably be found that one would hardly be content to work so little, and the work would extend into the period of leisure. But for the majority this is not the case. For many their work is dull and mechanical. Much office work is of this kind, while increased mechanization in industry, increased standardization and mass production means that there is more unskilled work and more people will have to stand by a machine repeating the same mechanical operation all day. The compensation that society must give to those condemned to such soulless occupations is more leisure, so as to provide them with the chance of doing some of the things they really want to do. And I believe once education has stimulated the innate desire, the majority will want to employ part of their leisure in making things and in various forms of creative activity or in some kind of engrossing study.

Many psychologists think that the desire to construct is an instinctive activity. William McDougall includes the instinct to construct in his famous classification of fourteen instincts.[1] This classification is widely accepted, with certain modifications, as

[1] *Introduction to Social Psychology.*

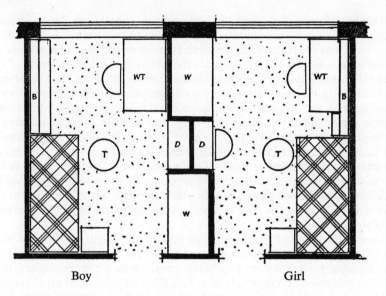

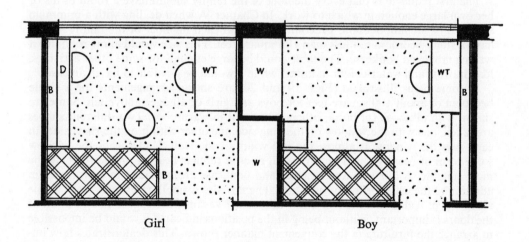

FIG. 19. Single bedrooms of 100 square feet for boys and girls with space for leisure pursuits.
These are designed with built-in furniture. (*See* p. 106.)

KEY B = Bookcase.
D = Dressing Table.
T = Table.
W = Wardrobe.
W.T. = Writing table.

a workable basis for psychological and philosophical speculation. Among philosophers who accept McDougall's recognition of an instinct to construct is Samuel Alexander, who considers it as the basis of the aesthetic impulse or feeling.[2] The impulse to study, especially some scientific subject, satisfies the widely recognized instincts of curiosity.

I make this apparent digression to try to demonstrate that the most satisfying use of leisure is found in the exercise of some constructive, creative, or inquisitive activity. Most young men and women who have received a fair degree of education usually want to do something of this kind. They may want to write, to paint, to carve stone or wood, to play a musical instrument, or even compose music, to make furniture and related things of a similar kind, or make dresses if they are girls, or they may wish to pursue some form of scientific study. One strong desire, which usually comes a bit later, is to make a nice garden and cultivate plants. To those who object that to play a musical instrument is interpretative rather than creative, I would reply that the term-re-creative is more accurate. The composer creates, the performer re-creates from a group of signs.

In planning the house of the future more and more thought will have to be given to the use of leisure, and facilities should be provided for these leisure pursuits. It is true that the facilities for some would be better provided in a community centre, club or technical or cultural institute which, in a well-planned residential area, should not be more than about a mile from home. But for the majority of leisure pursuits of a creative or studious character the house should provide the facilities.

The first requisite is that every member of the family should have a room of his or her own large enough in which to work. In Chapter V, when dealing with a minimum standard of accommodation, I recommended that each member of the family should have a study-bedroom not less than 100 square feet. This size would allow room for a writing table and bookcase. The table could be large enough for some other activities, like drawing and water-colour painting, while it would be possible to fix up an easel.

In some plans illustrated (Figs. 19 and 20) are shown arrangements for a single bedroom of about 100 square feet for boys and girls of all ages above ten. Some are shown with all loose furniture, others with built-in wardrobes. Two different shapes are taken, one with the window on the long side, the other with it on the short side. In each case the window is almost the full width of the wall. Underneath the window some form of heating could be arranged, electric tubular heating probably being the most suitable. A fair size writing table and bookcase are provided in each room, in addition to the usual bedroom furniture. There is also a small occasional table. While all this is provided there is still a fair amount of vacant floor space. The position of the doors is important. Without being in the positions indicated it would be impossible to arrange the furniture in the convenient manner shown. This demonstrates how important it is that the furniture should be planned with the planning of the house.

The second principal facility for leisure could be a room specially equipped for certain pursuits. If the reader will glance at plans S4, 5 and 6 illustrating Chapter XVII, he will note that in 6 a workroom has been added off the dining room and back entrance unit. The purpose of adding this is to provide facilities for leisure pursuits. It can be equipped for all kinds of activities, and four suggestions are made in the plans in Fig. 22. Plan A shows it equipped for carpentry and metal work. This includes two fairly large benches and copious tool chests. To equip a house with a workshop like

[1] *Beauty and Other Forms of Value* (London, 1933), p. 27.

this solely for carpentry would mean that a man's hobby is carpentry which may include making and repairing some of his own furniture, making model boats, aeroplanes and many other things of this kind. Such a workshop could also be used for chemistry. It would be too elaborate for just odd jobs that generally require doing from time to

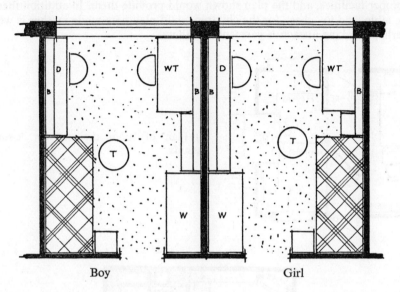

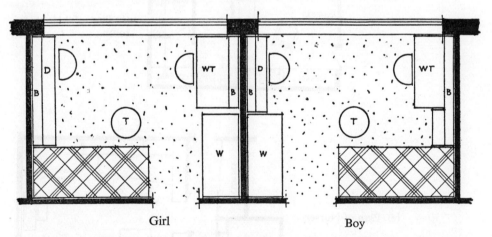

FIG. 20. Single bedrooms of 100 square feet for boys and girls with space for leisure pursuits. These are designed with free-standing furniture. (*See* p. 106.).

time in the house. Yet it is desirable that even for this a small bench should be provided. This would best be included in the utility room or covered entrance unit.

In B the room is equipped for the housewife. It cannot be said that it is wholly for leisure, because the equipment consists of work table and sewing machine. If a woman is not good at work like this and does not like it, she will naturally do as little as possible, although it may be economically incumbent that she should do some. But some women like making their own clothes and have a talent for it. But whether such work is done from economic necessity or from desire, or partly from both, it is agreeable to have proper facilities, and the plan shown would provide them. In addition there is a writing table, and toy chest, for the children could play here while mother is working and perhaps making attractive garments for them.

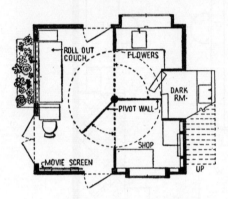

(a) Plan of room designed for leisure pursuits.

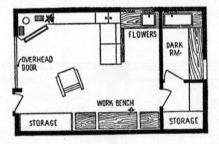

(b) Plan of 'Hobbies' room.

(c) Plan of Nursery.

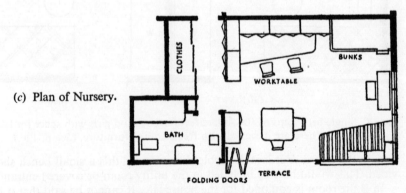

FIG. 21 (a), (b) and (c). Planning for leisure pursuits.

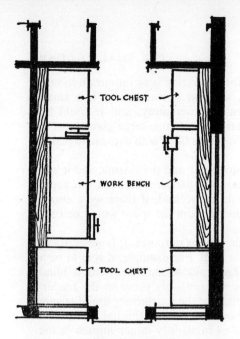

A—Room equipped for carpentry and
metal work.

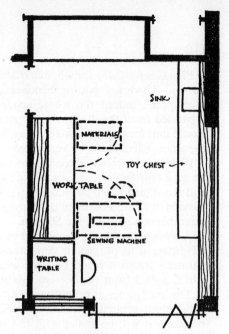

B—Equipped for the housewife.

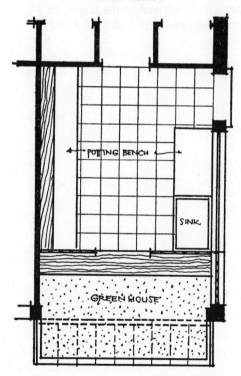

C—Gardening and plant cultivation.

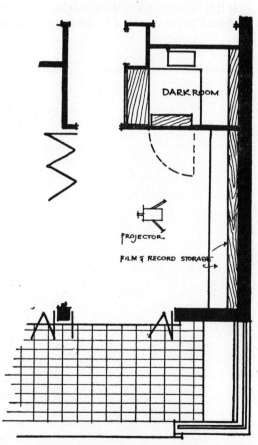

D—Photography and the cinema workrooms.
(*See* pp. 106 and 110.)

Fig. 22.—*Planning for leisure pursuits.*

Plan C is for those for whom gardening and plant cultivation is an important leisure pursuit. There are potting benches and a sink, while at one end there is a small greenhouse, indeed the whole space could form a conservatory, and it could be separated from the dining room merely by a glass wall and one large glass door. It would thus form an attractive annex. If the conservatory is filled with decorative plants the whole effect could be very pleasing.

Plan D is for those whose leisure pursuit is photography and the cinema, and it will be seen that facilities are provided. There is a movable partition between this room and the dining room so that the whole space could be utilized. If there were also a movable partition between the dining room and living room the space would be considerable in a house of the S6 plan.

A work room of this kind could be equipped for various purposes. It is generally of advantage if its purpose is determined before it is built. For example, if it is to be a painter's studio it could be built with a very large window and fitted with a blind which pulled from the bottom. Many other uses will probably occur to the reader.

The importance of providing facilities in the house for the satisfactory use of leisure cannot be overrated. With large families in small houses in the past this has rarely been possible. It will be easier with the smaller families in slightly larger houses in the future, but it is desirable that the facilities should form part of the original plan of each house. If it is not always economically possible to provide them at the outset, or if it is better to leave the provision of them for the actual occupant of the house, they should be planned as a future addition or extension as shown in the S plans 4, 5 and 6.

(*a*) Before planning. The sink is fitted low and there is a shortage of workspace and storage capacity, resulting in an untidy kitchen, which does not conduce to efficiency or economy of labour.

PLATE LVIII (*a*) *and* (*b*). *Kitchen transformed.*

(*b*) After planned installation. Sink is correct height. Provision is made for storage and adequate work surface. Wiring, pipework, etc., is buried to improve appearance. (Hotpoint planning service.)

(*a*) Ezee planned kitchen incorporating electric cooker, work counter, with storage cupboards over built-in Hoover washing machine and $3\frac{1}{2}$ cu. ft. Prestcold refrigerator.

PLATE LIX (*a*) *and* (*b*). *Planned kitchens.*

(*b*) Planned kitchen with refrigerator, generous wall cupboard storage, and water storage heater fixed to wall. The sink and counter top and wall cupboards are finished in formica.

(a) Kitchen in which full utilization is made of all available space for storage, both on wall above, and space below counter-cooker-sink level. Note washing machine on right of sink.

(b) Redwing planned kitchen. This arrangement has generous counter or worktable space, with wall cupboards and refrigerator. The kitchen is open on the left to dining space. The counter tops are finished in formica.

PLATE LX (a) and (b).
Planned kitchens.

PLATE LXI. *Kitchen planned by W. H. Paul.* A snack counter, for quick breakfasts, etc., can be seen on left.

CHAPTER XVI

SAFETY IN THE HOME

T HAT home should be the safest place on earth is probably the feeling of everybody, but at present it is far from being so. Yet with a little more thought and
care in design of both the house and the equipment and in the behaviour of the
occupants the home could be the safe place that everybody wishes it to be.

In Great Britain there is an average daily death roll from accidents of 45; 14 people
are killed on the roads, and 24 in and about the home, with some 20 of these actually in
the home.[1] Thus about 7,000 people die each year from accidents in the home, the actual
figures for five recent years being 6,050 in 1950, 6,522 in 1951, 6,249 in 1952, 7,029 in
1953 and 7,723 in 1954. There are no reliable figures for non-fatal accidents, but it is
estimated that each year there are between 1 and 2 million injuries sufficiently serious
to require hospital treatment. It is obvious that this is a very costly item in the national
economy because of the loss of industrial production and the cost to the community
of hospital treatment. It is therefore an obligation on the part of everybody to do his
utmost to reduce these accidents to a minimum. Perhaps the worst aspect is the suffer-
ing that these accidents cause. About two-thirds of the fatal accidents occur among
older people over the age of 65, but a large proportion occurs among young children,
indeed fatal accidents in the home is the third largest cause of death among children
between the ages of 1 and 5.

Some analysis of the causes of fatal accidents in the home has been made by the
Home Safety Department of the Royal Society for the Prevention of Accidents. The
year 1954 in England and Wales had a particularly bad record with 6,617 fatal
accidents, but 1953 might be taken as an average year with 5,895 fatal accidents in
private homes (of which 663 were in residential institutions). The main causes were as
follows:

	All persons	Males	Females	Age groups Under 5	5-14	15-44	45-64	65 & over
Falls	3,525	1,082	2,443	41	11	75	253	3,145
Poisoning	759	353	406	43	8	116	205	387
Burns and Scalds	598	200	398	104	44	36	83	331
Suffocation	543	301	242	431	7	37	32	36
Miscellaneous	470	221	249	112	37	82	77	162
Total, home accident deaths	5,895	2,157	3,738	731	107	346	650	4,061

The section with which the design of the house is involved is of course the first
which represents about 60 per cent of all fatal accidents. Heating equipment is

[1] The other items to make up the total of 45 are: 1 on the railways, 1 in air and water
transport, 2 in factories, 1 in coal mines and 2 in farms, quarries, etc.

involved in the section concerned with burns and scalds, while accidents with electric current is an item in the miscellaneous section.

The analysis of falls is as follows:

				Age groups				
Type of fall	Total deaths	Males	Females	Under 5	5-14	15-44	45-64	65 & over
Falls on stairs	738	282	456	7	2	29	107	593
Falls from ladders	44	40	4	—	—	4	13	27
Other falls from one level to another	360	165	195	30	8	31	42	249
Falls on same level	1,374	371	1,003	2	1	8	51	1,312
Unspecified falls	1,009	224	785	2	—	3	40	964
Total falls	3,525	1,082	2,443	41	11	75	253	3,145

Apart from unspecified falls the two largest categories are falls on stairs and falls on the same level. The commonest causes of the latter are polished floors, especially mats on polished floors, and grease on kitchen floors. It should be a rule in the home that no floor should be polished so as to involve the slightest risk of falling, I know many people like the effect of polished wood floors and place mats on them, but such floors are dangerous and should be avoided. A cork floor looks equally attractive, is softer and much safer. Some people have mats over polished linoleum, which is equally unsafe. A safe and attractive floor, in addition to cork, for living room or dining room is the fitted carpet and it looks as well as any other form. It is expensive of course. A little less expensive and almost as good is the carpet of a standard size which approximately fits the room with edges of polished wood or linoleum that are not walked upon. For the bedroom a carpet or cork carpet with a matt surface or one of the new plastic surface coverings which should not be polished. It is a good principle that all floor surfaces in the home if not carpeted should have a matt and not a polished or shining surface. If mats are used these should never be on a polished surface.

Grease on the kitchen floor, another common cause of serious falls, is a matter of care by the housewife. If grease does get on the floor it should be cleaned off at once, not left until the housewife thinks she has a moment to spare, otherwise she might wake up in hospital. But again, the possibility of an accident from grease on the floor is affected by the material. The principle of polished or shining surface and matt surface applies. Polished quarry tiles and shining linoleum, two common kitchen floors are obviously more dangerous than a cork surface on linoleum with a matt surface. A plastic safety flooring has been devised available in sheets or tiles consisting of poly-vinze-chloride, in which is incorporated aluminium oxide abrasive which is permanently non-slip wet or dry.

In *Bulletin No. 11 of National Building Studies on Floor Finishes for Houses,*[1] a list is given comparing the properties of floor finishes which includes non-slip characteristics. Cork carpet and cork tiles are given as very good, mastic asphalt, asphalt tile, bitumen felt, cement rubber-latex and cement resin emulsion, concrete tiles, granolithic covered linoleum and magnesium oxychloride, thermoplastic tiles, softwood boards and blocks are given as good. Clay tiles and terrazzo are given as good except

[1] By H. M. Llewellyn and F. C. Harper (D.S.I.R. London, 1950).

when polished and rubber sheet and tile as good except when wet. Cement-bitumen composition blocks, pitch mastic and hardwood strips and blocks are given as fair.

A contributing cause of accident on stairs is bad design, and the two principal factors appear to be stairs that are too steep and winders that cannot be easily manipulated. Stairs in the home should always be easy going because members of the family are usually preoccupied when going about the house.

Steep stairs are a common fault in many houses built in the thirties. They were often made steep to accord with economy in space and to fit into a design. Stairs with risers of $7\frac{3}{4}$ inches, and going (face of riser to face of riser) only 8 inches, which is not uncommon are much too steep. The going should not be less than 9 inches (with 1-inch projection for nosing) with a riser of not more than $7\frac{1}{2}$ inches.[1]

Winders are another cause of accidents and should be avoided whenever possible when designing a house. It is also important to have stairs well lighted. There should always be a switch both at the top and bottom of the stairs, while, because the light is in the hall or landing it should not therefore be of low illumination, not 20 or 30 watt as it often is, but 60 or 80 watt. Older people are more likely to fall and eyesight deteriorates with age, thus adequate illumination in every part of the house, but especially on stairs, is essential for safety.

Of deaths in 1953 due to burns and scalds in the home 499 are classified as caused by fire and explosion of combustible material, and 99 are classified as caused by hot substance, corrosive liquid and steam. Thus the domestic fire appears to be the cause of at least two persons dying a day during the winter months, when most of these accidents occur. Statistics do not appear to be available as to the type of fire, but exposed sources of heat, the coal, gas and electric fire without adequate guards are all major causes. Gas and electric fires, since the Act of 1952, must be sold with much better guards, and some of the modern solid fuel appliances include adequate guards, but there still remains a large number of heating appliances in houses which are potential dangers. The open fire, should never be left without an adequate guard, especially if there are young children or old people in the house. To be adequate the guard must be fixed in position and completely cover the fire, while it must have a fine mesh.

Especial care should be taken with electrical equipment in the bathroom because water and damp materials are good conductors of electricity. Portable electrical equipment should never be taken into the bathroom, while high temperature radiant heating should be avoided. As there is always a possibility of touching the switch with wet hands it is advisable to place it on the ceiling and manipulate by pulling a cord. Heating in the bathroom should be adequate by means of a heated towel rail, either hot water on the principle of a radiator or an oil filled electric towel rail.

[1] British Standard 585: 1944 for wooden stairs gives the going as not less than $8\frac{1}{4}$ inches and a pitch of not more than 42° which means a rise of about $7\frac{1}{2}$ inches. I think even this is a little too steep.

CHAPTER XVII

SOME POSSIBLE SMALL HOUSE
STANDARDS—PLANS

STARTING from the assumptions that the small house should satisfy requirements derived from the habits of family life, considerations of health, the provision of cultural and recreational amenities, the reduction of labour to a minimum and consequent efficiency of organization, and the provision, within inevitable economic limits, of the house as a setting for a full life, it is possible to evolve certain standard units. The serviceability of those standards depends largely on the extent to which requirements have been examined and evaluated.

The value of the adoption of standards when 2 million dwellings have to be supplied as quickly as possible should be obvious. Standard designs make possible standard parts which can be mass-produced on a large scale and thus conduce to the rapid production of houses. But the first essential is that the standard should be good, and that variations of the standard should depend on varying requirements. Walter Gropius defines a standard in this connection 'as that simplified practical exemplar of anything in general use which embodies a fusion of the best of its anterior forms—a fusion preceded by the elimination of the personal content of their designers and all otherwise ungeneric or non-essential features'.[1] It is an excellent definition, and if such precepts determine the creation of house standards these should give wide satisfaction.

One may say that the two features which prompt variations are the different size of families and their varying habits and tastes. There is more consistency in the other requirements, such as concern health, the organization of strictly utilitarian departments like kitchens and bathrooms; whereas the rest of the house varies, these can be comparatively static, based, of course, on the evolution of well-thought-out standards.

Once the essential type of house is determined, variations in accommodation according to size of families can be made by additions to the smallest unit, many alternative variations suggesting themselves as the additions are made. All these additions and variations can be interchangeable, and a definite set of standardized constructional units can be employed in a large number of different forms. This is obvious to anyone who has played those games in which from a certain number of constructional members, many objects can be made. The spirit of the growth of the house from the smallest unit is essentially organic, though it is realized by mechanical means. It is rather like the cellular growth of the asexual organism which adds cells to its original structure as it grows. In designing variations on a theme for a hall, Erich Mendelsohn has indicated that the form of one suggests another, and the form of one cell breeds the form of another. In the case of the house, this cellular growth is dictated always by family needs.

These considerations have determined the planning of the units illustrated. One basic type W is chosen for a detached house (which accords with the understandable preference of so many) with a kitchen utility-room, and living room on the ground floor,

---

[1] *The New Architecture and Bauhaus* (New York and London 1936), p. 26.

1 MINIMUM HOUSE for FAMILY of 3.

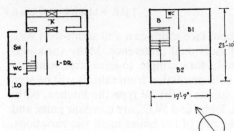

LIVING-DININGROOM
2 BEDROOMS FOR PARENTS AND 1 CHILD

5 HOUSE for FAMILY of 5 or 6.

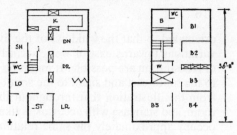

DINING NICHE, DINING ROOM, LIVING ROOM AND STUDIO
5 BEDROOMS FOR PARENTS AND 3 TO 4 CHILDREN

2 HOUSE for FAMILY of 3 or 4.

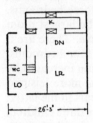
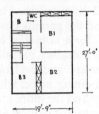

DINING NICHE AND LIVING ROOM
3 BEDROOMS FOR PARENTS AND 2 CHILDREN

6 HOUSE for FAMILY of 3.

DINING NICHE AND LIVING ROOM
2 BEDROOMS FOR PARENTS AND 1 CHILD (or CHILDLESS COUPLE)

3 HOUSE for FAMILY of 4 or 5.

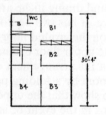

DININGROOM AND LIVINGROOM
4 BEDROOMS FOR PARENTS AND 2 OR 3 CHILDREN

7 HOUSE for FAMILY of 4 or 5.

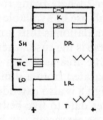
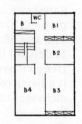

DINING ROOM AND LIVINGROOM
4 BEDROOMS FOR PARENTS AND 2 TO 3 CHILDREN

4 HOUSE for FAMILY of 4 or 5.

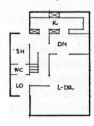
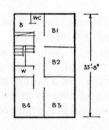

DINING NICHE AND LIVING-DININGROOM
4 BEDROOMS FOR PARENTS AND 2 OR 3 CHILDREN

8 HOUSE for FAMILY of 5 or 6

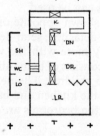
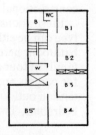

DINING NICHE, DINING ROOM AND LIVINGROOM
5 BEDROOMS — 5TH BEDROOM ADDED AT LATER DATE SEE 4 & 5

FIG. 23. *Variations on a suggested Standard (W) type of detached house.*

orientated so that the windows of the living room face south-east and south-west with variations towards east or west, according to individual preference. Many variations of fenestration are possible. It might be desirable, for example, to have large windows to the south-east and small to the south-west with protection from rain. It will be seen from the illustration that throughout the variations of the W type the kitchen, bath-room, and staircase with accessories like shed, lobby and W.C., are constant units, and occupy approximately the same relation to the rest of the house in all the variations. These kitchen-dining units and bathroom units will be described later. Each house has one flue for a coal fire in the living room.

The first plan is of a minimum sized house with living-dining room, for a family of three, one double bedroom for parents and a single bedroom for the child. The second unit is for a family of three or four. The length is increased by 3 feet, but here, instead of a living-dining room, is a living room and dining niche. There are three bedrooms, one for each person in the smaller family and the parents occupying the largest room in the family of four. The third variation is for a family of four or five. There are a living room and dining room, separated by a folding partition, and four bedrooms. The fourth variation is for a family of four or five, and the length is again increased by 3 feet. It consists of living-dining room and dining niche, whereby the more leisured and ceremonial meals are taken in the former and the more hurried meals in the latter. As in the third variation there are four bedrooms for parents and two or three children, in the former each person having a bedroom, in the latter the parents sharing the largest.

In variation 5 a larger type is shown for a family of five or six with living room, dining room, dining niche and study and five bedrooms. If the dining niche and dining room appear as a duplication, they could be made into one room. The study in this position could be utilized if desired in the other plans. Design 6 for a family of three is a variation of design 2 where living room and dining niche are separated by a folding partition to make full use of available space. It has two bedrooms with a roof terrace. The area of accommodation is thus larger on the ground floor than on the upper floor. In design 7 the reverse is the case, where the upper floor extends over the ground floor. Design 8 has the same area as design 4, but the arrangement of rooms differs as there is a living room separated from a dining room by a folding partition while the dining niche is as in 4. Design 8 is also extended to show that the upper floor of design 4 could be enlarged at a later date to five bedrooms in the event of an increase in the family. The same principle of extension can be adopted in all the houses on this type. In the houses with four or more bedrooms an additional washroom is provided.

It is possible to make numerous variations of this basic type and to continue enlarge-ments to the extent of accommodating families of eight, nine or ten. Whatever method of construction is employed, the number of standardized parts for so many different units can be worked out, and it will be seen that for many different variations the same constructional units can be used.

Illustrations are shown opposite of the different basic type S. As will be seen, this type can be either a detached, semi-detached or terrace house. The units of kitchen and bathroom here vary more with the variations of plan. The smallest unit (1) is for a family of four and consists of living-dining room and dining niche with three bedrooms for parents and two children. The next unit (2) for a family of four or five has an ex-tension outward of the kitchen and has living-dining room and dining niche and three bedrooms. Two of the bedrooms are double and are large enough to be divided by a

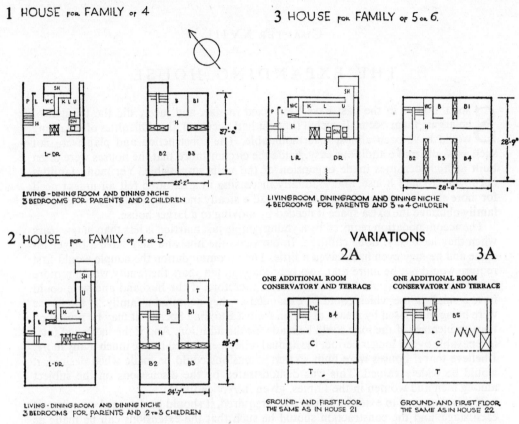

FIG. 24. *Variations on a suggested Standard (S) type of house* which can be detached, semi-detached or terrace.

partition, thus making a total of five single bedrooms. In design 3 for a family of five or six the kitchen is again varied, and there is a small dining niche as well as a dining room which is separated from the living room by a folding partition. There are four bedrooms and the largest bedroom can be divided into two, thus making five. Further variations could be made on these lines. It will be noted that in the bedrooms space is saved by utilizing the walls for wardrobes and avoiding projections. The relation in these designs between the dining room or dining niche and kitchen will be described when dealing with the kitchen-dining units.

A third basic type D is derived from the working kitchen type with living room and dining recess given as variation 2 in the Dudley Report, although it is a much more spacious plan. A utility room and entrance unit are added, while no bedroom is less than 100 square feet. Extension of this plan which includes a study, workroom and two bedrooms, making five in all, are shown in the plan marked D2.

CHAPTER XVIII

THE EXPANDING HOUSE

SMALL houses in the past have been fixed in size, and rarely did the thought of enlarging them occur. If such a thought had occurred, the difficulties of enlarging would have been almost insurmountable. The construction and plan were not such as would make additions easy, while the circumstance that the houses were often built at high densities made expansion of the units impossible. Yet many families occupying a small house, and gradually increasing in size, often felt an urgent need for more space. In cases where the father had a steady increase in salary or wages, the family obtained the extra space it needed by moving to a larger house.

The accommodation required by a young couple just married is less than in ten years when they have, say, three children. In ten years the husband may have a bigger income and he may even have saved a little. The accommodation the couple would first require would not be more than two bedrooms; in ten years the family would require four bedrooms. It would be of some value, therefore, if the husband and wife could have a small house which could be expanded as they acquired a family. If the house were being purchased by means of a loan from a Building Society, it may be presumed than an increase of the loan could be made for the addition. And if the increased total is repayable over a longer period, the annual repayments need not be much if any more. I believe that if houses were built so that extensions could be made when desired, it would be widely valued. This was demonstrated by the discussions on the subject among men and women in the Forces, given in Appendix II.

If it is proposed to extend a house when required, it should be designed complete at each stage, and the construction should be such that the extensions can be made as simply and efficiently as possible. It is much simpler, for example, to make extensions to a house with a flat roof than to a house with a pitched roof. This applies to both horizontal and vertical extensions. Further, where the walls, floors and roof are made of large factory-made sections, and the house is designed on a grid of, say, 3 feet for each of its completed stages, the extension will be simpler than if the house is of traditional brick construction.

The first eight plans shown of the W type of house, and the first three of the S type are variations according to family requirements, and built to each plan from the start. Plans of the W type 9 and 10, of the S type 4, 5 and 6, and of the D type 1 and 2 are made (Figs. 25 and 26) with the view to extension of the house when desired, each stage being complete. The designs are based on a grid of 3 feet. The same kitchen-utility room units described in the next chapter are preserved in all the types. It should be mentioned that in these types no bedroom is less than 100 square feet. Type W9 consists of living room and dining niche on the ground floor and three bedrooms on the first floor. This is extended by half its length in W10, the increase being made on the 3-foot grid. As a result a study is provided on the ground floor, the dining space and living room enlarged, part of which could be partitioned off to form a further room, while on the first floor two further bedrooms are secured and another bathroom,

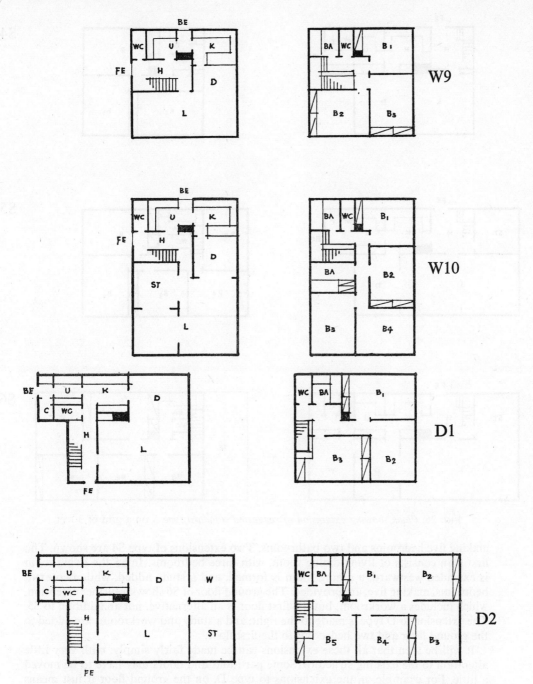

FIG. 25. *Plans showing expansion of two suggested standard types*, W and D, on a grid of 3 feet.

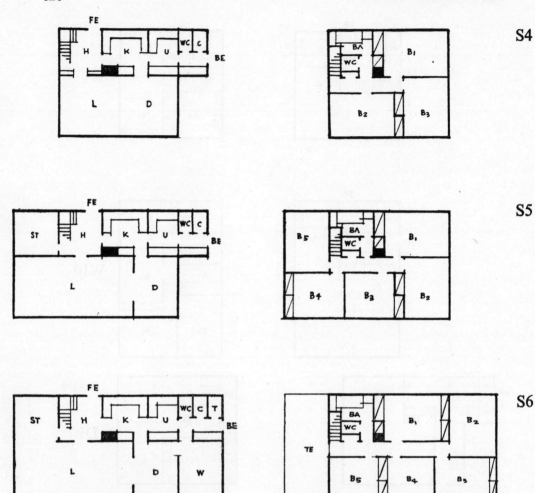

FIG. 26. *Plans showing expansion of suggested standard type S on a grid of 3 feet.*

making five bedrooms and two bathrooms. Two extensions of type S4 are shown. The first plan consists of living-dining room, with three bedrooms. In S5 the living room is extended westward, a dining room is formed, and a study added, while two extra bedrooms, making five, are provided. The ground floor of S6 shows a further extension, which includes a workroom, but the first floor is an alternative, not an addition to S5. The extension to D type is made to the right, and a study and workrooms are added to the ground floor and two bedrooms to the first floor.

It will be seen that all these extensions can be made fairly simply, with very little alteration to the existing structure. Some partitions and doors may have to be moved a little. For example, in the extensions to type D, on the ground floor it just means adding two rooms at the side. On the first floor the size of the front bedroom is reduced a little, a partition takes the place of the outside wall, while the wardrobes which were between the second and third bedrooms are moved. Other small adjustments are made with the partitions, slightly reducing or altering the shapes of the rooms. This should present little difficulty, for it should be remembered that the construction is designed with a view to these changes.

In types S2A and S3A further accommodation is made by the addition of a third floor to S2 and 3. This could be done quite simply if the houses are built with flat roofs. The arrangement provides a fourth bedroom for S2 and a fifth bedroom for S3. The bedroom occupies only a part of the area, the remainder being partly covered with glazing, to be used as a conservatory in S2 and as a sleeping porch in S3. In the latter, instead of a fifth bedroom, this extra room could be used as a workroom or studio for painting, carving, carpentry, photography and various crafts.

CHAPTER XIX

SOME STANDARD UNITS—KITCHEN, UTILITY ROOM, BATHROOM AND ENTRANCE UNITS

THE kitchen in the W type is a constant unit, remaining the same and occupying the same position in all the variations of the plan, being designed principally for families of from three to six. It is based on the combination of scullery—here called utility room—and kitchen, and is planned for the utmost convenience and efficiency. The arrangement is something between the old separate kitchen and scullery and the kitchen and scullery combined. There is less separation than the former and more than the latter. It is based on a thorough examination of the work done in the average kitchen of a small house, and the aim has been to provide an arrangement which will reduce labour to a minimum and conduce to the utmost ease of working. (Illustrated Figs. 16 and 27-30.)

The whole unit is long and narrow, extending nearly the whole width of the house, being 19 feet 6 inches by 7 feet 4 inches. Orientated approximately north-west to south-east its long side thus faces north-east. It consists of three main parts: at either end are the utility and cooking sections and in the centre is the small larder section; the whole being made complete in a factory and transported to the site in a convenient number of parts. The sections are shown clearly in the illustrations. The utility section is mainly the laundry part and is designed for washing and drying clothes. There is a wash boiler or washing machine, a sink for rinsing and other small operations, to which a wringer could be fixed if desired, and a drying cupboard with hot-water cylinder. The larder in the north-east external wall, with refrigerator underneath, projects well into the space, and effects a separation between the utility and kitchen sections. Opposite is the combined ironing table and broom cupboard.

The kitchen section is designed as a workshop, or rather studio for the creative work of preparing meals. An important feature of the design is a continuous wall table 2 feet 4 inches wide and 2 feet 8 inches high, which appears to be the most convenient working height for the average woman. On a level with this table on the north-east wall is the sink, by the side of which is a small circular vegetable sink, used also for rinsing. The draining board is on the left. By the end wall is the cooker, the top of which is at table level. Continuing and turning the corner the table becomes the serving portion, as it here adjoins the dining niche or room. The spacious hatch above this servery is closed with a roller shutter. Underneath the serving table is a sideboard which opens from both sides—from the kitchen and from the dining niche. Adequate shelves and cupboards are provided, including storage cupboards which are placed above reaching height, thus utilizing all available wall space. Utensils for preparing meals are either in the cupboard below or above the working table between the sink and cooker.

The plan on page 92 shows that the design is based on the sequence of operations in preparing a meal. The food enters by the utility door, and then goes to the larder or refrigerator. It is taken from there direct to the table to the right of the kitchen sink.

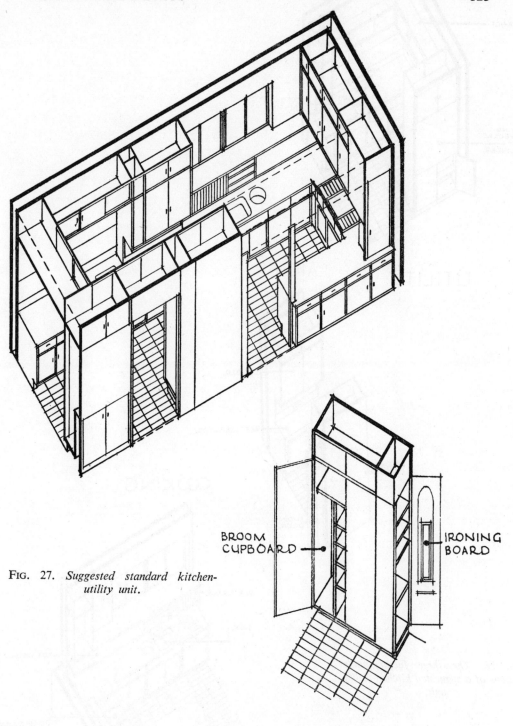

FIG. 27. *Suggested standard kitchen-utility unit.*

BROOM CUPBOARD

IRONING BOARD

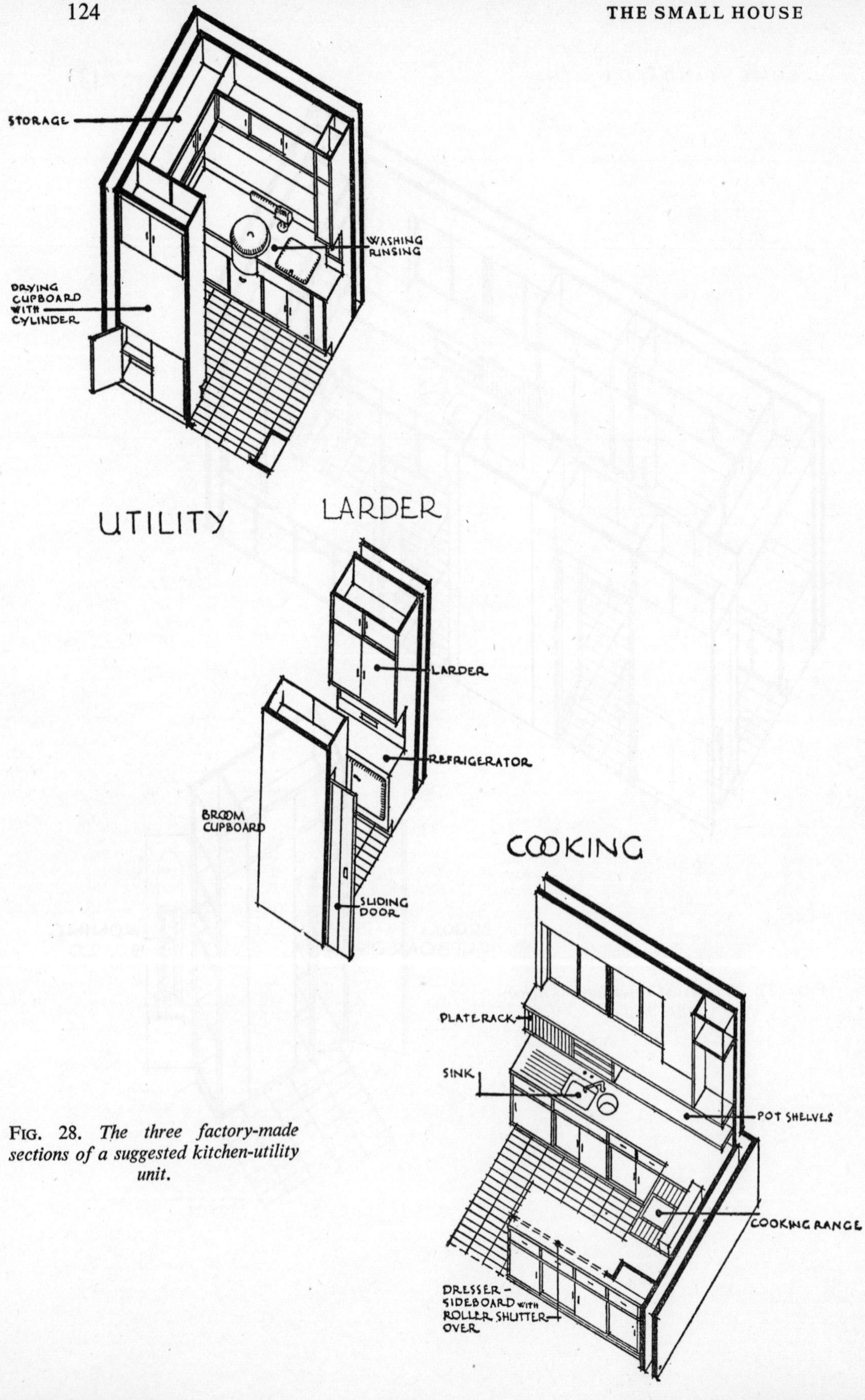

STORAGE

WASHING
RINSING

DRYING
CUPBOARD
WITH
CYLINDER

UTILITY

LARDER

LARDER

REFRIGERATOR

BROOM
CUPBOARD

SLIDING
DOOR

COOKING

PLATE RACK

SINK

POT SHELVES

COOKING RANGE

DRESSER—
SIDEBOARD with
ROLLER SHUTTER
OVER

FIG. 28. *The three factory-made sections of a suggested kitchen-utility unit.*

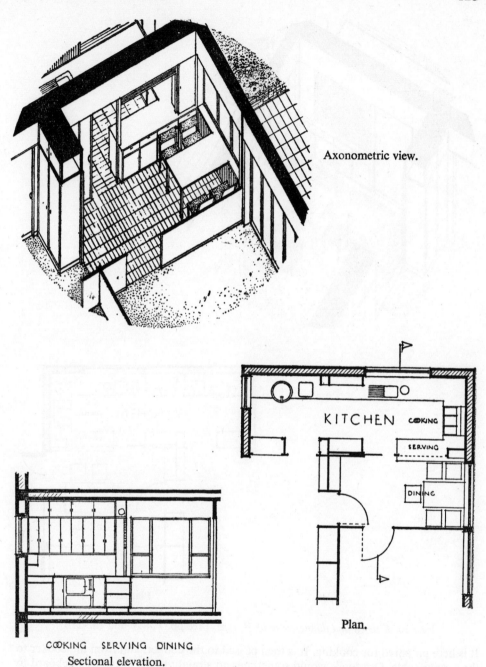

Axonometric view.

KITCHEN   COOKING

SERVING

DINING

Plan.

COOKING SERVING DINING

Sectional elevation.

FIG. 29. *Kitchen and dining-room of W type.* (*See* pp. 114-16 and 122-27.)

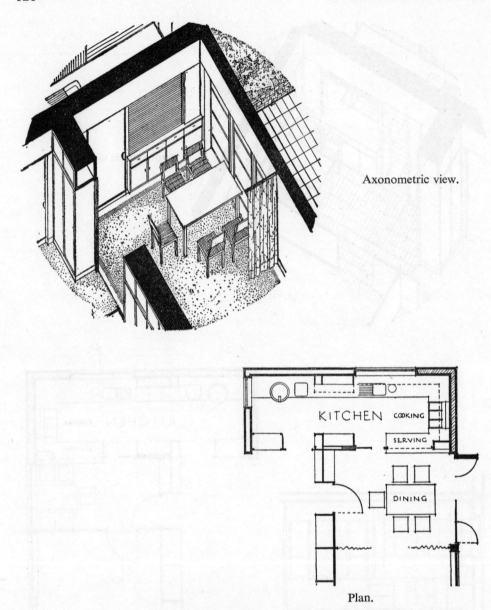

Axonometric view.

Plan.

FIG. 30. *Kitchen and dining-room of W type*. (*See* pp. 114-16 and 122-27.)

It is here prepared for cooking. It is then passed to the cooker, and from the cooker to the serving table. Dry foods would sometimes go straight to the spacious sideboard to be served direct. This sequence, and the narrowness of the kitchen reduce the work in preparing a meal to an absolute minimum. It would not be necessary to stand in preparing a meal. I would recommend a revolving stool with back, slightly higher than the ordinary chair, but preferably with adjustable height. As the space between the wall tables is only 3 feet, the housewife could sit on this stool and have the sink, cooker, working table and serving table all within easy reach as she turns on her stool.

A large window is on the north-east wall above the sink and work table, and another window is on the north-west wall in the utility section. The larder and storage cupboards are directly ventilated. Above the cooker is a cupboard, the lower part of which forms a hood, connected with a wall opening in which a fan draws off the steam and cooking smells.

I found that a large majority of men and women in the Forces wanted space for meals in or as near as possible to the kitchen, and that a high percentage of those in the groups of the Townswomen's Guild wanted space for meals in the kitchen (see Appendix II). It was agreed among the former that in obtaining this care should be taken not to interfere with the kitchen as an efficient work-room, and the solution appeared to be the provision of a recess at one end or a niche adjoining. In the W type an adjoining dining niche is provided, which in variations 3 and 7 is enlarged to a dining room, and in the first very smallest type is a living-dining room. But in all the closest proximity of kitchen and space for meals exists. The spacious serving table and sideboard is common to the kitchen and dining niche, and a door is at the side of this. A greater degree of convenience in taking meals, where despatch is a primary consideration, could not be achieved if the space for meals were actually in the kitchen. In this plan the disadvantages of such an arrangement are avoided.

In variation 4 is a living-room as well as a dining niche, and in variations 5 and 8 there is a dining room as well as niche. Here is the provision for the two ways of having meals dictated by the habits of family life—the hurried breakfast and the leisured evening and week-end meals. In the case of 5 and 8, for example, both would presumably be furnished for meals, and it would mean carrying things a little farther to the dining room; but whether both or only one are furnished for meals, the furniture transferred as required in the latter case, is a matter of individual choice.

It will be seen that in the relation of kitchen to dining space, and in the relation of these to the living room considerable flexibility is achieved in the interior design. The provision of a very large hatch, so that when the shutter is rolled up it appears as if the wall is eliminated, means that the kitchen and dining niche or room, as the case may be, becomes virtually one room. The sideboard would appear in the centre, and in the case of hurried meals the serving table could, if desired, be used as a kind of snack bar. The alternative of the existence or elimination of a wall provided by the large hatch and movable partition has numerous advantages. In addition to the meal space and kitchen becoming almost one room, with the shutter rolled up, the mother working in the kitchen can easily overlook her young children playing in the remainder of the ground floor. In the event of a party the kitchen can be completely shut off, the partition between meals space and living room removed, and thus a fairly large space obtained. The flexibility of removing walls will give the family much greater freedom in the use of its house.

In the S type the same kitchen unit is employed with abbreviations in 1, but fully in 2 and 3. In 2 the utility section is placed at right angles and the whole unit forms an L shape. In both the space for meals takes very much the form of a kitchen recess. In 3 the dining table in the recess is against the wall and can be passed under a low hatch

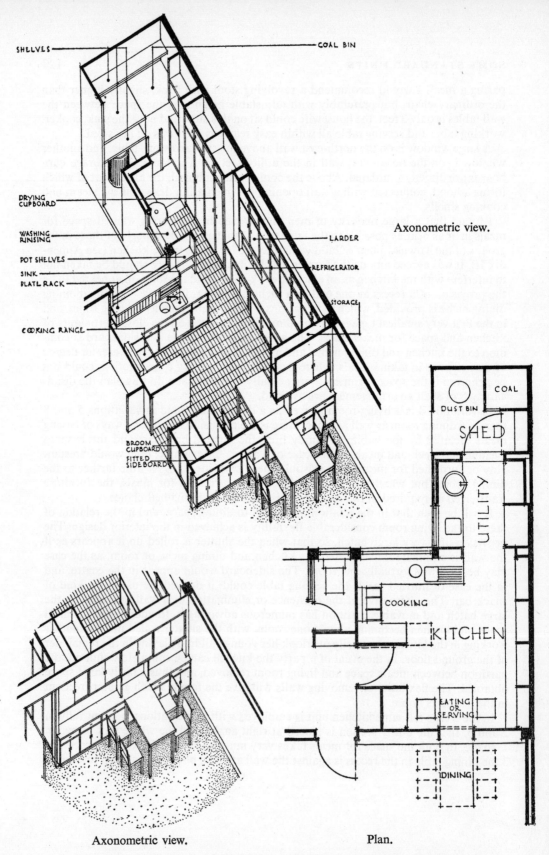

SHELVES

COAL BIN

DRYING CUPBOARD

WASHING RINSING

LARDER

POT SHELVES

REFRIGERATOR

SINK

PLATE RACK

STORAGE

COOKING RANGE

Axonometric view.

BROOM CUPBOARD

FITTED SIDEBOARD

DUST BIN

COAL

SHED

UTILITY

COOKING

KITCHEN

EATING OR SERVING

DINING

Axonometric view.

Plan.

FIG. 31. *Kitchen and dining-room of the S3 type*. It will be noted that the dining table passes under the hatch between kitchen and dining-room. *(See pp. 116 and 127.)*

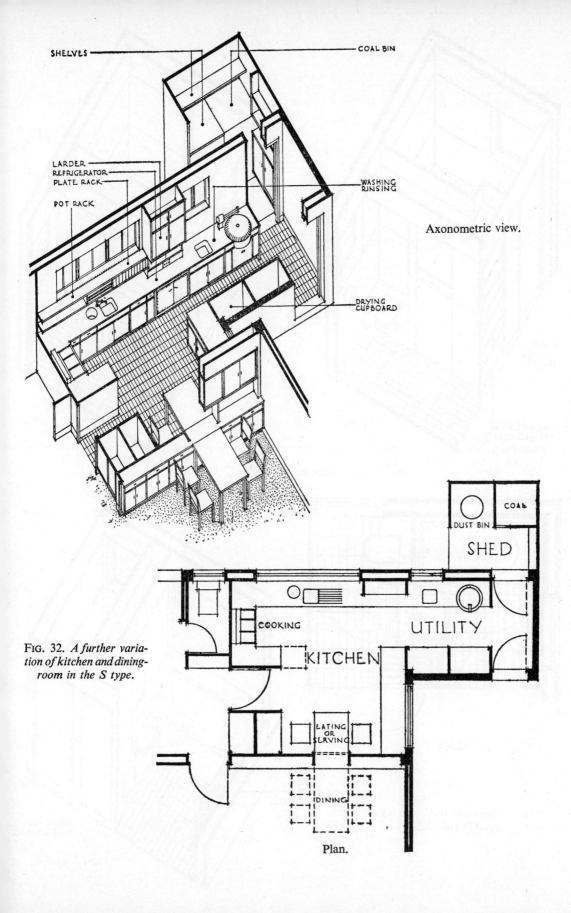

SHELVES — COAL BIN

LARDER
REFRIGERATOR
PLATE RACK

POT RACK

WASHING
RINSING

Axonometric view.

DRYING
CUPBOARD

FIG. 32. *A further variation of kitchen and dining-
room in the S type.*

DUST BIN   COAL

SHED

COOKING   UTILITY

KITCHEN

EATING
OR
SERVING

DINING

Plan.

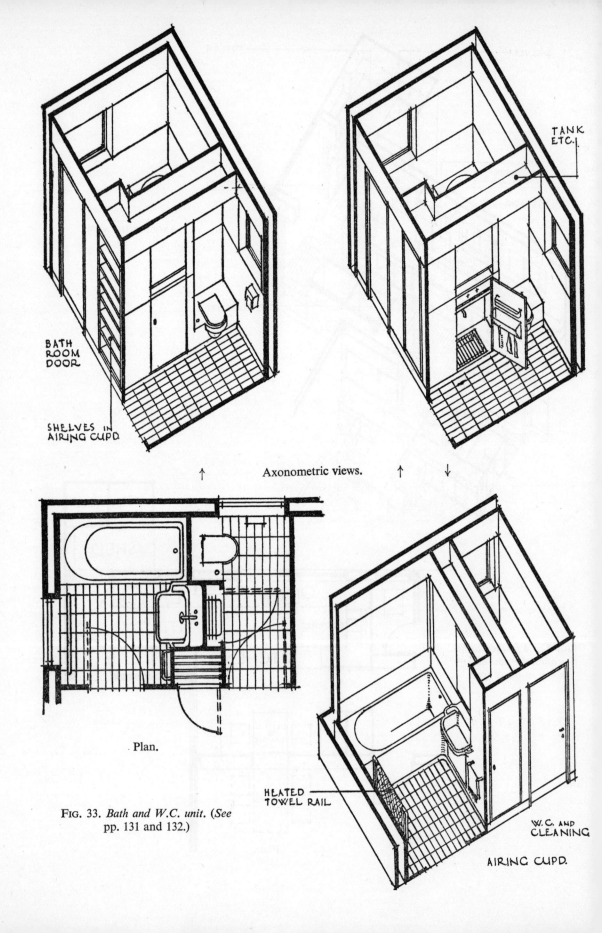

BATH ROOM DOOR

SHELVES IN AIRING CUPD.

TANK ETC.

Axonometric views.

Plan.

FIG. 33. *Bath and W.C. unit.* (*See* pp. 131 and 132.)

HEATED TOWEL RAIL

W.C. AND CLEANING

AIRING CUPD.

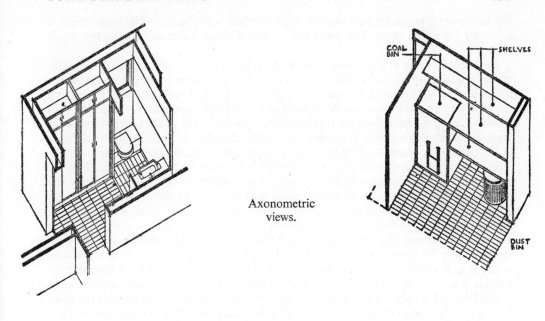

Axonometric
views.

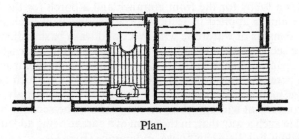

Plan.

FIG. 34. *Entrance unit designed for the W and S house types*. In the W type it provides a lobby
for the front entrance and a porch for the back entrance. In the S type it is applied in sections.
(*See* opposite page.)

into the dining room. Thus if meals are required in the dining room, the table already
laid can be passed under the hatch, and then moved back on the completion of the
meal (Figs. 131 and 132).

THE BATH AND W.C. UNIT

The bath and W.C. unit, which can be made complete in a factory and transported
in parts to the site, is built up from pressed sections designed to avoid dirt-collecting
surfaces and corners. The plumbing is of a simple type and can be easily reached. In

9

the bathroom a medicine cupboard is fixed over the wash basin, while underneath is a hopper for soiled linen. The towel rail is heated either electrically or by hot water (Fig. 33).

In the W.C. there is a cleaning cupboard in which a water tap is placed at a convenient height, with a floor sink underneath. This provision is very convenient for filling buckets for cleaning the first floor and avoids the bad habit of filling them from the bath tap. The floor sink can be utilized as a foot bath, especially for children, thus avoiding using the bathroom for this purpose. This cupboard has ample provision for keeping cleaning equipment. It occupies the space immediately opposite the wash basin in the bathroom, while abutting is the linen cupboard which opens on to the corridor. Above these cupboards and above the partition between bathroom and W.C. is the water tank, so introduced as to effect the utmost economy of space, and avoiding the necessity of having it amidst the rafters or on the flat roof. The merit of this whole unit is compactness. Much has been concentrated in a small space without, it is clear, producing any feeling of restrictive diminutiveness.

For larger houses, like the variations 4, 5 and 8 of the W type, there is provision on the first floor for an extra wash place, similar, as we shall see later, to that used as lavatory in the entrance unit, but instead of W.C. there is provision for a shower with flexible handshower, and drop-out basin in the wall. Thus there are shower, wash basin, foot sink combined in one small room. Such a room provides excellent facilities for a quick shower, for washing hair, shaving, footbath and other similar operations.

THE ENTRANCE UNIT

The entrance unit appears as a complete entity on one side of the house in the W type, and provides a lobby for the front entrance and a porch for the back entrance. In the S type the unit is applied in sections. The arrangement is clearly seen in the plans. The lobby consists of wardrobe with W.C. and wash basin adjoining. The back part is the storage section and holds a large coal bin, a dustbin, near which ventilation is provided, and space and shelves for garden and household repair tools. It is large enough to take a perambulator or bicycle. Access to the W.C., which lies between the lobby and storage section, can be from both or from the lobby only. In the case of the former it is convenient when working in the garden. The sections of this entrance unit are arranged in such a way that, in the event of a garage being added at a later date, they would provide a link between house and garage (Fig. 34).

The staircase, it will be noted, has no winders, and provides ample space underneath for a large cupboard, adequate to store a perambulator and a bicycle. Easy access is obtained from either the back porch or the hall. Again, in the arrangement of the entrance unit in relation to hall and staircase, compactness is the keynote, where much is contained in a limited space consistent with free and efficient movement.

(a) Sketch of hobbies room.

PLATE LXII (a), and (b). *Rooms for recreation and hobbies.*

(b) Section fitted for carpentry and metal work.

(a) Wood blocks.

(b) Brick and tiles.

PLATE LXIII. *Gardens.* In these illustrations of parts of small gardens the materials used for paving, paths and borders are wood blocks, flagstones, coral and cream bricks and tiles. (*See* p. 152.)

(c) Flagstones.

(d) Tiles and brick border.

CHAPTER XX

THE BASEMENT HOUSE

TOWARDS the end of last century in Great Britain the building of basement houses was gradually discontinued, and during the present century they have been the exception. This is contrary to the practice in the Scandinavian countries and in many other countries in Europe, Canada and the U.S.A., where a large proportion of basement houses continue to be built. In Scandinavia and Germany the great majority of houses built during the present century have been with a basement, while in 1946 a nation-wide survey of the U.S.A. showed that 59 per cent of all houses had basements.[1]

In the larger urban houses of the nineteenth century the basement was generally the place where the servants lived and did the work of preparing food, cooking and cleaning, while they slept in the attics. Basements were rarely inhabited by the well-to-do employers of the servants. In the smaller houses with basements, inhabited by the lower middle classes, who generally had no servants, families often spent much of their lives in the basement because both the kitchen and dining room were situated there. Social reformers and housing experts asked therefore whether these dark and sometimes damp basement rooms were good places for human habitation. This, together with the cost of excavation and construction were probably the main reasons for the discontinuance of the basement house in Great Britain.

Yet there are distinct advantages in the basement, not for habitation as in Victorian days, but as a place for heating plant, washing and drying clothes, storage and workshop, very much as it is used in many European countries and in America. In the report on Domestic Heating in America, already cited, the prime function of the American basement is stated as housing the heating plant and fuel supply, but 'it is also used as the place where clothes washing and often clothes drying is done. It is used for general storage and frequently as a childrens' play space and as a workshop'.[2]

The basement as a place for the heating plant has many advantages, assuming, as it should be assumed, that general background heating of the whole house is desired.

Some forms of heating, particularly the gravity warm air system, function better with the furnace in the basement, while it makes the whole area under the ground floor warm and contributes to making the habitable part of the house dry; while fuel storage can be far more conveniently related to the fire than if it were in the kitchen. It has also the advantage of separating the boiler fire from the place where the food is prepared. In a very large number of houses, especially those built since the First World

[1] Of these only 14·5 per cent were 2-story houses, of which 13 per cent had basements and 1·5 per cent were without basements. Of the 11·5 per cent 1½-story houses 10·5 per cent had basements and 1·0 per cent were without. The remainder were 1-story houses, of which 35·5 per cent had basements and 38·5 per cent were without basements. See *Domestic Heating in America* by J. C. Pritchard, C. C. Handisyde and R. H. Rowse (London, 1946), p. 32.

[2] Op. cit. p. 32.

War, when the separate scullery was eliminated and combined with the kitchen or kitchenette, a boiler fire is in the kitchen, a custom which is not conducive to cleanliness, because there is always dust with ash removed from the solid fuel boiler.

A space in the basement for washing clothes can be designed as such, and with space for other cleaning it would thus form a utility room, which would include a sink and draining board, a washing machine or wash boiler, ironing table and space for drying clothes, which could be arranged near the boiler. This is an important provision, for although the housewife may prefer to dry clothes out-of-doors, it cannot always be done in the winter months of cold, frost, fog and rain, and it is therefore a great advantage to have the facility provided indoors.

A workshop in the basement is also a valuable provision, because most men like a convenient place with a bench for doing odd jobs. Many men like to make various useful fittings for the house, like built-in cupboards, shelving, pelmets and so on, and a workshop in the basement conveniently tucked out of the way is excellent.

Storage space can be used for a variety of purposes, from fruit and wine to travelling cases and sports gear. Lack of storage space is not an uncommon complaint in English houses especially those built since 1914. In slightly larger houses part of the basement could be a garage separated from the house part by a brick wall or concrete wall.

Thus a basement used for heating plant, for storage, for washing and drying clothes and for a workshop, in no sense habitable like the old Victorian basement, and similar to American domestic basements, which are much valued by those who have them, could be a real asset in the modern home.

The basement rooms need not be more than 8 feet high, of which 2 feet should be above ground to allow for a frieze of windows to give light. This would mean that the ground floor would be nearly 3 feet above ground. If the house is built against the slope of a hill, one side of the house might be on ground level with the other a basement 5 or 6 feet below ground, which is an excellent utilization of the slope.

The deterrents of damp and cost have little validity today. Modern methods of construction, like the cavity wall and scientific waterproofing are such that keeping a basement thoroughly dry should present little difficulty. In the last century basements were dug by hand labour and the work in excavating one basement was a matter of days. Now, with mechanized excavators a basement for a small house could be excavated in less than an hour. There are many excavators, like the drag shovel, of about $\frac{1}{2}$-cubic yard capacity, made by manufacturers of earth moving equipment that can excavate for the basements of houses very simply and speedily.

Basement houses also constitute a small advantage in the matter of estate planning in a country where land space is limited, and where the great majority of families greatly prefer the family house with a garden to a flat. In building the basement house the accommodation is divided into three floors instead of two. With the latter a storage shed is often in the garden, and a garage often takes up garden space. It is obvious that an estate of basement houses could allow for a little more compact development than one of two-story houses, with the same garden space, and that, say, fourteen houses to the acre could be secured instead of twelve, and with better accommodation in the fourteen.

The advantages of the basement as outlined in this chapter are experienced and realized by large numbers of families in Europe and America, yet we, with less land space than most countries, have largely abandoned it for domestic purposes. Its

FIG. 35. *Standard (W) type of detached house with basement.*

advantages are surely so apparent that it is surprising that there has not been a revival on the lines indicated. The authors of the report on *Domestic Heating in America* considered that the advantages of basements were such that the whole question of such accommodation should be reviewed as a new possibility. Yet little has been done, and it is difficult to find any reason other than lack of enterprise.

CHAPTER XXI

SITE PLANNING AND THE RESIDENTIAL AND NEIGHBOURHOOD UNITS

IT has been customary in planning housing estates to arrange minor roads according to some preconceived pattern, and to fit this pattern as nearly as possible to the site with the houses facing the roads. In the nineteenth century this preconceived pattern was generally formal and geometric, and for industrial housing and London suburbs it was often an arrangement of parallel straight roads. In the latter part of the century a less formal pattern was introduced, as the result of mediaeval influence, and we find curved roads, small squares off the roadway and culs-de-sac included. The general pattern is more or less irregular. We are conscious of this change if we contrast the straight rows of houses in any indutrial city of the north, or the inner suburbs of London, with some of the later estates, like those of Bournville, Earswick, Hampstead Garden suburb or the Garden Cities of Letchworth and Welwyn. We can see this change vividly if we contrast an early housing community at Essen, like that of Grunenberg, built in 1875, with a later community like Dahlhauser, built in 1907. In the former all the roads and houses form a pattern of straight lines and rectangles, in the latter the roads are curved, and the alignment of the houses along the roads is frequently broken by recessed groupings.

It is clear that in the formal and geometric planning of housing estates, the pattern of the streets determined the orientation of the houses. The majority of the houses were generally what is designated as the parlour and non-parlour types with three bedrooms, two of a reasonable size and one little more than a boxroom. In the parlour type there was a front and back room. If such houses faced on to a street running east to west, then only the south side of the house had sunlight. The people living in houses which faced roads running north to south were more fortunate because one side had the morning sun and the other side the afternoon sun. In the days of rigidly formed street planning people did not value sunlight, as we have learnt to value it, and when the summer sun shone into their parlours they pulled down the blinds to protect the furniture and carpets. In such planning the street is regarded as the essential unit.

The change to more irregular planning did not necessarily mean that more consideration was given to the orientation of the houses. In many cases it was mainly an effort to get away from the deadness and monotony of formal planning. It should be noted, however, that this formal planning results in depressing monotony when the house units are mean and squalid, having no claims to beauty. When the house unit is an agreeable or beautiful one, then the repetition along a straight street does not result in the same dreary monotony, indeed, that repetition enhances the beauty, but even here there is a limit to the enjoyable extent of repetition. With the more informal arrangement along curved roads the terrace blocks were generally shorter, and there was a considerable mixture of semi-detached houses. The aim was to introduce variety, but there was also the romantic inclination, prevalent at the time, to revive the picturesque informal character of the mediaeval village.

It was these circumstances rather than the satisfactory orientation of houses that determined the patterning of the roads. That is not to say that the orientation was not considered. A common practice was to have houses of various types and to place them along the roads where they would get the most sunlight. Thus in a road running north to south, the ordinary parlour six-roomed house is suitable, but along a road running east to west it is better to have a through living-dining room or a living room and dining room and two bedrooms on the south side with the kitchen on the north.

In thought of this kind, which has almost always dominated estate planning, it is assumed that the street is the unit of planning in residential areas. Architects defend this practice because they say that the street must be comprehended as an architectural whole, and that is one of the reasons why architects generally prefer houses combined in terrace blocks, except when they have to live in them. Mr. Trystan Edwards in his book *Good and Bad Manners in Architecture*,[1] and Mr. Thomas Sharp in his book on *Town Planning*,[2] are at pains to demonstrate that the street must be a continuous whole, and that this is better achieved by terrace blocks than by detached houses. Streets in the centre of a town and in shopping areas must obviously be comprehended as a unified architectural whole, and this should apply to rows of houses aligned on the footway with no front garden, as with much Georgian housing in towns, and with the straight streets in industrial towns. But with the more recent irregularly planned estates, where roads are often curved, and where houses have front gardens, the landscape element enters into the general architectural composition. Looking down one of the streets in Letchworth or Welwyn Garden City, or in one of the outer suburbs of London, one is not conscious of a formal architectural composition of harmonious lines and masses but rather of relations between roads, trees, shrubs and houses. The intervals between detached or semi-detached units, provided these are good and provided they are not too narrow, often contribute to a satisfactory relation of trees, or shrubs and houses, and often afford a play of light and shadow not possible with the long flat façade of the terrace block. The fact too that there is a great dislike of terrace houses, and general preference for semi-detached houses (*see* Appendix II, p. 174) should prompt architects to concentrate on this unit and compose it successfully in groups in relation to trees and gardens.

Residential areas exist for the families living in them, thus planning should begin with family needs. The logical deduction is that the unit of planning is the house and not the street. We have rarely planned in this way, and yet it is the true functional way. Taking the detached or semi-detached houses as the units, it is possible to group these according to the sun and then plan the minor roads accordingly. This could be done either by grouping the houses as blocks of flats are sometimes grouped, away from the roads with service approach ways sufficient for small vehicles, or arrange the roads conveniently to serve the houses. The point is that the best siting of the houses is determined first, and it should not be beyond the ingenuity of the planners to arrange the roads accordingly. Both formal and irregular planning is possible. A good example is the siting of the houses built during the war in Aluminium City, Pittsburg. In this scheme, for which Walter Gropius and Marcel Breuer were responsible, the houses are planned on a hilly wooded site. Each row of houses is sited with a southern aspect, only some face on to the road, others abut it endwise, while others are grouped away from

[1] London, 1924, Chapter III.
[2] The Pelican Book published in 1940, pp. 91-108.

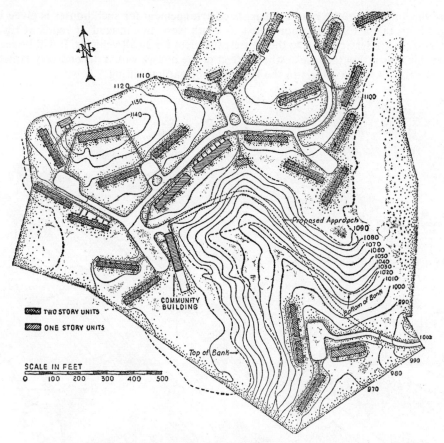

FIG. 36. *Site plan of Aluminium City, Pittsburg*. Designed by Walter
Gropius and Marcel Breuer. The houses are planned on a hilly wooded site,
and each row is sited with a southern aspect—some facing the road,
others endwise to it. (*See* p. 138.)

it and are reached by short branching service ways. The road winds through the group,
its course being determined by convenient proximity to the houses and by the contours
of the land (Fig. 36).

A formal geometric arrangement of roads is, however, possible with a satisfactory
siting of houses, that is if such a plan is desirable, although if the same house units are
used and they are to be placed on either side of the roads, they would not all face on
to the roads in the same way. But the mere facing of houses on to roads is not of
architectural importance when there are front gardens, and a generous inter-mixture
of trees and shrubs. If one takes the suggested standard type W (which is described in
Chapter XVII) through which the north-south axis runs diagonally, a good plan for
the roads would be to arrange them north-east to south-west and south-east to north-
west. The houses would all be sited in the same way, those on the north-east to south-
west roads would abut endwise, and those on the south-east to north-west roads would

have the long side to the roads. A suggested arrangement for such houses is given in Fig. 37. In this a road runs north-east to south-west, but instead of roads at right angles there are service ways to the houses, sufficient for small vehicles. It will be seen from this illustration that the aesthetic effect of the houses would depend very largely on the relation of the houses to the landscape or garden setting.

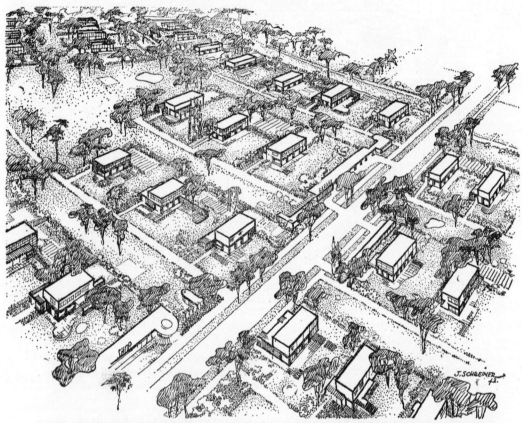

FIG. 37. *Detached houses sited according to the sun*. The living room in each house faces south. The road runs north-east to south-west. The service ways, of sufficient width for small vehicles, are at right-angles to the road. Garden design would be of major importance. The types of houses shown here are similar to the W type described in Chapter XVII.

With more conventional types of houses fairly satisfactory, if not ideal, arrangements are possible. The best conventional type for satisfactory siting is perhaps the house with a garden front to the south in which living room and dining room and two bedrooms face south. But such types could only satisfactorily be sited on one side of a road running east to west, so that the fronts of the houses face north. This arrangement is adopted for a large number of the houses in the neighbourhood unit illustrated, and it will be seen that they face on to a small service ways running between the minor roads, and at the ends of the gardens are strips which form children's playgrounds.

Other houses in the area, which would be of a different type, face the roads running north to south, so that they get the morning sun on one side and the afternoon sun on the other; but it will be noted that there are no houses in which the garden front is towards the north, an orientation which cannot be too strongly condemned.

Good housing is something more than well-designed and convenient houses well sited. It involves a good environment, a good setting in the neighbourhood, with educational, shopping and recreational facilities conveniently related to the house. In town planning it is customary to divide a planned area—such as a community or town—into neighbourhood units, and these into residential units. Let us consider the planning of a new town, and work outwards from the home.

One of the functions of family life is the rearing of children, therefore next in importance to a well-designed and convenient home is a good junior or primary school in the immediate vicinity of the home, so that the children from five to eleven years, which are the ages indicated in the Education Act of 1944 for attendance at a Primary School, shall be able to reach school after a short walk, which should not exceed half a mile, in reasonable safety, and without crossing a main road. Speaking of the importance of the school in determining the character of a residential unit, Professor C. B. Fawcett says that next to the home the school is the most important factor in the education of the young, and that therefore the residential settlement-unit is the primary communal service in the neighbourhood.[1] Professor Fawcett thinks of a primary school for a residential unit of 1,200 to 2,400, but this is not in accordance with general town planning practice, in which a primary school is planned as the centre of a neighbourhood unit of from 5,000 to 10,000, and in which residential units are comprehended. It is important, however, to calculate as accurately as possible on the basis of educational demands, the approximate size of a neighbourhood unit, and the approximate size of a satellite town or community.

In determining the size of a neighbourhood unit, calculations must be based on the numbers of children of school age relative to the total population, and this can be determined approximately by reference to the numerical changes in population and to the average expectation of life at birth. The population of Great Britain at the 1951 Census was nearly 49 million and has increased since then at the rate of about 175,000 a year, a rate of increase that seems likely to continue until 1960 when the population will probably be about $50\frac{1}{2}$ millions. The average expectation of life is likely to increase. Before the war it was sixty-one, which represents an increase of about thirty in a hundred years. It is now about 70[2] and for the purposes of planning we can thus take the average expectation of life at that.

The number in a neighbourhood would be determined by the size of school classes in a primary school. The maximum size of classes for children from five to eleven years in a primary school given in Ministry of Education regulations is forty.[3] We may therefore think of classes of from thirty to forty. The stationary population necessary

[1] C. B. Fawcett, *A Residential Unit for Town and Country Planning*, (London, 1944), p. 29.

[2] In the Ministry of Health report for 1953 longevity for that year is given as sixty-seven for men and seventy-two for women.

[3] This would appear to some as rather high, especially as in the Fisher Act of 1919 a desirable size of class is given as twenty-four, but we have to consider what is realizable, and it is unlikely that a lower maximum could be achieved in the immediate future.

therefore to maintain these classes would be thirty or forty multiplied by seventy, which would be from 2,100 to 2,800. That would be for a single-stream school which is recommended by Professor Fawcett, because the whole unit is not too large for the Principal to take some interest in each of the pupils. But there are other advantages in the double- or triple-stream schools occasioned by the fluctuating age groups in the neighbourhood. The triple-stream school would mean a population in the neighbourhood of from 6,300 to 8,400, which approximates to sizes often recommended for neighbourhood units. The Community Centres and Associations Survey Group of the National Council of Social Service recommends a neighbourhood unit of 2,000 dwellings,[1] thus comprising between 7,000 and 10,000 persons, but this calculation is based on 3·5 minimum to 5 maximum household which is too high. A more accurate basis is 3 to 4,[2] which gives a neighbourhood of 6,000 to 8,000. In the theoretic basis for communities and satellite towns in the County of London and Greater London Plans the neighbourhood varies from 5,000 to 10,000. It is stated that 'if the planning of a neighbourhood unit could be based upon a population constituted so as to be an exact reproduction, according to social class and income, of the population as a whole, the best size would be either 5,000, to contain one school for children aged five to seven and one for children aged eight to eleven, or alternatively a population of 10,000 containing two of each such schools'.[3] Presumably one-stream schools are envisaged, and it is thus difficult to see how these figures are determined. We have seen that on the basis of the proportion of children of school age to population with classes of thirty to forty one-stream schools would mean neighbourhood units of 2,100 to 2,800. The calculations of the authors of these plans are based either on too large classes or on an insufficient proportion of child population to the whole.

The triple-stream primary school seems to me the most desirable. It is to feed three types of secondary school, modern, technical and grammar, and it is possible towards the end of the period at the primary school to group the children in the three classes according to the secondary schools they are likely to attend. But I am aware that this is a doubtful advantage and may be attended with disadvantages. There is, however, the question of the changing character of the population. In a new estate there are a large proportion of newly married couples, and families with small children. In twenty years the majority of the same families would probably still be living there, but most of the children would have grown up and the number attending the primary school would be greatly reduced. The triple-stream school may have classes about the maximum of forty, but in twenty years' time these classes may be reduced to twenty or even less, and it might be advisable to make it a double-stream school. Such a school allows for flexibility. There is, however, the objection that the triple-stream school is too large for the principal to take an interest in each pupil, but this would be obviated by the division of the school into two sections, one for children from five to seven years, and the other for children from eight to eleven.

I have suggested that to serve a triple-stream primary school the neighbourhood

[1] *The Size and Social Structure of a Town* (London, 1943), p. 8.
[2] See the analysis based on the 1931 Census given in Appendix II of the *County of London Plan, 1943*, p. 172, and in Appendices 24 and 25, pp. 211-12 of the *Greater London Plan, 1944*. The average size of household according to the Census 1951 sample table is 3·21.
[3] *Greater London Plan, 1944*, para. 282.

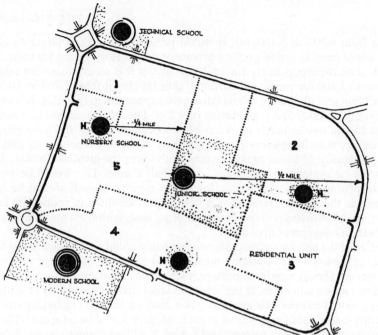

FIG. 38. *Neighbourhood unit.* In this plan the Junior school serves all five residential units, and is not more than half-a-mile walk for any pupil. Higher educational facilities are provided in conjunction with other neighbourhood units.

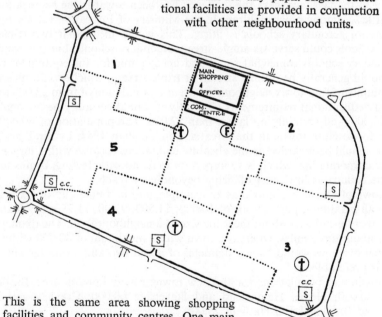

This is the same area showing shopping facilities and community centres. One main shopping centre is provided for the neighbourhood and a small centre for each residential unit.

would be from 6,300 to 8,400, but it would probably be a little larger to allow for children whose parents would prefer a private or preparatory school for their children. If we calculate twenty to thirty for each age group this would mean an addition of from 1,400 to 2,100 for the neighbourhood, thus making it from 7,700 to 10,500. The neighbourhood unit illustrated would correspond approximately to this. It is calculated on a minimum of 8,000 and a maximum of 9,250. The maximum size of a neighbourhood unit should not be much in excess of this because one of the main purposes in limiting its size is to have every part within easy reach of the school so that with an average net density of about twelve houses to the acre the greatest distance from the centre to the circumference would not exceed half a mile. This would be too far for the toddlers from three to five years, for whom nursery schools should be provided increasingly in the future, therefore it is wise to provide these in residential units into which the neighbourhood is divided: five as illustrated, with from about 1,600 to 1,850 in each being a convenient division.

As the size of the neighbourhood depends on educational requirements and facilities, so the size of the town or community must depend partly on this factor; although here other factors are almost equally important, such as the adequacy of the central shopping area, and of various amenities. If the sexes are separated for secondary education each community would require two grammar, two modern and two technical schools, but if co-education is adopted, one school in each category would be adequate. The general rule for older children is the former, and I think it will continue to be so. A few years ago there was a tendency towards increasing co-education, but I think this is less so now. In the U.S.S.R. there was once considerable enthusiasm and widespread adoption of it, but in the last few years the tendency has been towards the segregation of the sexes, at least among older children. In the Ministry of Education rules a maximum size class for secondary schools is thirty. This would mean that two triple-stream primary schools could serve six single-stream secondary schools, but this would make the secondary schools somewhat small and uneconomic for the equipment required. They should generally be double stream or triple stream, which would mean a town or community of four to six neighbourhoods, or a population of from 28,000 to 57,000. To satisfy educational requirements efficiently it should certainly be no smaller than about 28,000, and certainly no larger than 57,000. The population of 60,000 recommended for satellite towns in the Greater London Plan 1944, by Sir Patrick Abercrombie, should be regarded as the absolute maximum, because with a larger satellite town the corporate life, which is so important to democratic feeling, begins to be lost, while the country is in danger of being beyond easy reach.

The town of Ongar is planned as an example, and it is made up of six neighbourhoods with maximum populations of 10,000; 11,500; 9,400; 11,750; 8,600 and 8,200, with an area for industry about the same size as a neighbourhood. The diameter of the towns is about three miles, whereas a town with a maximum of 40,000 with the same residential densities would have a diameter of about two and a quarter miles, which I think is preferable.

The maximum populations for the new towns round London are: Basildon and Harlow 80,000; Hemel Hempstead and Stevenage 60,000; Crawley and Welwyn 50,000; and Bracknell and Hatfield 25,000.

The school is the chief factor in neighbourhood environment, but the need of cultural activities in the neighbourhood should not end with the school period, but end

PLATE LXIV. Small gardens such as shown here and on Plate LXIII call for little maintenance yet provide numerous attractive features—flower beds, pool, lawn. Neatness with minimum of maintenance for maximum of effect is greatly assisted by use of hard materials for paths and borders.

(*a*) Road in Letchworth—the first garden city commenced in 1903. Planned by Sir Raymond Unwin and Barry Parker, it was the first realization of the ideas of Sir Ebenezer Howard. Letchworth was the prototype of the new towns.

PLATE LXV (*a*) *and* (*b*). *Houses in settings of trees and shrubs.*

(*b*) Houses in Welwyn Garden City, the second garden city established in 1920 and planned by Louis de Soissons, R.A.

only with death; and thus there should be a community centre in each neighbourhood to provide cultural and recreational facilities. In a pamphlet on the subject produced by the Ministry of Education[1] it is suggested that the community centre might be part of the same building as the school. In America this is already being done, the building being designed partly as a school for children in the day-time and partly as a community centre for use in the evening. Parts of the building can be used for both purposes, and parts are kept separate generally at either end of the building. Examples of this are the Rhinebeck Central School, New York, and a combined nursery school and neighbourhood centre at Berea, Ohio.[2] The community centre would, of course, provide facilities for adult education and games, and would include a hall for meetings, the local dramatic club and film society, and there should be an adequate restaurant. In addition one would expect to find in a well-planned neighbourhood a good shopping centre, and two or three churches of various denominations; also I think the area is sufficiently large to support a cinema. What is fundamental is that the neighbourhood should be a precinct enclosed by main roads, with only minor roads in the actual area on which no through traffic is admitted. In the neighbourhood plan illustrated (Figs. 38 and 39) the five residential units are grouped around the primary school which is in the centre, surrounded by open space. A little to the east is the community centre, and there forming a square with a quadrangle is the shopping centre, with one outer side facing the main road.

Planned on the basis of a population of 8,000, with allowance for expansion to 9,250 the accommodation of this neighbourhood is divided as follows:

	Persons	Persons per family	Families
8 per cent in 6-story flats	640	3	213
12 per cent in 3-story flats	960	3·4	266
75 per cent in 2-story houses	6,000	3·4	1,668
5 per cent in bungalows	400	2	200
100 per cent	8,000		2,347

The bungalows for an average of two persons would be mainly for old people. These bungalows would not be segregated, but mixed with the two-story houses, as this is, generally although not always, preferred by old people.

The densities are as follows:

	Families to the acre	Acres
213 families in 6-story flats	18	12
266 families in 3-story flats	15	18
1,668 families in 2-story houses	10	167
200 families in bungalows	20	10

[1] Community Centres, 1945.
[2] See Architectural Forum, June 1954.

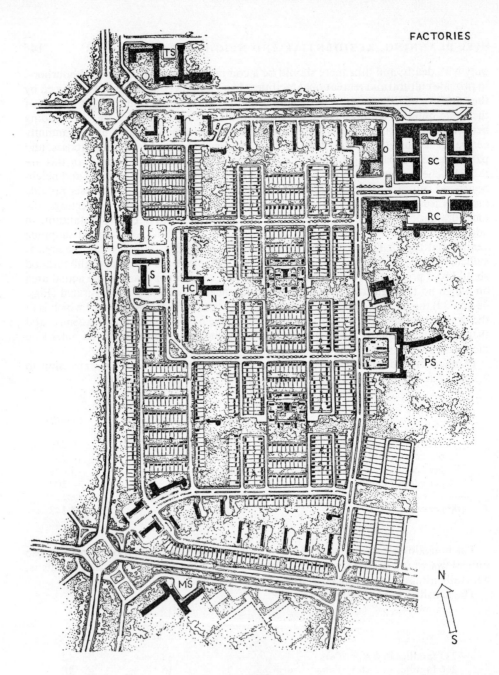

KEY

T.C. = Technical School.	M.S. = Modern School.	R.C. = Recreation Centre.
S. = Shops.	P.S. = Primary School.	Cottage groups for old
H.C.= Health Centre.	O. = Offices.	people are provided.
N. = Nursery School.	S.C. = Shopping Centre.	

FIG. 39. A development of the plans shown in Fig. 38 showing western parts of the area. The five residential units are grouped around the primary school. To the east is the community centre and north is the shopping centre with one side facing the main road.

	Acres	Persons per acre
2,347 approx. 8,000 persons net residential density families	207	38·7
Ten houses to the acre in the third item is an average.		
They would vary from 12 to 6 to the acre.		
Plus 20 per cent for schools, shops, civic buildings, etc.	41·4	
	248·4	32·2
Plus open space, 4 acres per 1,000	32·4	
	280·8	28·4

The allowance of only four acres of open space per 1,000 population is based on the assumption that in the town or community of which this neighbourhood forms a part there would be on one side the town centre with central garden or other open space, and on the other side the green belt of the town.

Allowance for increase in number of persons per family is:

	Persons per family	Persons
6-story flats	3·0 to 3·4	85·2
3-story flats	3·4 to 4	159·6
2-story house	3·4 to 4	1,000·8
		1,245·6

8,000 plus 1,245 equals 9,245 persons per neighbourhood, which should be regarded as the maximum.

10

CHAPTER XXII

A GARDEN

MOST families like a garden. I am thinking of the family as including one or more children, but many childless couples, and many older couples whose children have married and left them, also like a garden. It is a fairly universal wish among most of the races of mankind, although the large flat-dwelling population of Europe has not generally had opportunities to gratify this wish. It is increasingly recognised that if we are to give families the living conditions they desire we must plan so as to give more families a house with a garden. This can be accomplished only by an ambitious policy of planned dispersal from the congested centres where families either endure slum conditions or are crowded together in tall blocks of flats. This policy is being partially instrumented by the building of new towns in the country, like Stevenage, Crawley, Harlow, Hemel Hempstead, Basildon and Bracknall round London, the establishment of which follows the principles that determined the planning of the garden cities of Letchworth and Welwyn.

Among the majority who like a garden, interest in it varies considerably from the man or woman whose main hobby is gardening to those who just want a large, pleasant and perhaps colourful open-air room in which to sit in the summer, and a space for their children to play, but who have not the inclination to do much work there. Between these extremes there are numerous degrees. A very large number like a pleasant garden, they like flowers and trees and shrubs, and they desire to keep the garden neat and are prepared to do a little gardening, but it is not their main leisure occupation. Father is willing to devote Sunday mornings, an occasional Saturday afternoon and an occasional evening in the summer to gardening, while mother, taking much delight in flowers, can do some planting and help a little to weed and keep the garden tidy. It is to this couple, who, I believe, represent the majority, that this chapter is mainly addressed, not to the man and woman whose hobby is gardening and who will read books and journals on the subject and who will have ideas of their own. I will imagine that the family is looking for a new house on new land, such as would occur in a new town.

No houses planned collectively or in groups (as distinct from a house individually planned when all kinds of variation are possible) should be built with the garden front facing north, but should this bad orientation, which occurred so frequently in the past, be repeated, then it is the house to avoid unless other advantages are considerable. In discussing orientation in the chapter on Siting and Sunlight it was pointed out that rooms would get some sunlight during the summer months if they faced from north-east to north-west, but this would be reduced to approximately east to west for winter sunlight. It was pointed out that bedrooms should get the morning sun and face roughly east or south-east, while as the living room is used during the later half of the day it would be most desirable if this faced south-west or west. But if a living room faced from south-east to west it would get a fair measure of the day's sunlight. The desirable orientations can be completely achieved only in detached houses, as indicated in some

(a) The Orchard, Welwyn Garden City.

PLATE LXVI (a) and (b). *Houses in settings of trees and shrubs.*

(b) Cottages, Bursland, Letchworth.

(*a*) Eighteenth-century house in Mount Sorrel.

(*b*) Group of cottages at Buckminster.

PLATE LXVII (*a*) *and* (*b*).

(*a*) Houses at Harefield, Southampton, built by the 'Reema' system of concrete construction. Gable ends link up better with neighbouring blocks than hipped ends. *Architect of 'Reema' Houses, W. F. Smith, A.R.I.B.A.*

PLATE LXVIII (*a*) *and* (*b*). *Housing estates.*

(*b*) Block of two houses (three bedroom and two bedroom types) at Hemel Hempstead. The wall connecting with the neighbouring house gives a unity to the group. *Architect: H. Kellett Ablett, F.R.I.B.A.*

(*a*) Housing at Crawley. View of the corner of The Link and Buckman's Road, West Green. This is part of the site for which a Housing Medal was awarded in 1951. *Architect: A. G. Sheppard Fidler, F.R.I.B.A.*

PLATE LXIX (*a*) *and* (*b*). *Housing estates.*

(*b*) Three-story blocks of flats at Harlow awarded Housing Medal in 1954. *Architect: Frederick Gibberd, C.B.E., F.R.I.B.A. (Executive Architect: V. Hamnett, A.R.I.B.A.)*

suggested standard plans given in Chapter XIV. With the semi-detached house it is more difficult, but it is fairly easy to arrange two bedrooms and the living room facing south, as the plans of the Howard and Coventry houses demonstrate.

It is most desirable if the living room faces on to the garden and has direct access to it by means of french windows, or better, by means of sliding glass walls. Thus the garden front is best facing between south-east and west.

Small houses with gardens should generally be built at densities between ten and fourteen to the acre, twelve to the acre being a fairly good average. In new towns there is no necessity to build higher densities than fourteen to the acre, and there should be controls to prevent it. In congested cities it is proposed in various plans to build terrace houses at higher densities, but this is necessitated by congestion and the high cost of land; it does not, however, represent what is socially desirable.

In planning a garden I propose to take three plots as examples—one (A) 28 feet by 105 feet, which represents a density of about thirteen to the acre; another (B) 32 feet by 110 feet, which is about eleven to the acre, and the third (C) 36 feet by 105 feet, which is about ten and a half to the acre. In the calculation of densities 10 per cent is allowed for minor roads. I will assume that the couple has selected a house built on new land, and that the garden front faces between south-east and west, with the living room opening to the garden, and that the size of the plot approximates to one of the examples. In addition two examples of gardens with sloping ground, one down and one up from the house, of approximately the same size are considered.

Being new land it will probably be uneven and covered with weeds and grass. Having dug over the whole area the next stage will depend on the plan of the garden it is proposed to adopt. The more thought that is given to the plan at the outset the easier probably will be the work later on. If the ground is fairly flat it is simple to have the garden all on one level, but a garden with different levels may be desired. It is often pleasant to have the lawn and flower-beds on a slightly lower level than the paving near the house. If the ground slopes either up or down from the house, the garden should be stepped. Effective utilization can be made of sloping ground by various designs of terraces and steps. It is generally unsatisfactory to leave the ground sloping steeply, as it is neither good for growing, as the moisture runs away, nor is it very convenient for use.

Three plans are given for level ground for plots A, B and C in Figs. 40 and 41. In plan A, which is a plot 28 feet by 105 feet, there is a small front garden about 12 feet from the footway to the house. Allowing 23 feet for the depth of the house, this means a garden at the back of 70 feet by 28 feet. In plans B and C a garage separate from the house is included, but this could with advantage be connected with the house by covering the path between them. This connection of garage and house in one unified design has obvious aesthetic advantages. In plan B, where the plot is about 32 feet by 110 feet, the front garden is slightly larger than in A, and the garden at the back is about the same length. In plan C with a plot 36 feet by 105 feet the garden at the back is also about the same length. The garden front in B faces south and in A and C, west. It will be seen that in all the plans a lawn is the principal and central feature. It must be remembered that the garden for the small house is conceived as an open-air room, and provides facilities for sitting in the summer and for young children's play. To have a central lawn is the simplest and most satisfactory way of planning the small garden, and this arrangement allows for infinite variations. In both A and B plans herbaceous

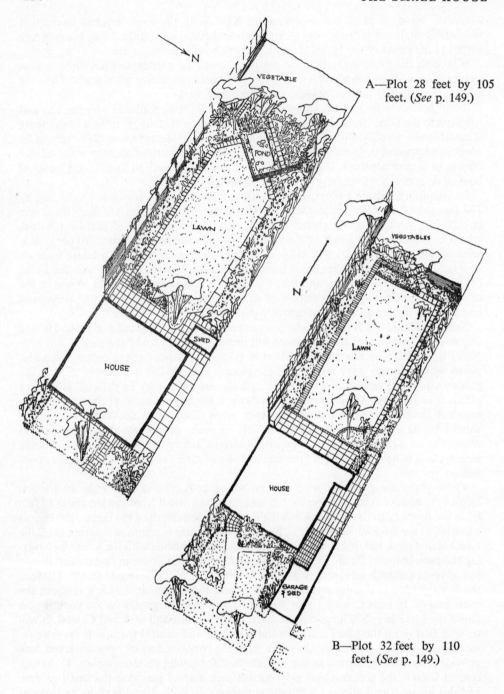

A—Plot 28 feet by 105 feet. (*See* p. 149.)

B—Plot 32 feet by 110 feet. (*See* p. 149.)

FIG. 40. *Garden Plans.*

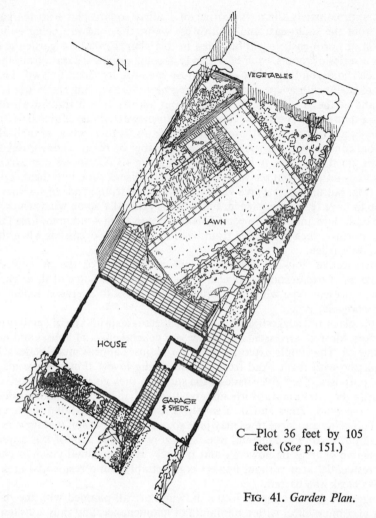

C—Plot 36 feet by 105
feet. (*See* p. 151.)

FIG. 41. *Garden Plan*.

borders are on either side of the lawn, and a space for vegetables is at the end of the
garden. A little more elaborate is plan C which the greater width allows. Plan D in
Fig. 42 shows a further variation for ground that slopes up from the house, while E
is a sectional drawing of a scheme for a garden which slopes down from the house.
In two of the plans a small water-lily pond is at the end of the lawn, which is always
an additional attraction in a small garden, but it might be unwise to include it when
there are very young children.

A detached house, like the standard type W suggested in Chapter XIV, is best set
in a more square shaped garden than those so far considered. One possible scheme is
given in the perspective sketch in Fig. 43 (F) which occupies a plot about 70 feet by
55 feet which is about ten and a half to the acre. The best orientation for this house is
with the living room walls facing south-east and south-west. In the sketch the house

occupies approximately the north corner of a fairly square plot with the garden extending from the south-east and south-west walls, the roadway being either to the north-west or north-east. It will be noted in this plan (F) that the garden is designed partly as a series of rooms, each of which is in some degree separate from the others. Three such rooms, on three sides of the house each has its separate lawn. This can be done more easily with a squarish than a long plot. Surrounding the house is a paved terrace, and at the part where the living room adjoins it is a framework forming a generous extension of the living room. This framework could either be partially or wholly covered in, or used partly for climbing plants. If this section of the walls of the living room consists of glass screens they could either be removed or moved along the framework on the terrace. A smaller sketch in Fig 43 (G) shows one arrangement. In this frames project from the walls and the wall screens slide into them. There is no top covering, but the screens give valuable protection from wind. In summer families often like to have tea in the garden, but there is generally some wind which is apt to blow the tablecloth and light objects. This protection from wind minimizes this inconvenience. Further, such protection from wind increases the occasions when the family can sit in the garden.

The perspective drawing Fig. 44 of different houses of the W type, showing various stages of expansion, are placed in similar gardens. Some of these gardens are of a more informal type which the square plot allows to a greater extent than the narrow rectangular type.

In all the plans and suggestions for gardens there is a sprinkling of small ornamental or fruit trees, for trees are essential if a pleasant general effect of houses and gardens is to be achieved. The simple exteriors of modern houses appear much better when seen in conjunction with them. And trees, besides being lovely things, serve many other desirable purposes. They give shade in the summer, they give additional privacy, they attract birds, they are sound absorbents, and, like aeolian harps, they are musical instruments for the wind. Trees and shrubs help considerably in wedding the house to the garden. Too many and large trees may take so much from the soil that flowers may not grow well, but smaller ornamental trees should not do this. And if it is a question of the alternative of trees or flowers—and it rarely is—I personally would choose the trees. A residential area without flowers is regrettable, but a residential area without trees looks bleak and barren.

The suggested gardens shown in the drawings are all planned with the purpose of getting a maximum effect with a minimum of maintenance, and thus considerable use is made of hard materials. The provision of these hard materials may mean more work at the beginning, but the maintenance is very much less than if they were not used. Consider, for example, the edges of grass and flower borders. These would require constant attention to keep them neat and tidy, but if an edging of hard material, like coloured concrete or brick, is used, level with the grass, then it remains neat with much less attention. Also paths keep neat if they are of hard material, and some very attractive paths with interesting patterns can be made in this way. Some suggestions are given in the sketches illustrated (Fig. 45). One is a pattern of bricks, two are of coloured concrete combined with strips of bricks, while two others consist of concrete edging enclosing coloured tiles in one and wood blocks in the other. Further types will probably suggest themselves. Stone is a very attractive material for a garden path, but is a little more expensive than the types shown. Sandstone, like hard York or some of the

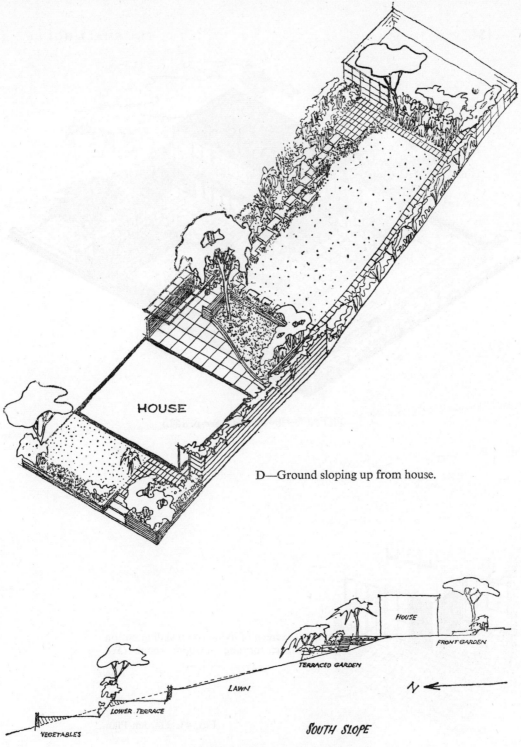

HOUSE

D—Ground sloping up from house.

HOUSE

FRONT GARDEN

TERRACED GARDEN

LAWN

LOWER TERRACE

VEGETABLES

SOUTH SLOPE

E—Ground sloping down from house.

Fig. 42. Garden Plan.

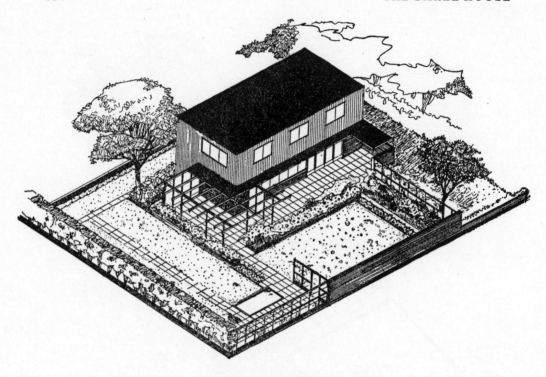

F—Plot 50 feet by 70 feet. (*See* p. 152.)

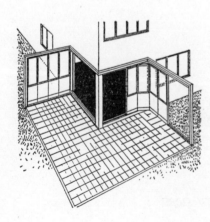

G—Screen of living-room sliding out on terrace, forming out-door room. (*See* p. 152.)

FIG. 43. Garden Plan.

millstone grits like Darley Dale, or some of the red varieties, like Woolton or Coreshill, are suitable and weather very beautifully. A path with grass adjoining should be of the same level as this makes the cutting of the grass edges easier than it would otherwise be.

For steps, stone or concrete are the best materials. The slabs for the paths or steps should not be less than 2 inches thick, otherwise they are liable to crack. It would be better if they could be a little thicker. In the garden that slopes up from the house stone steps are shown on the left. Some sketch suggestions are made for steps of an informal character.

It often happens in a small garden that a clothes line is required from the house to a point near the end of the garden, and above the lawn. It is not generally convenient to have the line near the edge of the lawn because the wind may brush the clothes on to the herbaceous border. When the grass is wet, as it often is in autumn, winter and spring, it is not pleasant for the housewife to hang clothes whilst standing on the wet grass. It is thus useful to have slabs of stone let in the grass, on the same level. The effect is quite pleasing and such stepping-stones would be appreciated by the housewife. They should be of concrete or stone and not less than 2 inches thick. A good size is 1 foot 6 inches square, with 9 inches between each slab. Clothes drying on a line in a garden is not generally a beautiful sight. It does not matter if it is kept to one or two mornings a week, say Monday and Friday, but sometimes with so many married women at work washing is seen hanging out on a Saturday and even Sunday. It is not very pleasant when one is sitting in one's garden on a summer Sunday afternoon to see one's neighbours' washing hanging on the line. It would be better if every house had a drying cupboard, although some consider that garments drying in the wind gives them a freshness that no other means does. Devices can be constructed to make drying in the open less unpleasant. One device (shown in the illustration) seen in the garden of a house at Lillehammer in Norway consists of a trellis work about 8 feet high forming a rectangle across which lines are strung and the clothes hang within the enclosure. If painted white with a few low climbing plants it looks very neat.

The division between gardens in this country is generally by means of timber fences. For front gardens privet hedges with a low wall along the footway are sometimes used. I think it may be said as a general rule that timber fences are not very satisfactory, as they do not last in good condition for a long period, and few things look worse than derelict timber fences. The tendency is now to substitute more durable materials. Few things look better than a brick wall surrounding the garden, but if it is high it will shut out sunlight. Also it is thought that an open fence is better for growing flowers as the air and sunlight are from all directions, but for some plants and for growing fruit a south or south-west wall is probably the best. A brick wall is, however, more expensive than a timber fence. I think that concrete and wire fences will be increasingly used, because being more durable they keep in good condition for a longer period than timber fences. Most of the concrete fences so far designed are of the open character very much in imitation of wood fences, but it is hoped that gradually designs more expressive of the material will emerge. Concrete is, after all, reconstructed stone, with tensile strength given by the reinforcement, and the starting-point should be the stone wall rather than the timber fence. If in designing concrete fences an open stone wall given a certain tensile strength can be imagined, then they will develop on more expressive lines.

Some of the most attractive fences can be made with a combination of different materials. For example, a low brick wall surmounted by a concrete framing makes a

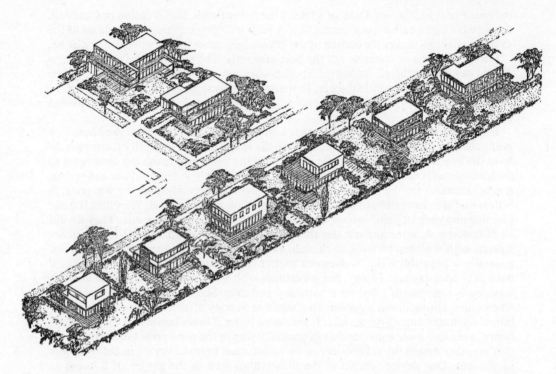

FIG. 44. *Houses of W type*; of various stages of expansion, set in similar gardens. (*See* p. 152.)

good fence, especially if it is desired to have climbing plants. Another good type consists of concrete posts at regular intervals with horizontal wires or wire trellis, or wattle or matting between. It is best to have holes in the concrete posts for securing the wires or other materials. With the introduction of new materials for building other types will suggest themselves. One of these is corrugated asbestos board held together by rods and buried endwise in the ground. The privet hedge, which some people appear to like, has two serious disadvantages. It requires constant cutting to keep it neat, while flowers do not grow well near it. In this latter respect a wall or fence is much better.

The question arises whether it is necessary to have fences or hedges between gardens and whether more informal demarcation, like flowering shrubs at intervals, is not preferable. The answer to the question depends on circumstances. In an ideal community where everybody is a good neighbour and follows the injunction of 'do unto others as you would would they should do unto you' there is no doubt that open gardens are preferable to walled or fenced gardens. There is always the risk, however, that small children might more easily wander and get lost. To obviate this yet preserve the same open effect short concrete posts with wire netting could divide herbaceous borders of adjoining gardens. This would hardly be seen during the summer and would prevent young children and dogs straying. In many areas there are no walls or fences in front gardens, noteworthy examples being found at Welwyn Garden City. Front gardens open to the footway without dividing fences, with shrubs and flower-beds, look far

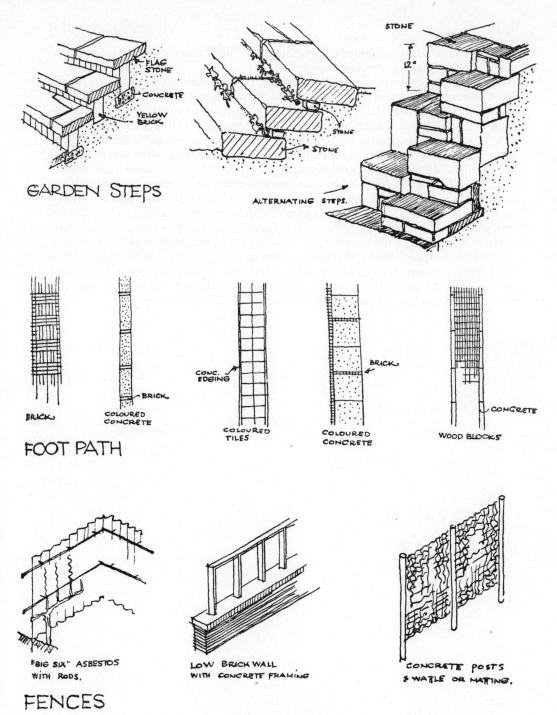

GARDEN STEPS

FLAG
STONE
CONCRETE
YELLOW
BRICK

STONE
12"
STONE
STONE
ALTERNATING STEPS.

FOOT PATH

BRICK
COLOURED
CONCRETE
BRICK
CONC.
EDGING
COLOURED
TILES
BRICK
COLOURED
CONCRETE
CONCRETE
WOOD BLOCKS

FENCES

"BIG SIX" ASBESTOS
WITH RODS.
LOW BRICK WALL
WITH CONCRETE FRAMING
CONCRETE POSTS
& WATTLE OR MATTING.

FIG. 45. (*See* p.152.)

better than the formally divided compartments. In Sir Charles Reilly's 'village green' plan, the front gardens are the village green.

Open front gardens like those at Welwyn will, I think, be more adopted in the future, but whether the fences and hedges between back gardens will be eliminated in the same way is extremely doubtful. Privacy is dear, and rightly so; the small garden is an open-air room, and most families like the added seclusion that a wall or fence gives. There is no doubt that the general effect looking across gardens, would be better without fences, as in the open treatment shown in the perspective drawing of the W type houses, but the deciding factor in any development of this kind must be the wishes of individual families. In an estate of houses designed mainly for owner-occupiers fences need not be provided until the wishes of the owners are ascertained, and alternative types could be presented, or an allowance of cost to enable the owner to provide his own fence. If neighbours get on very well together it will often be found that they will agree to dispense with a dividing fence. This has frequently been done in the case of the dividing hedge or fence between front gardens. But generally, I think, families will want fences between back gardens, and the essential is that they should be of good durable material that will remain sound for as long as the life of the house, and will weather attractively and be a pleasing background for flowers and shrubs.

CHAPTER XXIII

THE APPEARANCE OF THE HOUSE

EVERYBODY would like to live in a beautiful house. Beauty is a matter of opinion, it is a value we ourselves place on objects, as we can very easily discover by the differences of opinion on what constitutes a beautiful house. Some people think they live in one, while others do not agree with them. We all know the little suburban villas built in thousands in the nineteen-thirties with sham half-timber work, bay windows, sharply pitched roofs, often with small front gable ends with little ornate bits here and there and pretty porches and front doors with coloured lights—many people think such houses are lovely, and not quite so many perhaps think they are hideous. Many think they are infinitely preferable to the plain and simple houses built by local councils, while others prefer the council houses. Wide differences of opinion exist among architects. Some like the perpetuation of the English mediaeval types and see little beauty in plain flat-roofed houses, while there are architects who prefer the latter. What then shall be the guide? The guide can only be certain aesthetic principles, the application of which must largely be left to the individual. There may not, it is true, be agreement about the validity of these principles, but room for disagreement must be less the more they are rooted in human instincts and impulses.

The instinctive desire for order as opposed to chaos and disorder can hardly be a matter of dispute, for it is connected with self-preservation, the desire for security and the powerful emotion of fear. Order is associated with security, and disorder with insecurity. Thus an important instinctive basis of aesthetic delight is a desire for security and order. But the question arises, what constitutes this sense of order? In architectural criticism the terms synthesis, integration and organic unity are often used, and these terms give some indication of the nature of order in architecture.

The essence of order or unity is that the parts shall by their character demonstrate their connection with other parts and with the whole. If the whole already exists and a new part is introduced then the first aesthetic necessity is to make that part harmonize with the other existing parts constituting the whole. A residential neighbourhood of a new town is built somewhere in England. The existing whole for that new neighbourhood is what exists to the eye from the neighbourhood area, and the new houses are so many new parts which must be aesthetically related to the landscape and to each other. That is the first consideration.

It may appear that this is rather a circuitous way of arriving at the simple principle that houses should harmonize with their landscape setting, but in arriving at it in this way some of the elements of that harmony are made clear. Before discussing further these elements there is one apparent difficulty that must be overcome. Contrast is also an artistic principle, and is the opposite of harmony. But the difficulty is in terms rather than in meanings. Harmony as defined by the *Oxford Dictionary* is the 'combination or adaptation of parts, elements, or related things, so as to form a consistent and orderly whole'. Unity is defined as one-ness. Contrast is an accentuation of differences. Although contrast is a recognized artistic principle, it operates on a smaller and more

159

limited scale than harmony or unity. If the prevailing effect of a general view or object were several strong contrasts, it is very doubtful whether it would be aesthetically pleasing. Contrasts can only exist satisfactorily within a general harmony or unity, they help to provide that variety in unity which is the old Greek definition of beauty. There must, for example, be something in the character of contrasting parts to show their relation to each other. Orange and blue are contrasting colours and these can be the dominating colours in a picture. The colour values are enhanced and intensified by the contrast, yet there must be some formal and quantitive relation between the colours if the general effect is to be pleasing. Again, the general lines of a picture may be horizontal, but with a few contrasting verticals, which, however, must be carefully related so as to achieve a harmony of the whole.

If a neighbourhood of a thousand houses is built in the country, and a general harmony is to be achieved, the character of that landscape must be considered. In most parts of England where a new town is likely to be built—one can think for example of the sites of any of the new towns round London—the country consists of low hills and valleys varying to flatness. The prevailing colour of fields and trees is given—bright emerald and yellow in spring, becoming deeper in summer, and mingling with red and gold in the autumn. Here, then, is the setting with which the houses must harmonize.

First there is the form. The lines of the country are mainly horizontal, with but slight deviations, and the landscape when comprehended as it can only be from a distance, is one of broad simple masses. Thus we have three elements : horizontality, breadth and simplicity. These then should form the guide in designing the exteriors of our houses.

In the more general effect where varying distances play a part, the long horizontal masses of the landscape suggest long low masses in building as being most harmonious. A continuous row of cottages with long horizontal roof lines and eaves generally appears to be fairly harmonious with the country, while a number of detached or semi-detached houses where there are no long horizontal masses, but breaks at short intervals, is much less harmonious. The long low effect belongs more to cottages which are built with what is termed a 'narrow span' plan which gives a longer frontage than those built with a 'wide span' plan, where the frontage is much narrower, with greater depth from back to front. When these are built as semi-detached houses and the roof is steeply pitched with hipped ends and short ridge, it is like a pyramid on a square box. The advantage of the 'narrow span' roof, and the disadvantages of the 'wide span' roof are stressed in a book on *Housing in the Peak District*, published by the Council for the Preservation of Rural England, in 1934. It is pointed out that the former has been used almost invariably by the old builders of the Peak district, and that 'this type of plan is likely to result in a house of pleasant proportions'.

With the 'narrow span' a block of four houses, where a fairly long horizontal line can be obtained is better than a block of two or one, where the line is necessarily shorter. That makes it the more necessary that the blocks of two or one must be satisfactorily related, so that there can be some continuity of the horizontal lines. This does not mean that the line of one block should be continued in the next as if they were all one long block with clefts at intervals, but that the drop or break should not be so much as to destroy the continuity. Indeed that break, if well calculated, can be an advantage as providing an accent. Examples of such continuity with breaks as accents are provided in houses at Harefield, Southampton (Plate LXVIII (*a*)), and in the housing at Harlow by Mr. Frederick Gibberd, illustrated (Plate LXIX (*b*)). In these houses (*a*) House at 9 Heath Avenue, Mansfield. *Architect: J. Mein, A.R.I.B.A.*

(*b*) 'Grey Court', house built of rubble stone near Wetherby. *Architect: J. Stanley Wright.*

PLATE LXX (*a*), (*b*) *and* (*c*). The architects were awarded housing medals for these three houses in 1954.

(*c*) 'Green Acres', Troutbeck. *Architect: John C. Gill, A.R.I.B.A.*

(*a*) Exterior of the house at night with views of the interior.

PLATE LXXI (*a*) *and* (*b*). The Heal House, Hayes, Kent, completed in 1955, designed by the architect, *D. R. Hickman, A.R.I.B.A.*, for his own occupation. This house has been planned so that additions can be conveniently made.

(*b*) View of hall and stairs with glimpse of kitchen.

PLATE LXXII. *L.C.C. housing*, Alton estate, Roehampton. Interesting staggered treatment of terrace houses, with very low pitched roofs, $8\frac{1}{2}°$ on one side and $16°$ on the other. The roofs are constructed of a layer of mineral-surfaced bituminous felt 3-in. thick, covering 1-in. cement and sand screed on 2-in. wood-wool, on pre-stressed concrete purlins.

(a) The traditional and the new in domestic architecture at Virginia Water. The house on the left was designed by Amyas Connell, Basil Ward and Colin Lucas, A.F.F.R.I.B.A., in 1938. Note: The houses are brought slightly closer together than in actual view.

(b) House at Frognal Way, Hampstead.

PLATE LXXIII (a) and (b). Modern design in the thirties. Architects: Amyas Connell, Basil Ward and Colin Lucas, A.F.F.R.I.B.A.

it will be seen that the 'narrow span' plan gives a sufficiently long frontage for horizontal massing, an effect that accords with the line of the distant landscape. Another way in which this horizontal cohesion can be obtained is by connecting the blocks by walls, or garage buildings as is done in the housing at Hemel Hempstead by Mr. H. Kellett Ablett, illustrated (Plate LXVIII (b)).

A low horizontal effect according well with the landscape and agreeable in itself should have the right degree of horizontality and should have a certain variety to give interest. If I have suggested that the block of one or two houses might be too short, unless very well designed to achieve the desired effect, a block of four or more may be too long unless it has notes of varied interest. In the illustration of four cottages at Letchworth (Plate LXVI (b)) where there is an unbroken eaves line and hipped ends, it is a question whether the line is not just a little too long, and whether they would have been a little more interesting with a small gable on the front here and there. The hipped ends seem to isolate rather than to connect the blocks. Contrast the cottages at Welwyn, illustrated (Plate LXVI (a)). Here there is a similar low horizontality, but the blocks are generally not quite so long, consisting of two or three houses, and in one case front gables break the horizontality, while the gable ends seem to connect the blocks better.

With the flat-roofed houses shown in the illustrations (Plate LXXIII (a) and (b)) the same principles apply. For the most part they are selected as examples of just the right proportion, but it is possible that one or two may be a little short and they would be improved with added length, while others may appear a little too long without a break. It is all a matter of artistic calculation which the architect is not always able to exercise as fully as he may wish because of practical exigencies, but generally he can do so sufficiently to achieve a considerable degree of harmony with the setting.

As previously suggested, a sharply pitched roof with long diagonals of between 40 and 60 degrees ascending skyward is apt to destroy harmony with the landscape. It is better to have a low-pitched roof not more than 25 degrees and a long ridge so that the diagonals are not prominent. And gable ends are generally better than hipped ends for, in addition to connecting with adjoining blocks better, the gabled ends reduce the accent on the diagonals. It is best of all to have a very low pitched or flat roof. The house at Mansfield shown in the illustration (Plate LXX (a)) is a good example of the former with gable ends. This harmonizes well with the horizontal lines of the landscape. Vertical lines, as in a church tower, are in decided contrast, but the steep slope of the pitched roof is neither harmony nor contrast. I know that a number of old houses and cottages in the country districts, in the Cotswold villages, for example, are admired for their beauty and harmony with their surroundings. I would suggest that the harmony is created by the local materials used in building, especially the local stone, and by the touch of time, and not by the pitched roofs. The best roofs are those which are low and near the horizontal or very steep and near the vertical, but never those approximating to 45°.

Simplicity and broad masses in houses rather than elaboration and ornament seem to secure harmony with landscape setting. These qualities conduce to a sense of peace and repose which one likes to associate with home, but they are also agreeable from the more exclusively aesthetic aspect. This is particularly so in the more intimate relation of the house with natural surroundings, especially with trees and shrubs and plants. Can you remember glimpses of a house with broad plain walls behind a group of silver birches or other trees with similar delicate foliage? The effect is similar with most trees in spring, when the buds are changing to full foliage. If you can remember you will probably have noticed how beautifully patterned the trees are against the plain walls, and in the ensemble it is the trees that provide the lovely ornamental effect. If the house has a fussy and ornate exterior nothing like the same beauty is achieved. The Airey house, one of the new houses being adopted by some local authorities, has a very simple exterior. It has a flat roof with concrete walls designed with weather-boarding effect, which give a horizontal pattern. I remember seeing some of these simple box-like houses mingled with a group of trees, and I remember thinking how much more pleasing they looked than large numbers of comparatively ornate and fussy pre-war suburban houses.

Windows well placed on a plain wall, in which there is a satisfactory relation of void to solid conduces to a sense of order. Simplicity helps to reveal that order. Ornament may do the same if it grows out of the form and emphasizes it, but if it is just ornament for ornament's sake, and just stuck on without relation to the basic form, then it obscures and often destroys any effect of order. If windows have some relation in size, as would be the case if they are all multiples of a common unit, and the spaces between them have some relation to each other, if the lines of one window are continued in the next, all this conduces to an agreeable sense of order.

If the form of the house should harmonize with its setting, it is equally important that a similar degree of colour harmony should be achieved. Any default in colour harmony is even more apparent than the formal harmony, because surrounding colour is generally more insistent than surrounding form. In the past, up to the early nineteenth century, where local stone was available it was customarily used in the houses of the villages or small towns, and a very pleasing general harmony was achieved. This harmony is all the more complete when local stone slates are used, as in the old houses in the Peak district and in the Cotswolds. Generally, however, where blue or grey slates have been used, the roofs harmonize less satisfactorily than the walls. Green slates from Cumberland or Westmorland are much more agreeable. Stone is available mainly in the western and northern districts of Britain; in the south-eastern area, where building stone is comparatively rare, brick is more frequently used. Because of developments in transport and the more economical production and use of other materials like brick and concrete, these have been largely used in place of local stone. Whether they have suceeded in harmonizing with surroundings and with existing old buildings depends largely on the colour of the bricks and the concrete. Often when these are harmonious the effect is spoilt by harsh blue-grey slates or red tiles.

It will be found that soft colours of neutral shades and low saturation are the most agreeable, and that strong positive colours are generally to be avoided. The soft colour of stone, the greyish fawns or greyish yellows of the Bath or York stone groups are examples.

The most suitable bricks, especially if they are used in a district of old stone buildings, should be brownish, or fawn or yellowish grey. Red bricks strike a discordant note. They are less objectionable in urban areas, but even here the colour is too strong. From an aesthetic standpoint it would be better to have some kind of covering, like cement rendering, or stucco or roughcast or limewash, which can all be treated a soft stone colour.

In the case of concrete walls, an agreeable soft colour can be obtained by the use of aggregates and sands of pleasing hue, while pigment can be mixed with the concrete. One particularly pleasing colour is that of the concrete walls of the Airey house which are a pale brown. The slabs of which the walls consist are pre-cast, and this colour is obtained by brushing quartzite and spar into the surface of the slabs while they are wet.

The roofs of most houses which are sufficiently recent not to be wedded to their surroundings by the touch of time, are very unsightly, and when seen in relation to a beautiful landscape constitute to the sensitive percipient a painful experience. In many cases it takes a great deal of weathering for these roofs to be wedded at all pleasingly with their surroundings. In Kent there are a considerable number of houses scattered about the countryside in small groups. Many of these have harsh bluish grey or purple slates which even after a considerable time do not harmonize with their surroundings. In the valley of the Medway there are groups of houses with these roofs and they are discordant splashes of colour in the landscape. There are several cement works on the banks of the Medway between Chatham and Maidstone, and the broad masses of greyish white or cream harmonize far better with the landscape than do these slate roofs.

In Minehead in Somerset many of the houses built in the last thirty years have red tiled roofs. I remember one summer's afternoon descending into Minehead, and I cannot forget, after the glorious country of the hills, the unpleasant shock of the harsh red roofs bespattering the lovely landscape. Here is an aesthetic crime.

The most agreeable colour for the roof is similar to that of the wall, a soft, pale greyish brown or greyish yellow. The best slates are of such hues or the green variety already mentioned, but these are expensive. Green tiles, which are sometimes seen, are better than red and if softened with the mixture of pale brown can be pleasing. Concrete tiles, which are increasingly used, can be one of the solf colours mentioned. Unfortunately, many of them are being manufactured in various shades of red; such is the power of custom and tradition. Whatever colour is used the texture of the slate or tile should not be smooth and polished so as to reflect light, it should on the contrary have a rough texture. The slates which are classified as 'seconds' and 'thirds' are rougher and thicker than the 'first' quality, but are far more pleasing, and also of course, more economical.

Best from the aesthetic standpoint, and from almost every other standpoint too, is the flat roof,[1] although it must be admitted that the pitched roof is still more popular even among architects. If both walls and roof are concrete then they can be the same colour, and if the houses are to be built in a district where there are old stone buildings it would be pleasant if the surface aggregate were of the same local stone. If the flat roof is used as an open-air room, then it can have plants and flowers and shrubs which will connect it with the garden below. Indeed, climbers could be trained in a very pleasing manner to connect the room on the roof with the garden below and thus assist in this merging of house and garden[2] while a water-lily pond could be incorporated in the roof garden.[3] The flat roofed house provides some of the best conditions for

[1] I should again remind the reader of its advantages enumerated by Walter Gropius in *The New Architecture and the Bauhaus* (London, 1936), pp. 23 and 24.

[2] It is important as a matter of detail that creepers should be kept a little away from the wall and trained on a trellis.

[3] Walter Segal when designing the Tretol building at Hendon stipulated that the flat roof should be constantly covered with water as protection.

11

satisfactory harmony with the landscape. The horizontal mass which can be suitably emphasized is undisturbed by diagonals, while the colour of both walls and roof can be approximated to the local stone. I stress the importance of the landscape setting because I hope that although building our new towns and neighbourhoods compactly, we shall yet build them sufficiently openly for the contours of the ground to be felt and glimpses of the wider landscape to be obtained occasionally. That is one reason why the horizontal masses should not be too long and should be sufficiently separated to allow for glimpses of landscape between. This is well seen in the arrangement of the blocks in the housing at Crawley, illustrated (Plate I) whereby they are brought more into relation with the landscape behind.

I have tried to suggest some of the principles which should contribute to making the small house beautiful. Why is it then that the ornate fussy pseudo-picturesque houses with sham half-timber work, mentioned at the beginning of this chapter, which were built in hundreds of thousands in the suburbs of the big cities during the nineteen-thirties were more popular than the house of simple restrained appearance that would result from the aesthetic principles enumerated? Why is it that these fussy, often vulgar-looking houses were preferred? The answer is that the preference was not principally an aesthetic one, the preference was for other reasons. If the people choosing the houses had been capable in their evaluation of appearance of divorcing all other considerations but the aesthetic—that is, harmony with setting, and combination of the parts into a unified whole, then their preferences would have been different, but the majority were incapable of so doing. Pretentiousness, picturesqueness, which often has little relation to formal beauty, old-world character no matter what the surroundings of the house, were some of the prime considerations. Further, the plain simple exterior was so often associated with the council house, while the more ornate fussy house was more often associated with the house built for sale, and these considerations had some effect on the snobbish elements so strong, either consciously or unconsciously, in most people. I do not say this critically or disparagingly. Snobbery is a very natural impulse and is often closely associated with romantic feelings; but I mention it as one reason for the sort of houses that were preferred in the nineteen-thirties.

If our towns and residential neighbourhoods of the future are to be beautiful, it is desirable that in choosing a house people should be mainly influenced by aesthetic reasons rather than for socially pretentious or old-world, romantic reasons. I think but a small minority can be expected to decide for aesthetic reasons only; but if plain walls and long horizontal lines appear in slightly larger individually designed houses, like some of those illustrated, and these begin to appear in increasing numbers, this will have its effect on small house units repeated in large numbers. Such influence was beginning to be noted before the war. It is very much like fashion in dress—a style is first adopted by the few and then the many follow. This demonstrates how very important it is that the individually designed house should be good. It is really the research laboratory where improvements are made and tried out from which the small unit for repetition can benefit much.

Chapter XXIV

COST

A<small>N</small> important question that will occur to the prospective householder in considering the ideas and designs presented in this book is: What will a house built accordingly cost? Shall I, with a very modest income and a family to support, be able to afford such a house? Or a Housing Committee of a local authority may ask: Can such a unit be provided at a reasonable cost, because economy is one of the first matters we have to consider?

As it is the wish of the majority ultimately to own the house they live in (see Appendices II and III) I will deal mainly with the house built for sale. Still, the question of cost is equally vital to the government and local authorities, because they are under an obligation in spending public money to see that the houses are built as economically as possible. Subsidies should be regarded as a temporary expedient, for it is sound economy that all houses pay for themselves. This can only be achieved when costs of houses and wages are so related that people can afford to buy the houses by means of a mortgage in the usual way, or pay a rent based on the cost of the house.

The unit on which I have concentrated in this book is the detached or semi-detached house with a garden, because conclusive evidence demonstrates that it is the type that is most widely acceptable. I think this is generally realized by local authorities and speculative builders, because there is a tendency to build chiefly the two-story semi-detached house.

Let us consider the cost of a house for a family of five according to a fairly good standard of accommodation. The Dudley house for a family of five has a floor area of about 900 square feet minimum, with three bedrooms. One of these bedrooms is 70 square feet, which is too small. In the suggestion made in Chapter IV the ideal number of bedrooms is five, but a reasonable compromise is four, none of which should be less than 100 square feet, while one double bedroom should be 130 square feet. This is a total of about 430 square feet, as against 330 square feet for the Dudley house. This would mean a house of a total area of about 1,100 square feet, part of which could be a garage on the ground floor. But if the house were designed to allow for a slight overhanging of the first floor to make a veranda underneath, it would be possible to get the accommodation in 1,000 square feet. This could also be achieved if one of the bedrooms were on the ground floor, which has certain advantages, one being convenience in case of illness, and another being possible change of function with changes in the family, such as the eldest getting married, and father acquiring a study.

Let us, then, take a house with a floor area of 1,000 square feet, which should represent the minimum for a family of five. At what cost could it be built, and what is the most economical way of building consistent with efficiency and good appearance? It is helpful firstly to consider costs for traditional methods of building and then consider other possibilities.

In Appendix II of the Dudley Report the 1939 cost of a house of 755 square feet is given as £335 and of a house of 825 square feet is given as £400. It is estimated that a house embodying the Dudley recommendations with an area of 900 square feet would cost £467. Of the increase on the house of 825 square feet £22 10s. at 6s. a square foot is due to increase of size and the remainder to improved equipment. If then another 100 square feet is added at 6s. a square foot it would result in a cost of £497 for a house of 1,000 square feet. If another £28 is allowed for some improvements in fittings and equipment it means a house of 1,000 square feet costing £525.

It must be emphasized that these calculations are for a house in which close attention is given to economy of construction, with straight walls, low-pitched roof and none of the bay windows, ornamental gables and picturesque elaborations which were so often an additional expense in the house built by the speculative builder; although he did sometimes build as economically as the local authority when he concentrated on the simple straightforward construction.

In estimating the freehold price of a house to a purchaser four main factors have to be borne in mind. The costs of (1) land, (2) building materials, (3) labour and overheads, (4) builder's profit. It should be mentioned, by the way, that the last item is the least important in assessing any differences in the cost of houses built by a local authority and the speculative builder, because in the former case the majority of the houses are built by contractors to a local authority, in which there is a margin of profit. Further, in houses built for local authorities the overhead expenses are generally more than on houses built by the speculative builder, as there is often a duplication of work. The profit of a contractor to a local authority may be generally less than that expected by the speculative builder, but the difference is far less than is often thought, for the margin of profit expected by the latter is not usually high, generally in the region of 10 per cent. I think it can be said then that the cost to the purchaser of a house of 1,000 square feet in 1939, in which there is the strictest attention to economy consistent with efficiency would be as follows:

Cost of building the house	£525
Prime cost of land—one-tenth of an acre at £800 an acre. (This was not an unusual price on the outskirts of Greater London.)	80
Cost of development of land (including provision of sewers and services like water, gas, electricity, making up carriage ways and footpaths) one-tenth of an acre at £700 an acre	70
Overheads and interest on loan	100
	£775
Builder's profit—10 per cent	78
	£853

By the end of 1956 the cost of materials had increased by about 170 per cent above 1939 prices, and the cost of building labour by about 160 per cent. If half is allowed for materials and half for labour the rise in cost should be about 165 per cent, but the actual building cost is over 200 per cent owing to various unspecified causes, one of which is undoubtedly defective organization in building. At 200 per cent increase the 1956 cost for a 1,000 square foot, three-bedroom house would work out as follows:

Cost of building the house	£1,575
Prime cost of land—one-tenth of an acre at £2,500 an acre	250
Cost of development	210
Overheads and interest on loan	300
	£2,335
Builder's profit—10 per cent	230
	£2,565

This would be a minimum. The majority of semi-detached houses of about 1,000 square feet on the outskirts of London would be a little more, probably nearer £3,000.

In the third report of the Girdwood Committee on the cost of House-building (1952), the cost in October 1951 of an average local authority house of 1,050 square feet is given as £1,690, of which £1,450 is for building cost, £190 for cost of land and site development and £50 for architect's and surveyor's fees. Since 1951 it was the policy of the government to produce houses more economically by reducing the total area, chiefly by reducing the circulating space, that is, the hall and landing, while maintaining the sizes of rooms. The average tender for a three-bedroom house of 1,031 square feet in the third quarter of 1951 was £1,403. A year later, in 1952 the tender for a house of 932 square feet was £1,391, in 1953 the tender for a house of 914 square feet was £1,382, in the third quarter of 1954 the tender for a house of 919 square feet was £1,381 and in 1955 the tender for a house of 914 square feet was £1,432. The cost in the four years was thus effected by reduction of space, while an increase of cost actually occurred, as £1,403 for a house of 1,031 square feet is £1 7s. 2½d. per square foot, £1,381 for a house of 919 square feet is £1 10s. 1d. per square foot[1] and £1,432 for a house of 914 square feet is £1 11s. 4d.! The average final cost for the years 1952 and 1953 was 1·75 per cent higher.[2]

From this it would seem that a house of 1,000 square feet in October 1955 would be approximately £1,567. Some increase took place in the year, so that the figure of £1,575 given in the calculations would not be far out. For larger houses it would be wise to add at the rate of £1 10s. to £1 12s. a square foot.

The approximate cost of £1,575 for a traditional three-bedroom house of 1,000 square feet is for simple traditional construction, with cavity brick walls and pitched timber roof covered with tiles, making a total price of about £2,500. This price is more than the majority can comfortably afford to pay. A deposit of 10 per cent for the majority of young married couples cannot easily be found, while the repayment of £2,250 with interest of 6 per cent over a period of twenty years is a large slice of incomes from £500 to £1,000, which is the income range of a very large number of clerical, professional and more highly skilled industrial workers between the ages of 23 and 35, which is the period when the majority contemplate setting up home, buying a house and having a family. At 6 per cent the repayment of £2,250 over twenty years is £197

[1] See Report of the *Ministry of Housing and Local Government* for the period 1950-51 to 1954 (London, 1955), pp. 13 and 132, and for 1955 (London, 1956) p. 111.
[2] Final cost figures for 1954 and 1955 were not available at the time of writing.

a year, twenty-five years it is £177 and over thirty years it is £164. The man of thirty with a wife and one child and a desire for three children receiving £750 a year would naturally hesitate to pay £177 a year in house purchase, yet the majority desire to own the house in which they live. It is an important social service to endeavour to reduce the cost of house building so as to bring houses within the means of the majority. Is it possible, then, to effect a reduction in the cost so as to put house purchase within the reach of the majority?

There is little prospect that either the costs of materials or the labour will decrease in the future, indeed all the indications are that such costs will increase. Yet if house building were merely the sum of these two costs plus cost of land, site development and 10 per cent for the builder's profit, houses would cost less today.[1] There is a margin due partly to defective organization not satisfactorily accounted for. It might be suggested, therefore, that some reduction in costs might be effected by (1) the more widespread adoption of methods of construction which allow for a great degree of standardization, mass-production, pre-assembly in the factory and dry assembly on the site, and (2) by improved organization.

For the house, the more work that can be done in the factory, and correspondingly the less work that is done on the site, the more this method of manufacture with its vast economical possibilities can be employed. The possibilities have already been discussed in Chapter III. All that needs to be said here in emphasis is that if people want good houses to be provided economically so that they can realize their wish and buy rather than rent a house, then one way is to support with encouragement experiments and methods of building that are designed to provide houses more rapidly and economically, and not be retarded by conservative adherence to traditional methods in which there cannot exist the same promise of economical provision of improved accommodation.

The other principal way in which economy in building can be effected is by improved organization of the building trade which should increase the output per man. It is instructive to compare wages and building costs here with those in the United States of America. The Government mission that went to the United States in 1944 to study and report on building methods gave some illuminating facts about relative building costs and wages in the two countries. If the British figure for each item was standardized at 100 the relative cost of building in the United States was 75-175, the hourly rate of wages for craftsmen was 350-80, for labourers 215-45 and the cost of materials was 110-60. It will be seen then that the cost of building is little more than in this country, whereas the wages of craftsmen are three and a half times as much. The relative position has not changed much since then.

No very clear reason was given in the report for these differences, and I feel that they should be regarded with caution, especially as they are accompanied with somewhat vague comments. There is room for a more thorough investigation of the matter. One or two comments made by the mission are, however, of some significance. It was stated (para. 67) 'that the average output per man-hour is greater in the United States than in Great Britain'. This 'cannot be wholly accounted for in the speed at which the individual operative works, or by the assumption that he is a better workman than the British operative. The reasons are more fundamental and can be traced to the different tempo existing in—and, indeed, expected of—the whole industry, and made possible

[1] See articles in *The Builder*.

by improved organizations.' The mission was 'impressed with the speed which is notice-able at all stages of an American building job, and with the steady "pacing" of the work from its inception to its final completion.' Reference is made to the co-operation between the American operative and the designers and organizers who constantly strive after greater economy and efficiency. The operative, it is pointed out, makes full use of the better organization and tools provided. There also appears to be a greater degree of specialization among craftsmen than in Britain, while there seems to be more stimu-lation of the craftsman's interest in his work.

These various factors can all be regarded as organization. After the dislocation of war it took some time to recover the efficiency of pre-war organization in the building trade, but even on the basis of pre-war standards there would appear to be considerable room for improvement on some of the lines indicated in the mission's report. Factory work permits far more thorough organization than site work. One reason is that the former can proceed throughout the year uninterrupted by adverse weather conditions, and again it will be seen that an increase of factory work and a corresponding decrease of site work would be a major contribution to economy. With dry assembly methods and early roofing it would be possible to continue the factory efficiency on the site to a far greater degree than has been possible in the past.

An interesting example of organization designed to secure rapid and economical building of houses is provided by the planned sequence of operations in the Smith system of house construction to which reference is made in Chapter III. This is effected by the organization of teams. In the erection of the shell of the house there are the two principal teams, the bricklayers and carpenters. Following the construction of the concrete rafts, the gantry of the first pair is erected. Then the team of bricklayers erects the wall to the first floor, while the gantry for the second pair is being erected. Each stage takes six hours. Six of the stages may be indicated as follows:

1. Bricklayers erect first floor level of first pair and then move to second pair.
2. Carpenters lay first floor framing of first pair and bricklayers erect to first floor level of second pair and then move back to first pair.
3. Bricklayers erect walls to eaves level of first pair and then move to second pair. Carpenters lay first floor framing of second pair.
4. Carpenters fix roof framing to first pair and middle of gantry is removed, while bricklayers erect walls to eaves level of second pair.
5. Carpenters fix roof framing to second pair and bricklayers erect wall to first floor level of third pair and move on to the fourth pair.
6. Carpenters lay first floor framing of third pair while bricklayers erect wall to first floor level of fourth pair and then move back to third pair to erect wall up to eaves level and so on.

The cycle of operations for four pairs of houses is shown in the diagram illustrated opposite.

When the continuity is maintained the shell of one pair of houses from the concrete raft to the roof joists is completed and ready for tiling in twenty-four hours; while working on several houses in the sequence indicated the shells of four pairs of houses ready for tiling are completed in fifty-four hours, an average of thirteen and a half hours each. But the average is actually less because by the end of the fifty-four hours the bricklayers have erected the wall to the first floor level of the fifth pair which thus makes an average of twelve and twelve-seventeenths hours each.

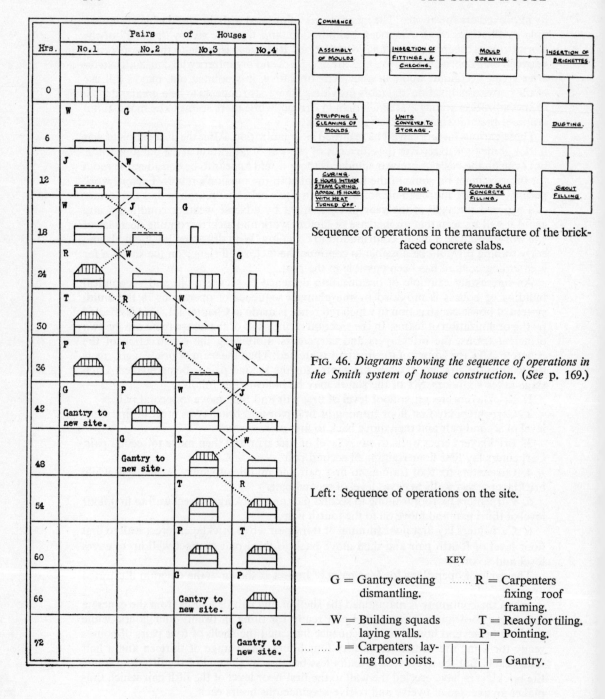

Sequence of operations in the manufacture of the brick-faced concrete slabs.

FIG. 46. *Diagrams showing the sequence of operations in the Smith system of house construction.* (*See* p. 169.)

Left: Sequence of operations on the site.

KEY

G = Gantry erecting dismantling.

W = Building squads laying walls.

J = Carpenters laying floor joists.

R = Carpenters fixing roof framing.

T = Ready for tiling.

P = Pointing.

‖‖‖ = Gantry.

For the best results to be obtained there must be a constant flow of units from the factory to the site, and it is therefore of advantage for the factory to be fairly close to the site. Also for this system to operate with the greatest economy and efficiency not less than fifty houses should be erected in one area. Say, for example, 500 houses are to be erected on a site. A factory of temporary character can be erected in the neighbourhood, plant and equipment can be set up, and immediately the manufacture of the units commences these can be transported to the site in an even flow. Thus it is largely a question of correct planning of successive operations from the assembly of the moulds for the manufacture of the brick faced concrete wall slabs to the completion of the shell.

An example where, by improved tools, considerable time and labour can be saved on the site, which would contribute to added economy in building, is provided by the use of a portable air compressor set developed by the Hymatic Engineering Company of Redditch. This has been developed as the result of experience gained in the manufacture of air compressors for aircraft. The set weighs a little over fifty pounds, it is a self-contained unit not requiring any outside source of power, and can thus be used anywhere. Among its uses are drilling holes, routing mortar for pointing, stone chiselling, spray painting, screw-driving and sheet metal shearing. It would be difficult to estimate the speed of operations performed in relation to hand work, but having used it for some tools I would estimate that it should be possible to make at least six holes in brickwork while one is made by hand, and that ten screws could be driven to one by hand. Fatigue would also be less at the end of the day using the air compressor. If, therefore, operations of this kind can be done many times as quickly, the economy is obvious. It also enables the builder more easily to organize his job into specialized units, as is done in engineering. In this way a man can become expert in the operation of particular tools and can move from house to house on a building site and perform his particular operation in each instance.

APPENDIX I

HOUSE PRODUCTION IN GREAT BRITAIN BETWEEN THE WARS

AFTER the war of 1914-18 it was apparently felt that no start could be made with housing until peace had been signed, so that no actual beginning on a big scale was made until October 1919, about eleven months after the Armistice. In June 1920, about 22,000 were under construction, and for the period 1919-23 the peak was reached in August 1921, when nearly 90,000 houses were being built. This is a miserable record, and it contributed to the social unrest which existed after the First World War. The reasons for this failure were many, but I am convinced that the principal was the absence of a comprehensive programme and of resolute Government control to effect its realization. After 1924 the provision of houses improved immensely. Here is the record between the two wars of the number of houses completed in Great Britain.

Year	England and Wales	Scotland	Great Britain
1919-1922	210,237	20,586	230,823
1923	78,738	8,129	86,867
1924	109,491	6,267	115,758
1925	159,026	10,049	169,075
1926	197,584	15,407	212,991
1927	273,229	22,407	295,636
1928	166,415	20,243	186,658
1929	203,443	19,515	222,958
1930	161,699	12,464	174,163
1931	194,944	12,468	207,412
1932	201,976	17,544	219,520
1933	218,313	23,963	242,276
1934	313,669	24,900	338,569
1935	318,644	25,900	344,544
1936	339,528	23,801	363,329
1937	337,134	21,528	358,662
1938	340,878	26,473	367,351
1939	280,597	25,529	306,126
1919-1939	4,105,545	337,173	4,442,718

Of this total 1,366,623 were provided by local authorities and the remainder by private enterprise.

The record for Scotland is not so good as that for England and Wales as the number is less than one-third of the houses existing in 1911, while that for England and Wales is more than a half. In proportion to population the housing shortage in Scotland was much greater in 1939 than in England. In recent years, however, housing output in Scotland has greatly improved on pre-war totals, the output for 1952-55 much exceeding the highest pre-war figures, being 30,947 in 1952, 39,548 in 1953, 38,653 in 1954 and 33,669 in 1955; whereas in England and Wales the high totals of 1934-38 have not been equalled since the war.

ACCOUNTS OF DISCUSSIONS AMONG MEN AND WOMEN IN
THE FORCES ON TYPES OF HOUSES THAT ARE WANTED, AND
RECORDS OF VOTING ON THESE PREFERENCES

T HE method I have generally adopted is to put the question in the form of asking the
members of the audience to state their preference for one of alternatives, but sometimes for one of three alternatives. After stating the question I give the arguments
for and against each alternative as far as I am able. The question is then open to general
discussion, and at its conclusion the question is put. In the course of an hour's lecture
and discussion I can rarely put more than three questions, or in the course of a two-hours'
lecture and discussion more than six questions. Following are some of the questions,
accounts of discussions and results of voting.

*1. Would you prefer to live in a flat or a house with a garden? In expressing your prefer-
ence would you bear in mind the possibilities of flat development?*

In the preliminary statement of advantages of each type of dwelling, I have concentrated
on the advantages of flat life, as all audiences are far more conscious of the advantages of
the two-story house with garden. I have generally spent twenty minutes enumerating the
advantages both personal and general if people in towns would live in flats. I have (A)
enumerated amenities, which can be provided in a limited space economically. I have
pointed out that tall blocks of flats can be orientated north-south so that windows face
east and west, thus getting a maximum amount of sunlight; that if with high densities of
population like 200 or 300 to the acre the blocks are built high, as much as eight or ten
stories, they would be well separated from each other so that façades are not enveloped
in shadow. Gardens, playgrounds for children, swimming pools, tennis courts and allotments
could be provided in the grounds; a nursery school and clinic could be provided for each
1,000 population; central heating, lifts, a restaurant, crèche and rooms for games could be
provided in each block, and all interior walls be constructed of insulating material. I have
mentioned (B) that as population is at present distributed with large industrial concentra-
tions with high densities, it is impossible to build small houses with gardens in these areas.
If these were provided a large number of people would have to move to other less congested
areas in accordance with a policy of dispersal. Building flats would make the problem
of lateral extension less urgent, as pointed out in paragraph 202 of the Scott Report. I have
mentioned lastly (C) that by agreeing to live in flats they are more likely to live near their
work which would have the economical advantage of small, or no transport costs.

I have put the question as follows: '*Assume that you live in an area that has been
bombed, and the whole district (including remaining houses, etc.) is to be rebuilt. You
can either stay and live in a good modern flat and be near your work, or you can move to
the outskirts and have a house and garden and be away from work.*' (I may say that in a
comprehensive policy of dispersal industry should be dispersed as well as the population,
so the alternative of being away from work would probably not apply. But I mentioned
it as I wanted to stress the advantage of flats.) But in spite of all these arguments in favour

of flats, nearly everybody wanted the house and garden, and were willing to sacrifice quite a lot to get them. Here is the voting on the question among twenty representative groups.

	Number of audience	Vote for flats	Vote for houses
A	102	None	All
B	44 (24 women, 20 men)	3 women, 1 man	Remainder
C	78	2	,,
D	140	None	All
E	37 (21 men, 16 women)	1 woman	Remainder
F	42 (18 men, 24 women)	2 women	,,
G	43 (21 men, 22 women)	None	All
H	450	4	Remainder
I	500	5	,,
J	380	9	,,
K	72 (20 men, 52 women)	1 woman	,,
L	75	3	,,
M	42 women	1	,,
N	58 women	3	,,
O	112 (about half men and half women)	2 women, 1 man	,,
P	56 (34 men, 22 women)	1 woman	,,
Q	70	5	,,
R	26 men	None	,,
S	18 men	4	14
T	62 (32 men, 30 women)	3 women	Remainder

I should mention that generally a few of each audience, but not more than 2 or 3 per cent, did not vote, because they could not decide or because they were shy of being with so few in preference for flats. To make the proportion in favour of houses more accurate the first column should be reduced by 5 per cent.

2. Would you prefer a terrace house, semi-detached or detached house?

Before putting this question to the vote, the economical advantage of terrace houses over the other two types was considered. It was emphasized that it costs less to build this type. You could either have more accommodation for the same money in a terrace house than in a semi-detached house, or pay less for the same accommodation. The extra seclusion that a semi-detached or detached house gave, and the value of having three or four sides of the house free, and having access from the front to the back of the house without going through the house, were advantages which appeared greatly to outweigh economical advantages. Here is the voting:

	Number of audience	Terrace houses	Semi-detached houses
A	37 (21 men, 16 women)	None	All
B	42 (18 men, 24 women)	None	,,
C	43 (21 men, 22 women)	1	Remainder
D	450 (approx. men)	None	All
E	500 ,, ,,	4	Remainder
F	380 ,, ,,	3	,,
G	72 (20 men, 52 women)	None	All
H	75 men	,,	,,
I	58 ,,	,,	,,

The same economical advantages apply to the semi-detached over the detached house.

I found that these considerations influenced many towards a preference for the semi-detached house, and that many did not feel that the increased seclusion (which was not always desirable) was worth the sacrifice of accommodation or the extra cost. The voting was as follows:

	Number of audience	Vote for semi-detached house	Vote for detached house
A	37 (21 men, 16 women)	21	11
B	42 (18 men, 24 women)	12	19
C	43 (21 men, 22 women)	11	31
D	450 (approx. men)	170 (approx.)	280 (approx.)
E	500 „ „	105 „	390 „
G	32 men	9	18
I	58 „	10	46

It will be seen that 795 prefer the completely detached house, whereas 338 do not want the extra seclusion, or do not think it is economically worth it. But from the discussions on the subject very few of the 795 feel very strongly about it. There is a much stronger feeling against terrace house and flats.

3. Would you prefer a two-story house or bungalow?

The advantages of both types were stated. The main advantage of the bungalow is that, like the flat, everything is on one floor, and this and the elimination of stairs mean less work for the housewife. It was pointed out, however, that in the big city, in the rebuilding of congested areas, for example, space is limited, and also in the case of small towns, lands is likely to be limited. It would thus mean that to build bungalows where space is limited might mean that the garden area would be reduced. If, for example, the principle of twelve houses to the acre is adopted, then if bungalows are built it would mean that there would be less garden per house than if the two-story houses were built. Also, if it is desired to add an extra bedroom to the house to provide extra accommodation for an increasing family, this could be satisfactorily done—provided it were a flat-roofed house—by extending the room partly over the garden and supporting it on piers with a veranda underneath, without thus taking any space from the garden as would be the case with an extension to a bungalow. Also the two main divisions of the house into the family part consisting of kitchen, eating space and living room, and the more private and individual part consisting of bedrooms can more easily and completely be divided in the two-story house than in the bungalow. This would apply with added force if the ideal that every member of the family over the age of ten has a room of his own, in the form of a study-bedroom, is an ultimate objective of housing policy. If this ideal should become a housing objective, then the two-story house can more easily be divided than the bungalow into the two main divisions of the family part, and the private and individual part. These arguments seemed to have some influence, because there was a general preference for the two-story house as the voting demonstrates.

	Number of audience	Vote for two-story house	Vote for bungalow	Undecided
A	44 (20 men, 24 women)	28	12	4
B	37 (21 men, 16 women)	18	18	1
C	42 (18 men, 24 women)	35	7	None
D	43 (21 men, 22 women)	41	2	„
E	450 men	300 (approx.)	95 (approx.)	55 (approx.)
F	500 men	430 (approx.)	40 (approx.)	30 (approx.)

	Number of audience	Vote for two-story house	Vote for bungalow	Undecided
G	72 (20 men, 52 women)	71	1	None
H	75 men	70	3	2
I	58 men	52	6	None
J	42 women	27	15	,,
K	58 women	39	19	,,
L	112 (about half men and half women)	102	8	2
M	56 (34 men, 22 women)	27	20	9
N	70 men	57	10	3
O	32 (12 men, 20 women)	30	1	1
P	36 men	32	2	2
Q	27 men	26	1	None

4. Would you like a traditional house, brick built with pitched roof covered with tiles or slates and with the traditional English picturesque appearance, or would you prefer a modern house built with modern methods and materials like reinforced concrete, or steel or other frame with panels between, with a flat roof and with plain walls?

The audiences were reminded of the typical small suburban villa erected in the ten years before the war. Its construction of brick with the pitched roof represented hardly any advance in construction on the small house of 400 years earlier, whereas in most other types of building—office blocks, factories, public buildings—the method of construction had changed during the present century from stone or brick construction to steel framed or reinforced concrete framed construction. But not only in the method of construction was this house strictly traditional, but the aim seemed to be to give the house the appearance of being built 400 years ago. This was especially so in those built in the early nineteen thirties during the Tudor craze. The speculative builder thought that what the average person wanted was the picturesque Tudor house with appropriate ornament and half-timber work, which was, of course, sham. Even municipal houses, as far as appearance is concerned, seemed unduly influenced by mediæval cottages, but being simpler they were generally architecturally more pleasing than many small houses where the aim was too consciously picturesque or stylistic. In the modern house, on the contrary, full advantage is taken of modern materials and methods of construction, which make possible, for example, the flat roof. Certain advantages of the flat roof were pointed out, such as the greater freedom it gives to the planner, and thus the greater facility it affords to plan more strictly according to purpose and convenience; because in planning with a pitched roof if the plan is very irregular, the roof becomes complicated and expensive, whereas a flat roof will go over any plan quite simply, however irregular. Secondly, it was pointed out that a flat roof makes additions to the existing structure so much simpler and less expensive, while it reduces fire risk.

In the discussion that ensued, some objections were expressed to the flat roof on the grounds that it does not prevent damp penetration and that the thermal insulation is not always good. I pointed out that this was less a criticism of the flat roof than the way it has been constructed in some cases. Reinforced concrete construction is a new method, still in its infancy; it had been introduced to us by the French early in the present century and only a few had thoroughly mastered the science. The majority of builders were still very much amateurs at the game. Still, there had been technical difficulties with the flat roof, but these had been mastered years ago by the few experts, but not unfortunately by the majority of builders. Some of the technical precautions were discussed, like covering the bituminous weather proofing with a light material—white tiles or whitewash—to keep its temperature low in the sun so as to prevent blistering, and the desirability of cavity walls with the flat roof. Some objected to the flat roof on the grounds of appearance. In reply to these objections I contended that time had wedded many well-built and well-designed pitched roof houses to their surroundings, especially in country districts, where local stone had been used for the wall, and there were no such examples of flat-roofed houses in this country similarly graced by time. To make the comparison just we must try to divorce time. Consider the form of both types in relation to landscape setting. In England most of the country consists of flat or undulating scenery with low hills and the long lines of the landscape generally approximate to the horizontal. Harmony or direct contrast is agreeable, something between the two is surely less so. The flat roof is harmonious, the church tower or spire is in extreme contrast, but the pyramid of the pitched roof is neither. There are a few examples of flat-roofed houses in this country which, I pointed out, harmonize with the landscape, as well as any pitched-roofed houses I had seen. Generally I could not forbear likening the sham Tudor villa to a house in fancy dress, and rather regretted that it did not seem as ridiculous to most people as walking about today in Elizabethan costume; whereas the truly modern house was essentially a product of our industrial age, in which materials and methods made possible by modern industry were employed; and whether one liked its appearance or not, one had to admit that here architecture is a living art.

It will be seen that the arguments I put forward were nearly all in favour of the modern house. I mentioned that the equipment in a traditional house could be just as modern and up to date as in the modern house, although it is doubtful whether it would always be so conveniently installed. Also its very character would be more in harmony with the house that was the product of modern construction and materials. I think many were influenced by the arguments put forward. Some had already thought on these lines, and needed no persuading as the discussion revealed; others, however, were adamantly in favour of the traditional house, and some wanted as old a house as they could possibly get, the genuine Tudor in fact. The result of the voting was as follows:

	Number of audience	Traditional house	Modern house	Undecided
A	44 (12 men, 32 women)	1	42	1
B	26 men	18	8	None
C	32 (12 men, 20 women)	20	6	6
D	44 men	7	29	8
E	37 (8 men, 29 women)	5	27	5
F	52 men	7	38	7
G	49 men	3	44	2

With the exception of B and C a large majority in each audience was in favour of the modern house. I made a note with regard to audience C that they were rather below average intelligence. The discussion revealed that the men in particular were inclined to think mainly of difficulties in the way of developing new methods rather than of considering how they might be employed. There was also an element of suspicion that these new ideas were being developed not for the common good, but in the interest of a certain section of the community. There are always a certain number in each audience who think like this, but here it seemed to be the bulk of the audience.

5. Assuming that living rooms and bedrooms face in the circle E.N.E.—S.—W.N.W. would you prefer that windows be (A) very large to the extent of complete exterior walls in the form of glass screens, (B) of medium size, or (C) small?

The value of sunlight as a health-giving agency was emphasized. It was pointed out that the ornamental, fussy and often dark interiors of Victorian houses harboured dust which harboured germs and made these rooms unhealthy. Some germs live for a long time in such dark and dusty interiors, but when they are subjected to the sunlight they die. The ultra-violet rays of sunlight are, as is now well known, productive of vitamin D which increases resistance to disease. It is therefore of value to health to let as much sunlight into the house as possible, thus the value of large windows. To the objection that such windows might make the house cold in winter it was replied that the provision of double glass should not prove difficult or expensive, and this would minimize the cold. If central heating was employed a radiator would be under or near the window. When the sun shone in the winter, however, it would make rooms with large windows warm. It had been found that on a cold winter's day when the sun was shining, a room with a glass wall became quite warm, and it was possible to sit in it without artificial heating.

The voting showed a preference for windows as large as possible, influenced, a little, I think, by the arguments advanced.

	Number of audience	A. Large windows	B. Medium windows	C. Small windows	Undecided
A	44 (20 men, 24 women)	28	12	None	4
B	37 (21 men, 16 women)	31	4	„	2
C	42	19	17	„	6
D	43	22	19	„	2
E	72	60	7	„	5
F	58	52	6	„	None
G	21 women	7	13	1	„
H	42 women	25	16	None	1
I	58 women	56	1	„	1
J	38 men	9	27	„	2

6. If there is only one living room, would you like the kitchen to be large enough for meals, say in the form of a recess at one end or a niche adjoining?

This question provided much discussion. There was a general criticism that in houses consisting of a living room and kitchen on the ground floor, the kitchen was often not large enough for meals. The reaction of a woman living in a new house on the outskirts of Liverpool is typical. In this house is a fairly large living room with very small kitchen, and she complains that there is not space in the kitchen for meals. Not that she would like all meals in the kitchen, but it would be convenient to have some, like a hurried breakfast and the mid-day meal for the children coming in from school. She remarked that the children rushing in from school have their mid-day meal in the living room, which made it more difficult for her to keep the living room 'really nice' as she expressed it. There was general sympathy with this point of view. Most of those in the Army groups with whom I discussed this matter had had experience of either the parlour or non-parlour house of what might be called the old type with scullery and fairly large kitchen built generally between 1870 and 1910, and the more recent type without scullery, and with small kitchen built generally between 1920 and 1939. In the former there was space for meals in the kitchen, and a considerable number of meals were taken there. In the latter there was generally not space for meals in the kitchen, although the desire existed. People generally deplored this fact. They did not always want to carry things from the kitchen into another room for a small hurried meal, and often made do with the limited space in the kitchen. The habits of the average family suggest the desirable accommodation for meals. In the morning of an average working day when the man goes to factory or office, and the children to school, breakfast is a hurried meal, and at mid-day when children come in from school or the housewife provides only for herself, dispatch is usually a primary consideration, and it is convenient to have meals in or near the kitchen. But the evening and week-end meals, are of a more leisured character, and the living room is the place for them. There was general agreement with this line of thought. It was argued, however, that in providing space for meals in or adjoining the kitchen, there should be no interference with the kitchen as an efficient workroom. The old type of square kitchen with the table in the centre and scullery adjoining meant much labour for the housewife, the contraction of the kitchen and elimination of the scullery meant considerable reduction of labour. It was contended, therefore, that the space for meals should be at one end of the kitchen in the form of a recess or adjoining the kitchen in the form of a niche. This idea proved to be popular as the voting shows:

	Number of audience	Those who want provision for meals in form of kitchen recess or adjoining niche	Those who prefer all meals away from kitchen in living room or dining room	Undecided
A	44 (20 men, 24 women)	19	21	4
B	37 (21 men, 16 women)	35	None	2
C	42 (18 men, 24 women)	39	3	None
D	43 (21 men, 22 women)	42	1	"
E	58	56	2	"
F	78	68	8	2
G	21 women	21	None	None
H	42 women	19	21	2
I	58 women	16	38	4
J	75 men	55	15	5
K	38 men	33	5	None

The groups with the exception of A, H and I thus demonstrate a strong preference for the kitchen recess or adjoining niche, over the usual arrangement today. I remember in the case of group B there was a prolonged argument on the subject, some women speaking forcibly on the desirable separation of the place where meals are prepared and where they are consumed, cooking smells being advanced as one reason. But in the other groups this argument did not weigh strongly against the obvious convenience of the recess or niche for meals. It is interesting to note that these results agree fairly closely with those obtained by the Townswomen's Guild where 95·2 per cent in England and Wales and 94·17 per cent in Scotland wanted space for meals in the kitchen.

7. *Which do you prefer—a small kitchen and a scullery or utility room separate, or a large kitchen and scullery combined?*

There was considerable difference of opinion on this question. Both men and women were very much influenced by what was familiar to them. Those who liked the separation of kitchen and scullery pointed out that clothes are washed in the scullery, and in the winter are often dried there. They contended that such operations should not occur in the same place where meals are prepared. Monday morning is spent in washing clothes, and at mid-day it would be better to prepare and consume a meal away from the steam-laden atmosphere where the washing had been done. The reply to that was that the housewife finishes one operation—that of washing clothes—before she commences another—that of preparing a meal, and that steam can be easily dispersed by opening windows. But again that was countered by the argument that to finish one operation and clear the tools away before commencing another is not always convenient, and that to open windows on a cold day is to lose too much heat. It might be more convenient to suspend the operation, to break off from one and turn to another, and then return to the former. It was pointed out that it is not always possible to dry clothes out of doors in the winter months, and, in this event it would be better to dry them in a separate scullery than where food is prepared and cooked. It was agreed that it is convenient to have a sink and water handy in the preparation of a meal, and with the sink in a separate scullery it meant more labour. Those who wanted such separation were interested in the possibility of a sink both in the kitchen and scullery. The voting was as follows:

	Number of audience	Preference for small kitchen and scullery separate	Preference for kitchen and scullery combined	Undecided
A	44 (20 men, 24 women)	33	10	1
B	37 (21 men, 16 women)	24	8	5
C	42 (18 men, 24 women)	21	11	10
D	43 (21 men, 22 women)	18	19	6
E	72 (20 men, 52 women)	9	62	1
F	58 men	3	49	6
G	78 men	7	70	1
H	21 women	2	19	None
I	42 women	41	1	,,
J	58 women	21	34	3
K	70 men	45	21	4
L	38 men	6	29	3

It appears from this that there is about 2 to 1 vote in favour of the kitchen and scullery combined. But discussions with further groups might alter the balance. The vote is not sufficiently strong to indicate a general preference one way or the other. I believe that if they could see examples of some degree of separation of what might be called scullery and kitchen activities, but not sufficient to mean extra labour, a majority would prefer this arrangement. I am strengthened in this belief because a very good design of this arrangement was shown to group I and all but one voted for the kitchen and scullery separate. Nearly all wanted something like it.

It is interesting to note that these results do not vary much from those received in the questionnaire of the Townswomen's Guild in reply to the same question. In England and Wales 24·52 per cent wanted kitchen and scullery separate, 66·71 per cent wanted them combined, the remainder being undecided. In Scotland the relative percentages were 21·90 per cent and 74·28 per cent.

8. *Would you prefer (A) an all-electric house, (B) an all-electric house with the exception of a coal fire in the living room, or (C) a house with other forms of lighting, heating and cooking available?*

I am aware that the way this question is framed gives it a certain propaganda value for electricity, and many arguments in the discussion continued the progaganda. This must be borne in mind in assessing the value of the voting. It was argued that if the number of electricity undertakings could be reduced (from 580 to 78 as recommended in the McGowan Report), and be administered in regions; that if the same voltage was used throughout the country so that equipment could be extensively standardized, and thus mass-produced on a greater scale; that if we used water power to a greater extent, and that if we concentrated on electricity to the exclusion of all other forms of lighting, heating and cooking, it would reduce the cost of the service enormously. It was pointed out too that the elimination of flues would reduce cost of construction by about 10 per cent. It was agreed there was no alternative to electric lighting, and there seemed to be a general preference for electric cooking and heating with the important exception that most wanted a coal fire in the living room. They felt that a fireplace was unnecessary in any other room, especially in bedrooms, but they generally insisted that it must be in the living room. The cheerfulness of the coal fire on a winter's evening seemed of great value to most. Although there was a general preference for the electric cooker, some argued, especially women, that you could cook better by gas. The favourite argument in favour of the gas cooker was that heat can be regulated better.

	Number of audience	A All Electric house	B All electric house with coal fire in living room	C Other sources of lighting heating and cooking available	Undecided
A	140 (approx.)	8	98	14	20 (approx.)
B	75	3	66	6	None
C	53	4	28	7	14
D	50	19	19	6	6
E	220	77	126	8	9
F	72	16	48	8	None
G	21 women	None	20	1	,,
H	42 women	9	28	5	,,
I	58 women	6	43	6	3
J	112 men	4	41	44	23

Conscious of the propaganda for electricity in the way the question was put, in discussions subsequent to those of which the record is given, I changed the form. I still led the discussion in the way indicated, but gave greater prominence to gas, stressing the advantage of being able to regulate the heat so well in a gas cooker, and pointing out that some of the recent excellent gas fires were preferred by some persons to any other form of heating for the dining room and bedrooms. The revised form of question is as follows:

Electric lighting is assumed.

A. Would you like cooking and heating (including hot water) by gas, excepting coal fire in living room?

B. Would you like gas cooking, electric heating (including hot water), excepting coal fire in living room?

C. All-electric house, excepting coal fire in living room.

D. All-electric house.

(I should mention that I took the trouble to see that everybody knew precisely for what they were voting.)

	Number of audience	A	B	C	D	Undecided
K	146 men	None	80	52	14	None
L	44 men	,,	21	19	2	2
M	21 men	,,	4	6	11	None
N	21 men	,,	2	18	1	,,
O	20 men	,,	2	15	1	2
P	31 men	4	20	7	None	None
Q	33 men	None	3	27	1	2

	Number of audience	A	B	C	D	Undecided
R	32 men	,,	5	27	None	None
S	48 men	,,	7	32	6	3
T	27 men	,,	None	20	2	5
U	37 (8 men, 29 women)	,,	16	10	6	5
V	52 (half men, half women)	,,	11	31	7	3
W	49 (half men, half women)	,,	6	27	13	3

It will be noted from this voting that the great majority want an all-electric house, but with a coal fire in the living room. Out of a total of 1,304 who voted 809 wanted this, which is about 62 per cent. In the second group of 536 who voted 292 wanted this, which is about 55 per cent. The second preference was for this form, but with gas cooking, as in the second group, 177 voted for this which is about 33 per cent.

I discussed this question with a mixed audience of 150 American and Canadian soldiers. About 75 per cent of this audience wanted an all-electric house, and it is interesting to note that not one wanted a coal fire anywhere in the house.

The response of these audiences would suggest that there would be widespread accept-ance of houses with one fireplace in the living room only, and the remainder of the house all-electric.

9. Would you like a house to which additions or extensions could be made if desired?

The question proved the most difficult of all to answer, and it will be seen that a very large number did not attempt an answer. Consideration of the question required more imagination than any other because there is hardly any experience of this type of house, and it was rather probing into the unknown.

It was explained that by having a house to which future additions could be made, would be more consistent with building according to family needs, as the house could be enlarged as the family increased. It was more a case of fitting the house to the family than of fitting the family to the house as so often in the past; which in the case of an increasing family and a small house meant squeezing the family in, and in the case of a large house and an increasing family, filling it out as you proceeded. Economic advantages are apparent if an example is considered. A man of twenty-five marries. He has not saved much money and has a limited income. His initial requirements are a living room, hall and kitchen on the ground floor, and one bedroom and a bathroom on the upper floor. The cost would be less than a five-or six-roomed house. In six years time he has two children. He has saved more money and his income has increased a little. He can add an extra bedroom, which he now requires, quite economically if provision is made for this in the design of the house. In a few years when the children want rooms of their own he could add a further bedroom.

It was explained that if this method of building houses were adopted the house would be complete at each stage; that it would be designed for its maximum size, and for its minimum and intermediate sizes, and that it could have an agreeable appearance at each stage. It was pointed out that the flat roof construction would make the process of extensions simpler and more economical than would the traditional pitched roof construction. Also it would be of advantage if fairly large prefabricated units were employed.

Groups were a little puzzled, and a little apprehensive that the economical develop-ment of this type of house might result in unsatisfactory building. There was a certain amount of opposition from those engaged in the building trade, an opposition which I feel was not so much to the ideas as to the new methods of building that it might encourage.

	Number of audience	Preference for a house to which additions can be made	Preference for the old fixed type	Undecided
E	37 (21 men, 16 women)	10	12	15
F	42 (18 men, 24 women)	9	5	28
G	43 (21 men, 22 women)	7	28	8
H	450 (approx.) men	155	170	125 (approx.)
I	500 (approx.) men	216	149	145 „
K	72 (20 men, 52 women)	15	20	37
L	75 men	11	29	35
M	58 men	21	22	15
N	78 men	15	23	40
O	21 women	14	6	1
P	44 men	44	None	None
Q	32 (12 men, 20 women)	None	9	23
R	44 men	29	15	None
S	27 men	14	5	8
T	37 (8 men, 29 women)	14	14	9

The value of this record is that so many voted for a comparatively new idea of which they cannot have seen examples. It is clear the idea appealed to many. I may say that the majority in groups H and I were men under thirty.

Group P with its unanimous vote for the expanding house represents a noteworthy exception which merits a word of explanation. The audience was entirely voluntary and they discussed housing enthusiastically for three hours one evening (from 8 to 11 p.m.). The discussion on the expanding house lasted about an hour, and reached a really high level. After putting the arguments for the expanding house, I left the matter very much in the hands of the audience. At first, there was some criticism of the idea, and I thought the feeling of the meeting would go against it, but then there were some really eloquent speeches in its favour, based on the logic of the proposition, on the contention that here was something that was better than the fixed type, and that if we were to progress we should find ways and means of having this more convenient type for family life. The eloquence of these speeches, eloquence due very much to sincerity, converted the whole audience.

10. Would you rather rent or buy a house?

All the familiar advantages and disadvantages of buying and renting a house were discussed, but the most important factor always seemed to be economic security. To most people the only advantage of renting a house was one imposed by economic necessity. The discussions demonstrated that it is as much a question of being assured of a regular income as of the size of the income. In putting the question to the vote after each discussion it was therefore necessary to put it in two ways: would you rather rent or buy a house (A) assuming economic and social conditions to be those obtaining in the year 1938, and (B) assuming that you are assured in the future of a regular income sufficient to provide the necessities of life. Following are the results of voting in eight groups which are representative of many others:

Number of audience	A (Conditions as in 1938)		B (Assured of regular income, etc.)	
	Rent	Buy	Rent	Buy
43	21	22	None	All
87	7	80	„	„

Number of audience	A (Conditions as in 1938)		B (Assured of regular income, etc.)	
	Rent	Buy	Rent	Buy
38	5	33	1	Remainder
31	11	20	2	„
125 (approx.)	4	105	2	„
	(the remainder undecided)			
42	11	31	None	All
45	12	33	3	Remainder
41	4	37	2	„

It is apparent from these figures that there is a general desire for house ownership provided that families can be reasonably confident of a regular income in the future.

How far these records of preferences can be taken as a guide to the kind of houses we should build in the future depends on a thorough critical examination of all relevant factors. If studied in relation to modern technical developments and potentialities, to the evolution of house design, and to the recommendations of sociologists and the medical profession, they should prove of value.

QUESTIONNAIRE TO BRANCHES OF THE NATIONAL WOMEN CITIZENS' ASSOCIATION ON PREFERENCES REGARDING TYPES OF HOUSES, PLANNING, HEATING AND EQUIPMENT

THE objects of the National Women Citizens' Association are mainly to promote active and intelligent citizenship and to secure equality of liberty, status and opportunity for men and women. The members are drawn from all strata of society. The branches to whom the questions were put are largely in the south-eastern and north-western regions. The voting can be regarded as a fairly representative cross-section in these regions of serious, thoughtful and intelligent women. In answering the questions the branches gave considerable thought to the subject, devoting in some cases a whole meeting to their discussions. Branches A to H are in the south-eastern region, I is in the West Country, J is in the Midlands, and K to N are in the north-western region. The six branches O to T no voting was recorded, but general preferences were indicated.

The figures of the voting are necessarily approximate and were received by a show of hands. It will be noted that in several branches the total of voting for various alternatives is less than the number of the group, in some cases very much less. This means, of course, that several individuals were unable to reach a conclusion. It is apparent in the questions on the types of flooring and may be due to lack of experience of all the types of flooring mentioned in the questions.

1. Would you prefer a terrace house or semi-detached? To avoid misunderstanding it should be explained that by terrace house is meant a house in a block with no access from the front to the back without going through the house. It is less costly to build than the semi-detached house, with the result that for the same money slightly better accommodation could be provided in the terrace house (to the extent perhaps of a utility room adjoining kitchen) than in the semi-detached.

	Size of group	Terrace house	Semi-detached house
A	58	22	36
B	42	None	All
C	52	None	All
D	22	2	20
E	62	None	All
F	50	None	All
G	80	None	All
H	74	None	All
I	40	10 if back entry	30
J	80	None	All
K	42	12	30
L	24	None	All
M	68	14	24
N	38	None	All

In the branches from O to T there was general preference for the semi-detached house. It is possible that if it had been stated in the question that a passage way between houses under the first floor is a feature of many rows of terrace houses that this might have influenced a slightly stronger vote for the terrace house, but it is very unlikely that this would have disturbed the overwhelming preference for the semi-detached house. It will thus be seen that members of the N.C.W.A. generally shared the preferences of men and women in the Forces.

2. *Assuming that the bedrooms face towards the morning sun, and that the living room faces towards the south or west, would you prefer the windows to be (a) very large, so that the whole wall above say 3 feet from the floor is of glass, (b) medium size or (c) small?*

	Very large windows	Medium size windows	Small windows
A	8	50	None
B	16	26	None
C	None	All	None
D	2	18	2
E	24	38	None
F	30	10	None
G	16	24	1
H	None	64	10 no preference
I	None	All	None
J	None	All	None
K	24	16	2
L	10	14	None
M	2	54	None
N	4	34	None

O to S preferred medium sized windows and T very large windows. It will be seen that there was in most branches a decided preference for the medium-sized window, and very little wish for small windows. In one branch the feeling was expressed that large windows would make the room too cold, which is as much an argument for double glazing as for smaller windows.

3. *In the early years of the century small houses generally had a kitchen with a scullery. The kitchen was generally large enough for meals and included a solid fuel cooker and a dresser, while in the scullery was the sink and copper. Between the wars there was a tendency to combine kitchen and scullery in one room, and this became smaller. Since the last war there has been a tendency to revert to the older arrangement of a separate kitchen and scullery only now the latter is called a utility room. Which arrangement would you prefer—the kitchen and scullery, or utility room combined or separate?*

	Kitchen and utility room combined	Separate
A	26	18
B	38	4
C	34	20
D	10	12
E	24	38
F	All	None
G	24	28

	Kitchen and utility room combined	Separate
H	18	48
I	None	All
J	This branch was unanimously in favour of a good working kitchen, which is really a vote for combined kitchen and scullery.	
K	18	24
L	14	10
M	Remainder, about 29, indifferent	14
N	30	8

The preferences are fairly evenly divided. In some cases the answers depended on the size of the kitchen, and if this could be large there was a preference that it should be combined with the utility room. One branch, F, stated that it should be suitable for occasional meals, such as breakfast. Those in branch L, who wanted the rooms combined, asked that it should be large. Of the branches O to T, O asked for the rooms 'combined if large enough, otherwise separate'. P and T asked for them combined, while S asked for a large kitchen. It would appear, therefore, that if the two are to be combined in the one kitchen, this should be large, and certainly not the kitchenette of between the wars.

4. *Would you prefer (a) the living room and dining room to be entirely separate, or (b) the living room with the dining recess?*

	(a) A living room and dining room separate	(b) Living room with dining recess
A	32	22
B	No answer	
C	32	18
D	16	4
E	38	24
F	34	10
G	40	12
H	52	8
I	None	All
J	78	2
K	24	16
L	8	16
M	20	34
N	22	16

Five of the remaining six branches preferred the living and dining rooms entirely separate, while the other branch, P, suggested two rooms while children are at home, but living room with dining recess later in life. It will be noted that the preference is a little on the side of the dining and living room separate, whereas the modern tendency in design is to provide a dining recess in the living room. The best way to please both and also to suit the requirements stated by P group is to have a movable partition between the dining and living spaces.

5. If you wish the dining room to be entirely separate from the living room, would you (a) like it also to be entirely separate from the kitchen—with perhaps a hatch—or (b) would you like a kitchen with a dining recess?

	(a) Separate from the kitchen	(b) Kitchen with dining recess
A	30	20
B	12	14
C	All	None
D	10	10
E	All	None
F	All	None
G	52	No vote
H	40	8
I	All	None
J	All	None
K	24	16
L	No vote recorded	
M	No vote recorded	
N	20	18

The six branches O to T expressed preference for dining room separate from kitchen, and P, R and S emphasised the desire for a hatch. It will be seen from the answers to this question and No. 4 that the open plan is not generally accepted and that there is rather a preference for the rooms or units with different functions to be kept separate.

6. One tendency in modern houses (a) is to have one coal fire in the living room with the other rooms heated by electric or gas fires. Alternatives are to have (b) electric fires or gas fires in the living room, thus eliminating a coal fire entirely and (c) to have some form of central heating again without the coal fire in the living room. Which would you prefer? It should be mentioned that in (a) it could incorporate water heating by means of a back boiler and that (c) could be combined with the provision of hot water, the central heating supply being shut off in the summer.

	(a) Coal fire in living room	(b) Electric or gas fire in living room	(c) Some form of central heating, etc.
A	24	6	28
B	18	8	16
C	46	4	2
D	18	None	4
E	46	16	None
F	34	None	16
G	All	None	None
H	56	4	None
I	36	None	4
J	Undecided, but general feeling that electric and gas heating too expensive		
K	26	None	16
L	All	None	None
M	All	None	None
N	All	None	None

Of the other groups O and T wanted (*a*) coal fire in living room, P wanted coal fire in living room and added that if a back boiler is incorporated there should be an alternative way of heating the water during the summer months. S showed a preference for (*c*) some form of central heating, while Q and R did not express an opinion. The voting confirmed the traditional preference for the open coal fire in the living room.

7. *Various arrangements can be made for water heating. There is (a) solid fuel boiler in the kitchen or utility room (b) electric immersion heater supplemented by small sink storage heater (c) large gas storage heater supplying both kitchen and bathroom, or a smaller one for each. Which of a, b or c would you prefer?*

	(*a*) Solid fuel boiler	(*b*) Electric immersion heater supplement	(*c*) Large gas storage heater
A	28	30	2
B	All—supplemented by immersion heater in summer		
C	4	34	6
D	18	4	None
E	36	22	4
F	30	38	wanted immersion heater as alternative for summer use
G	40	6	None
H	20	16	None
I	24	12	4
J	All	None	None
K	22	12	6
L	14	10	None
M	14	20	None
N	36	2	None

Branches Q and T wanted (*b*) electric immersion heater supplemented by small sink storage heater. O, P and R wanted (*a*) solid fuel boiler, supplemented by immersion heater in summer. The voting in the other branches suggested that this arrangement would be popular with many. The solid fuel boiler in kitchen or utility room is a strong preference, and, with the answers of the majority to Question 6, suggests that the two flue house, one for the living room fire, and one for the boiler fire, is a fairly general preference.

8. *Would you prefer (a) solid fuel cooker (b) an electric cooker or (c) gas cooker?*

	(*a*) Solid fuel cooker	(*b*) Electric cooker	(*c*) Gas cooker
A	10	4	40
B	2	18	22
C	4	20	28
D	4	6	12
E	40	10	12
F	2	8	32
G	None	24	40
H	None	6	68

	(a) Solid fuel cooker	(b) Electric cooker	(c) Gas cooker
I	None	2	38
J	None	None	All
K	6	22	14
L	None	8	14
M	16	22	30
N	2	18	18

Groups O, P, R and T all expressed preference for the gas cooker, S preferred an electric cooker, while Q was equally divided. It will be seen from the voting that in most of the groups more preferred gas cooking to either electric or solid fuel.

9. *Do you like (a) a garden, or (b) would you be quite content without one?*

	(a) Garden	(b) Without one
A	58	2
B	26	16 would be without one if a garden room or conservatory were provided.
C	48	4
D	20	2
E	56	3
F	45	5 did not vote
G	All	None
H	All	None
I	All	None
J	70	10
K	40	2
L	20	3
M	41	No vote
N	All	None

Groups O to T all wanted a garden. The general preference for a garden was qualified in some instances by the stipulation that it should be small.

10. *What kind of floor would you like for the living room (a) a carpet on softwood boarding, (b) linoleum on wood boarding with rugs or carpet, (c) hardwood strip flooring or parquet floor with a rug or rugs, (d) cork floor with rugs?*

	(a) Carpet on softwood boarding	(b) Linoleum with rugs or carpet	(c) Hardwood or parquet	(d) Cork floor with rugs
A	35	None	23	None
B	20	None	22	None
C	46	None	6	None
D	12	None	10	None
E	40	None	22	None
F	18	None	25	5

	(a) Carpet on softwood boarding	(b) Linoleum with rugs or carpet	(c) Hardwood or parquet	(d) Cork floor with rugs
G	21	None	25	None
H	7	None	33	None
I	None	None	40	None
J	All	None	None	None
K	10	2	28	1
L	12	2	9	None
M	All	None	None	None
N	22	None	16	None

Groups O, Q and T expressed a preference for (a), whereas P, R and S expressed a preference for (c).

11. What kind of floor would you prefer for the bedroom, (a), (b), (c) or (d) the alternatives as in 10?

	(a)	(b)	(c)	(d)
A	32	2	8	None
B	42	None	None	None
C	38	12	None	None
D	22	None	None	None
E	40	None	22	None
F	19	None	10	7
G	38	2	19	5
H	5	None	11	None
I	All	None	None	None
J	All	None	None	None
K	22	7	8	2
L	16	2	6	None
M	All wanted bedroom floors sound proofed			
N	28	2	8	None

Groups O, P, Q and T wanted (a) and R and S wanted (c).

The answers to Questions 10 and 11 showed the popularity both for living rooms and bedrooms of the carpeted floor. There was some preference for the hardwood floor with rugs, probably because of the attractive appearance, although it is possible that the safety factor influenced a greater preference for (a), as the rug on the hardwood floor does suggest a risk of slipping. The very few who expressed any preference for the cork floor is partly due, I think, to lack of experience of this excellent type of flooring. The preference for carpeted floor, both for living room and bedrooms, suggests the strong liking for a sense of comfort, warmth and quiet.

12. What kind of floor would you like for the kitchen, (a) quarry tiles, (b) thermoplastic, tiles available in a variety of colours, having a slight resilience, (c) linoleum, (d) cork tiles, (e) rubber, (f) hard composition jointless floor?

	(a) Quarry tiles	(b) Thermoplastic	(c) Linoleum	(d) cork tiles	(e) Rubber	(f) Hard composition
A	17	10	14	3	14	None
B	7	22	None	1	12	None

	(a) Quarry tiles	(b) Thermo- plastic	(c) Linoleum	(d) cork tiles	(e) Rubber	(f) Hard composition
C	6	16	23	2	None	None
D	2	2	5	None	11	2
E	8	None	53	None	None	None
F	8	4	11	None	2	2
G	5	5	2	8	28	7
H	None	17	7	None	17	None
I	None	24	None	None	16	None
J	None	All	None	None	None	None
K	4	16	2	None	10	9
L	6	18	None	None	None	None
M	17	None	None	17	8	None
N	12	10	None	12	4	None

Groups O and P and T wanted (b), Groups Q and R wanted (a) and Group S wanted (e).

13. What kind of floor would you like for the bathroom, alternatives a, b, c, d, e or f, as in 12?

	(a)	(b)	(c)	(d)	(e)	(f)
A	None	3	12	14	19	None
B	None	10	21	10	None	None
C	18	None	31	None	3	None
D	None	2	16	None	4	None
E	9	None	53	None	None	None
F	None	3	19	11	9	None
G	None	None	7	3	33	None
H	3	9	None	3	24	None
I	None	2	2	5	31	None
J	None	68	None	12	None	None
K	None	17	1	10	10	4
L	8	None	4	7	4	None
M	None	None	None	31	31	None
N	None	None	None	None	All	None

Groups O and T wanted (b), group P wanted (c), groups Q and S wanted (e) and group R wanted (d).

In the answers to Questions 12 and 13 there did not seem to be any overwhelming preference for any particular type of floor covering for kitchen and bathroom.

For the kitchen a fair number expressed a liking for quarry tiles, thermo-plastic tiles, linoleum and rubber. In the bathroom, the greatest preferences were for linoleum, rubber and cork. It might be concluded that there was a general wish for clean, slightly soft resilient flooring for both kitchen and bathrooms, and if there was any difference in the flooring required in the two rooms it was that in some cases a slightly harder floor would be acceptable in the kitchen.

14. Place the following in the order of preference, (a) refrigerator, (b) washing machine, (c) television set.

It would not convey a great deal to record the voting to this question ; it is more useful to indicate general preferences. All the groups in the south-eastern area A to H gave first preference to a refrigerator, while Groups A, B, F, G and H gave second preference to a washing machine. Groups K, R, S and T also gave first preference to a refrigerator, but Groups I, J, M, N, O gave first preference to a washing machine. No group gave first preference to a television set, although it was a second preference in some cases.

15. *Do you think it is a good idea that a house should be built in stages and increased in size as the family grows? Do you think therefore that houses should be designed complete or in stages, the first with two bedrooms with provision for the addition of one or two bedrooms and a utility room and garage? It would mean that the house can grow with the family and the income.*

	Good idea	No
A	37	None (although not all voted)
B	Majority if life of family is not disturbed while additions are being made, or it could be done while family on holiday	
C	26	26
D	8	14
E	All	None
F	None	All
G	17	25
H	Preference divided, but proportions not given	
I	8	32
J	All	None
K	9	25
L	Majority	—
M	None	All
N	All	None

It should be explained that in the second column, which indicates those who did not think it a good idea, many expressed it by saying that they wanted the house designed complete from the start. This was also the view of Groups O, Q, S, whereas Groups P, R and T thought it a good idea. The interesting feature in this record is that so many thought it a good idea, because it is not a method of housing which is at all familiar in this country.

16. *Would you prefer to own the house in which you live, or would you prefer to rent it?*

	Own	Rent
A	47	7
B	All	None
C	48	4
D	All	None
E	All	None
F	37	2
G	All	None
H	All	None
I	All	None
J	All	None
K	36	6
L	16	6
M	45	17
N	All	None

The remainder all wanted to own the house. The voting confirms the great desire, seen also in the voting on the subject among men and women in the Forces, to own the house occupied. It is probable that underlying this preference, as also the preference for the house and garden over the flat, is the feeling of freedom that it gives. If the family owns their house, there is the feeling that they can make it more completely to their hearts desire—in the matter of decorations, fittings, built-in furniture and so on—whereas in renting a house there is always the sense of restriction, and the feeling that if improvements are made it is work done for the landlord. This wide desire for house ownership, of which it should not be difficult to obtain further confirming evidence, should prompt a national policy to make the means as easy and simple as possible, consistent of course with economic stability. Much more could be done to assist house ownership.

As in the questionnaire to the Forces, the value of the answers given by the branches of the National Women Citizens' Association can only be appreciated after a critical examination. Some of the items mentioned in some of the questions may have been a little outside individual experience, while there was a natural tendency to have a bias for the familiar, but on the whole the answers indicate an imaginative response to the questions.

BELFAST
REFERENCE
LIBRARY.

BIBLIOGRAPHY

(Only books published since 1930 are included)

1. GENERAL

HUGH ANTHONY
Houses—Permanence and Prefabrication (Pleiades Books), London 1945.

ERIC AMBROSE
Know your House (Thames & Hudson), London 1954.

ASSOCIATION FOR PLANNING AND REGIONAL RECONSTRUCTION
Housing Digest, an Analysis of Housing Reports 1941-5 (Art and Educational Publishers), London 1946.
This is a Digest of various reports on housing and of the results of housing questionnaires.

ASSOCIATION OF BUILDING TECHNICIANS
Homes for the People, by a Committee of the A.B.T. (Paul Elek), London 1946.

CATHERINE BAUER
Modern Housing (Allen & Unwin), London 1935.
This is the most comprehensive book in English on the sociological aspects of the subject.

ANTHONY BERTRAM
The House: A Machine for Living In (A. & C. Black), London 1935.

ALEXANDER BLOCK
Estimating Housing Needs (The Architectural Press), London 1946.

G. M. BOUMPHREY
Your Home and Mine (Allen & Unwin), London 1938.
The House Inside and Out (Allen & Unwin), London 1936.

BRITISH STANDARDS INSTITUTION
Summaries of British Standards for Building Materials and Components for Housing—
B. S. Handbook No. 3—1944, 1947, 1950, 1953 and 1955. The last edition—1955—is published in loose-leaf form so that further summaries can be conveniently added.

NOEL CARRINGTON
Design and Decoration in the Home (Batsford), London 1952.

COUNCIL OF SCIENTIFIC MANAGEMENT IN THE HOME
Meals in Modern Homes, London 1955.
An inquiry into the space-layout and equipment provided for preparing and serving meals in samples of post-war local authority houses, the housewives' use of these facilities and their satisfaction with them.

ELIZABETH DENBY
  Europe Re-housed (Allen & Unwin), London 1938.
  The countries covered in this survey are Sweden, Holland, Germany, Austria, Italy and
     France.

M. J. ELSAS
  Housing Before the War and After (Staples Press), London 1942, 2nd edition 1945.

WALTER GROPIUS
  The New Architecture and the Bauhaus (Faber & Faber), London 1936.

ALAN HASTINGS (edited by)
  Week-end Houses, Cottages and Bungalows (Architectural Press), London 1939.

MORRISON HENDRY
  Planning Your Home for Tomorrow (Faber & Faber), London 1950.

HOUSE BUILDING INDUSTRIES STANDING COMMITTEE
  Your New House, London 1946.
  The specifications, plans and elevations of the designs selected in the national com-
     petition organized by the House Building Industries Standing Committee.

ALEC JOHNSON
  This Housing Question (Lawrence & Wishart), London 1954.

LONDON COUNTY COUNCIL
  London Housing (London County Council), 1937.

JOHN MADGE (edited by)
  To-morrow's Houses (Pilot Press), London 1946.
  Articles by experts on modern building materials and methods of construction, lighting,
     heating and sound insulation.

MASS OBSERVATION (Report by)
  An Enquiry into People's Homes (Murray), London 1943.
  An enquiry into the opinions of people regarding their present living conditions and the
     homes they would like. This is the result of one of the most exhaustive enquiries of
     the kind ever undertaken, and covers many aspects of house planning and design, of
     conditions in the home and home environment.

RAYMOND MCGRATH
  Twentieth-Century Houses (Faber & Faber), London 1934.

GEORGE NELSON AND HENRY WRIGHT
  To-morrow's House (The Architectural Press and Simon and Schuster), London and New
     York 1945.

MINISTRIES OF HEALTH AND OF HOUSING AND LOCAL GOVERNMENT
  Design of Dwellings. Report of the Design of Dwellings Sub-Committee of the Central
     Housing Advisory Committee. Chairman: Earl of Dudley (H.M.S.O.), London 1944.
  Housing Manuals, London 1944 and 1949, second supplement 1952, third supplement
     1953.
  Housing Manual Technical Appendices, London 1944.
  The Cost of House Building, Third Report of the Committee of Inquiry 1952. The first
     report was made in 1948 and the second in 1950.

DEPARTMENT OF HEALTH FOR SCOTLAND
Planning our New Homes, Report by the Scottish Housing Advisory Committee on the Design, Planning and Furnishing of New Houses, Edinburgh 1946.
Rural Housing, Third Report of the Rural Housing Sub-Committee of the Central Housing Advisory Committee, Chairman: Sir Arthur Hobhouse, London 1944. Reconditioning in Rural Areas—Fourth Report 1947.
The Codes of Practice Committee of the Ministry of Works, composed of nominees of professional and scientific institutions, has published the 'Code of Functional Requirements of Buildings', in various chapters which are given in the sections of this bibliography. Two that should be given here are Chapter VII, 'Services' 1945, and Chapter X, 'Dirt and Vermin' 1945.

COLIN PENN
Houses of Today (Batsford), London 1954.

J. M. RICHARDS
A Miniature History of the English House (Architectural Press), London 1938.
Castles on the Ground (Architectural Press), London 1946.

WALTER SEGAL
Home and Environment (Leonard Hill), London 1947, second edition 1953.
Housing—A Survey of the Post War Housing Work of the London County Council 1945-1949, London 1949.

E. D. SIMON
Rebuilding Britain—A Twenty-Year Plan (Gollancz), London 1945.
Part I, Building ; Part II, Housing ; Part III, Planning ; Foreign Examples ; Part IV, Planning: Britain.

A. SHAW WARING
Approach to Better Housing (Leonard Hill), 1947.

H. MYLES WRIGHT (edited by)
Small Houses, £500—£2,500 (Architectural Press), 1932-7, second edition 1946.

F. R. S. YORKE
The Modern House (Architectural Press), London 1934.
The Modern House in England (Architectural Press), London 1937.

2. METHODS OF HOUSE CONSTRUCTION

BERNARD H. COX
Prefabricated Homes (Paul Elek), London 1945.

D. DEX HARRISON (edited by)
Building Science (Allen & Unwin), London 1948.
This consists of papers prepared for the Architectural Science Board of the R.I.B.A. and includes 'The Technique of Social Survey' by Dennis Chapman; 'Developments in the Design of Timber Structures' by Phillip O. Reece; 'Recent Developments in Lightweight Concrete' by T. W. Parker; 'Fundamental Principles of the Weathering of Building Materials', and 'External Rendered Finishes' by F. L. Brady; 'Concrete: its Appearance and Durability' by Norman Davey. The book also includes papers on heating and lighting, see heads 3 and 4.

DEPARTMENT OF SCIENTIFIC AND INDUSTRIAL RESEARCH (BUILDING RESEARCH STATION) AND MINISTRY OF WORKS
National Building Studies Special Reports.
No. 1. *Structural Requirements for Houses*, 1947.
No. 4. *New Methods of House Construction*, 1948.
No. 5. *Party Walls between Houses*, 1948.
No. 10. *New Methods of House Construction*, 2nd report, 1949.

JOHN GLOAG AND GREY WORNUM
House out of Factory (Allen & Unwin), 1946.

MINISTRY OF WORKS
House Construction by an inter-departmental Committee of the Ministries of Health and Works and of the Scottish Office, Chairman: Sir George Burt (Post-War Building Study No. 1), London 1944. *Second Report* (Post-War Building Study No. 23), 1946. *Third Report* (Post-War Building Study No. 25), 1948.
The Code of Functional Requirements of Buildings, Chapter II, 'Weather Protection', 1945.

RICHARD SHEPPARD
Prefabrication in Building (Architectural Press), London 1946.

3. LIGHTING

H. C. WESTON
'Basic Requirements of Lighting' in *Building Science* (Allen & Unwin), London 1948.

R. O. ACKERLEY
'Artificial Lighting Practice' in *Building Science* (Allen & Unwin), London 1948.

MINISTRY OF WORKS
The Lighting of Buildings, by the Lighting Committee of the Building Research Board. Chairman: Dr. C. C. Paterson (Post-War Building Study No. 12), (H.M.S.O.), London 1944.
The Code of Functional Requirements of Buildings, Chapter I a, 'Daylight'; I b, 'Sunlight', 1945; Chapter VII, 'Services—Lighting', 1945.

4. HEATING AND VENTILATION

PAUL DUNHAM CLOSE
Thermal Insulation of Buildings (Reinhold), New York 1947.

R. K. CORNELL
Heating and Ventilating for Architects and Builders (Paul Elek), London 1946.

MINISTRY OF WORKS
Memorandum on District Heating by the District Heating Sub-Committee of the Heating and Ventilation (Reconstruction) Committee of the Building Research Board, Chairman: Sir Alfred Egerton, 1947.
Domestic Fuel Policy, Report by the Fuel and Power Advisory Council, Chairman: Sir Ernest Simon, 1946.

MINISTRY OF FUEL AND POWER AND D.S.I.R.

Domestic Heating in America, A Study of Heating, Cooking and Hot Water Supply in Small Houses in U.S.A. and Canada, Report of a Joint Party from the Ministry of Fuel and Power and the Department of Scientific and Industrial Research, consisting of J. C. Pritchard of the Ministry of Fuel and Power, C. C. Handisyde of the Building Research Station, D.S.I.R., and R. H. Rowse, Fuel Research Station, D.S.I.R., 1946.

District Heating in American Housing, Report of a Mission to U.S.A. 1947, London 1949.

MINISTRY OF WORKS

Electrical Installations by a Committee of the Institution of Electrical Engineers, Chairman: J. R. Beard (Post-War Building Study No. 11), 1944.

Gas Installations by a Committee of the Institution of Gas Engineers, Chairman: R. J. Rogers (Post-War Building Study No. 6), 1944.

Heating and Ventilation of Dwellings by the Heating and Ventilation (Reconstruction) Committee of the Building Research Board of the Department of Scientific and Industrial Research, Chairman: Sir Alfred Egerton (Post-War Building Study No. 19, 1944.

Solid Fuel Installations by a Committee of the British Coal Utilization Research Association, Chairman: J. Stanleigh Turner (Post-War Building Study No. 10), 1944.

The Code of Functional Requirements of Buildings, Chapter VIII 'Heating and Thermal Insulation'.

'Centralised Domestic Hot Water Supply', C.P. 342, 1950.

'Open fires, heating stoves and cookers burning solid fuel', C.P. 403, 1952.

T. BEDFORD

'Basic Conditions for Comfort' in *Building Science* (Allen & Unwin), London 1948.

JONH BICKERDIKE

'Lighting' in *New Ways of Servicing Buildings* (Architectural Press), London 1954.

E. A. C. CHAMBERLAIN

'Developments of Solid Fuel Appliances for Small Houses' in *Building Science* (Allen & Unwin), London 1948.

KENNETH CHEESMAN

'Interior Finishes' in *New Ways of Servicing Buildings* (Architectural Press), 1954.

DEPARTMENT OF SCIENTIFIC AND INDUSTRIAL RESEARCH (BUILDING RESEARCH STATION)

An inquiry into Domestic Hot Water Supply in Great Britain, (National Building Studies, Special Reports 8 and 14), Part 1: *Distribution of Water Heating Appliances and their use in Winter, 1950;* Part 2: *The use of Water Heating Appliances in Summer and the relation between the Usage of Hot Water and the Appliances available.*

C. C. HANDISYDE

'House Heating' in *New Ways of Servicing Buildings* (Architectural Press), London 1954.

A. C. PALLOT

'An Outline of Heating Systems' in *Building Science* (Allen & Unwin), London 1948.

5. INSULATION (THERMAL AND SOUND)

MINISTRY OF WORKS
  Sound Insulation and Acoustics by the Acoustics Committee of the Building Research
  Board, Chairman: G. B. Sharples (Post-War Building Study No. 14), London 1944.

G. D. NASH, J. COMRIE AND H. F. BROGHTON
  The Thermal Insulation of Buildings—Design Data and how to use them, D.S.I.R. 1955.
  The Code of Functional Requirements of Buildings, Chapter III, 'Precaution Against
  Noise', 1945.

D. W. SAUNDERS AND A. POTT
  'Thermal Insulation', *Building Digest*, July 1947. An exhaustive bibliography is given.

6. PLANNING AND HOUSING

SIR PATRICK ABERCROMBIE
  Town and Country Planning (Home University Library—Butterworth), London 1933.

C. B. FAWCETT
  A Residential Unit for Town and Country Planning (University of London Press),
  London 1944.

STANLEY GALE
  Modern Housing Estates (Batsford), 1949.

MINISTRY OF HOUSING AND LOCAL GOVERNMENT
  Design in Town and Village, London 1953.
  This is divided into three parts: Part1: 'The English Village' by Thomas Sharp; Part 2:
  'The Design of Residential Areas' by Frederick Gibberd; Part 3: 'Design in City
  Centres' by W. G. Holford.

EBENEZER HOWARD
  Garden Cities of To-morrow, edited with a preface by F. J. Osborn (Faber & Faber),
  London 1946.
  This is the third edition of the book originally published in 1898 under the title of *To-
  morrow a Peaceful Path to Real Reform*. The text follows the second edition published
  in 1902 under the title *Garden Cities of To-morrow*. In this book are stated the principles and ideas which led to the building of the garden cities of Letchworth and
  Welwyn, principles which are determining to a considerable extent the building of
  new towns like Stevenage, Crawley, Harlow, Hemel Hempstead and others.

ELIZABETH AND GILBERT MCALLISTER
  Homes, Towns and Countryside—A Practical Plan for Britain (Batsford), London 1945.
  Contributions by various authorities on different aspects of the subject. Chapters especi-
  ally relevant to housing are 'Space, Standards and Planning' by F. J. Osborne and
  'The Place of Fuel in National Planning' by E. W. Smith.
  Town and Country Planning (Faber & Faber), London 1941.
  A survey of planning and housing from 1919 to 1939.

F. J. OSBORN
  Green Belt Cities (Faber & Faber), London 1946.

OFFICIAL PUBLICATION
   Site Planning and Lay-out in relation to Housing, a Report of a study group of the
      Ministry of Town and Country Planning included in the Dudley Report on the Design
      of Dwellings, H.M.S.O., London 1944.

THOMAS SHARP
   Town and Countryside (Oxford University Press), London 1932.
   English Panorama (Dent), London 1936.
   Town Planning (Penguin Books), London 1940.

TOWN AND COUNTRY PLANNING ASSOCIATION
   The five following books are selected from the Rebuilding Britain Series published by
Faber & Faber for the Town and Country Planning Association and edited by F. J. Osborn
with the exception of No. 13 which is edited by R. L. Reiss.
No. 1. F. J. OSBORN, *Overture to Planning.*
No. 5. CLOUGH WILLIAMS-ELLIS, *Plan for Living—The Architects' Part.*
No. 9. LEWIS MUMFORD, *The Social Foundations of Post-War Building.*
No. 10. ARNOLD WHITTICK, *Civic Design and the Home.*
No. 13. B. SEEBOHM ROWNTREE, *Portrait of a City's Housing,* 1945.

LAURENCE WOLFE
   The Reilly Plan: A New Way of Life (Nicholson & Watson), London 1945.
   A description and advocacy of Sir Charles Reilly's scheme of planning houses round
      greens, which he originally made for Birkenhead.

7. HOUSES IN THE LANDSCAPE

PERCY S. CANE
   Garden Design of To-day (Methuen), 1934.

COUNCIL FOR THE PRESERVATION OF RURAL ENGLAND
   Save Leicestershire's Countryside, Leicester.
   Housing in the Peak District, Sheffield 1934.
   Both of these books deal with the appearance of houses in relation to the surrounding
      country.

WALTER H. GODFREY
   Our Building Inheritance (Faber & Faber), London 1944.

OFFICIAL PUBLICATION
   The Architectural Use of Building Materials by a Committee of the Royal Institute of
      British Architects, Chairman: Edward Manfe (Post-War Building Study No. 18),
      (H.M.S.O.), London 1946.

8. MODERN ARCHITECTURE

MARTIN S. BRIGGS
   Building To-day (Oxford University Press), London 1944.

MAXWELL FRY
   Fine Building (Faber & Faber), London 1944.

OLIVER HILL
　　Fair Horizon—Buildings of To-day (Collins), 1950.
　　In this book some account is given of the work of eight pioneer architects: Frank Lloyd
　　　　Wright, J. J. P. Oud, Le Corbusier, Walter Gropius, Adolf Loos, Miës van der Rohe,
　　　　Gunnar Asplund and Alvar Aalto.

HENRY RUSSELL HITCHCOCK AND CATHERINE BAUER
　　Modern Architecture in England, New York 1937.

LE CORBUSIER AND PIERRE JEANNERET
　　Oeuvre Complète, three volumes, 1919-29, 1929-34 and 1934-38, (Gersbegr), Zurich.
　　Text in French with some of the notes in English translation. The volumes contain most
　　　　of the data regarding Le Corbusier's important contribution to modern house design
　　　　and construction.

J. M. RICHARDS
　　An Introduction to Modern Architecture (Penguin), Harmondsworth 1940.

HOWARD ROBERTSON
　　Architecture Arising (Faber & Faber), London 1944.

ALFRED ROTH
　　The New Architecture (Gersbegr), Zurich 1940.
　　Text in French, German and English. Seven of the twenty examples illustrated and
　　　　described are domestic.

ARNOLD WHITTICK
　　European Architecture in the Twentieth Century, volume I to 1924, vol. II, 1924-1933
　　　　(Crosby Lockwood), London, vol. I 1950, vol. II, 1953.
　　Volume I gives an outline of some of the main European developments in housing and
　　　　house design in the late nineteenth and early twentieth centuries, and also an account
　　　　of the experiments in house construction that were made after the First World War.
　　　　Volume II includes a review of developments in house design and construction by
　　　　some of the famous European architects from 1924 to 1933.

BRUNO ZEVI
　　Towards an Organic Architecture (Faber & Faber), London 1950.
　　The first part deals mainly with the revolt against and survival of modern architecture
　　　　in Europe; much of the second part is concerned with Frank Lloyd Wright's houses.

BELFAST
REFERENCE
LIBRARY

INDEX

Note—Page numbers in italic refer to Illustrations.

BELFAST
REFERENCE
LIBRARY